ROMAN LAW, CONTEMPORARY LAW, EUROPEAN LAW

The Civilian Tradition Today

ROMAN LAW, CONTEMPORARY LAW, EUROPEAN LAW

The Civilian Tradition Today

REINHARD ZIMMERMANN

OXFORD
UNIVERSITY PRESS

OXFORD
UNIVERSITY PRESS
Great Clarendon Street, Oxford OX2 6DP

Oxford University Press is a department of the University of Oxford.
It furthers the University's objective of excellence in research, scholarship,
and education by publishing worldwide in

Oxford New York

Athens Auckland Bangkok Bogotá Buenos Aires Calcutta
Cape Town Chennai Dar es Salaam Delhi Florence Hong Kong Istanbul
Karachi Kuala Lumpur Madrid Melbourne Mexico City Mumbai
Nairobi Paris São Paulo Shanghai Singapore Taipei Tokyo Toronto Warsaw

with associated companies in Berlin Ibadan

Oxford is a registered trade mark of Oxford University Press
in the UK and in certain other countries

Published in the United States
by Oxford University Press Inc., New York

First published 2001

British Library Cataloguing in Publication Data
Data available

Library of Congress Cataloging in Publication Data
Data available

ISBN 0–19–829913–3

1 3 5 7 9 10 8 6 4 2

Typeset in Palatino by
Cambrian Typesetters, Frimley, Surrey

Printed in Great Britain
on acid-free paper by
T.J. International Ltd. Padstow, Cornwall

Preface

This is the text on which my Clarendon lectures were based. They were delivered in October 1999 at the University of Oxford. I am very grateful to all those who came to the three lectures and who contributed to the seminar winding them up. I would also like to thank Mr John Louth and Oxford University Press for the arrangements relating to the lectures and for their kind and efficient cooperation in the production of this book. Above all, however, I would like to express my gratitude to Peter Birks for his generous hospitality, for his constant support, and for his unfailing friendship.

Quotations from German books, articles or court decisions are given, throughout the book, in an English translation; the translation is my own, except where otherwise indicated.

R.Z.

March 2000

Summary of Contents

Contents

List of Abbreviations

A	Appellate Division of the South African Supreme Court
ABGB	*Allgemeines Bürgerliches Gesetzbuch*
AC	Law Reports, Appeal Cases
AcP	*Archiv für die civilistische Praxis*
AD	South African Supreme Court Appellate Division Reports
ADHGB	*Allgemeines Deutsches Handelsgesetzbuch*
All ER	All England Reports
ALR	Australian Law Reports
American JCL	*American Journal of Comparative Law*
App Cas (HL)	Law Reports, Appeal Cases, House of Lords
art(s).	article(s)
B.	Baron
B & Ad	Barnewall and Adolphus' Reports, King's Bench
B & Ald	Barnewall and Alderson's Reports, King's Bench
B & C	Barnewall and Cresswell's Reports, King's Bench
BGB	*Bürgerliches Gesetzbuch*
BGH	*Bundesgerichtshof*
BGHZ	*Entscheidungen des Bundesgerichtshofs in Zivilsachen*
Burr	Burrow's Reports, King's Bench
BW	*Burgerlijk Wetboek*
C	Cape Provincial Division of the South African Supreme Court
CA	Court of Appeal
cap.	*caput*
CB	Chief Baron
Cels.	*Celsus*
Ch D	Law Reports, Chancery Division
CJ	Chief Justice
col(s).	column(s)
Cowp	Cowper's King's Bench Reports
CP	Common Pleas Division

CPD	South African Law Reports, Cape Provincial Division
D.	*Digesta*
DJZ	*Deutsche Juristenzeitung*
Doug	Douglas' King's Bench Reports
EDC	Eastern District Court Reports, Cape of Good Hope
El & Bl	Ellis & Blackburn's Queen's Bench Reports
El Bl & El	Ellis, Blackburn & Ellis' Queen's Bench Reports
ER	English Reports
ERPL	*European Review of Private Law*
Ex.	Exchequer
Gai.	Gaius; Gaius' *Institutes*
Gruch	*Beiträge zur Erläuterung des deutschen Rechts, begründet von J. A. Gruchot*
H & C	Hurlstone & Coltman's Exchequer Reports
HansOLG	*Hanseatisches Oberlandesgericht*
H Bl	H. Blackstone's Common Pleas Reports
HL	House of Lords
HLC	Clark's House of Lords Cases
HRG	*Handwörterbuch zur deutschen Rechtsgeschichte*, ed. Adalbert Erler and Ekkehard Kaufmann (1971 ff.)
ICLQ	*International and Comparative Law Quarterly*
Inst.	*Institutiones Iustiniani*
J	Judge
JA	Judge of Appeal
JhJb	*Jherings Jahrbücher für die Dogmatik des bürgerlichen Rechts*
JLH	*Journal of Legal History*
JR	*Juridical Review*
JuS	*Juristische Schulung*
JW	*Juristische Wochenschrift*
JZ	*Juristenzeitung*
KB	Law Reports, King's Bench Division
Ld Raym	Lord Raymond's King's Bench Reports
lib.	*liber*
Liv.	*livre*
LQR	*Law Quarterly Review*
LR HL	Law Reports, House of Lords
LR QB	Law Reports, Queen's Bench
Macq	Macqueen's House of Lords Reports

M & W	Meeson and Welsby Exchequer Reports
Menz	Menzies' Cape of Good Hope Reports
MR	Master of the Rolls
n(n).	note(s)
NDB	*Neue Deutsche Biographie*
NJW	*Neue Juristische Wochenschrift*
NLR	Natal Law Reports
no(s).	number(s)
OAG	*Oberappellationsgericht*
OLG	*Oberlandesgericht*
OPD	South African Law Reports, Orange Free State Provincial Division
OR	Official Reports, High Court of the South African Republic; *Obligationenrecht* (Switzerland)
Oxford JLS	*Oxford Journal of Legal Studies*
Paul.	Paulus
PECL	Principles of European Contract Law
PICC	Principles of International Commercial Contracts
Plowd	Plowden's Commentaries or Reports
pr.	*principium*
prALR	*Allgemeines Landrecht für die preußischen Staaten*
QB	Queen's Bench Division; Queen's Bench Reports
RabelsZ	*Rabels Zeitschrift für ausländisches und internationales Privatrecht*
RGZ	*Entscheidungen des Reichsgerichts in Zivilsachen*
RIDA	*Revue internationale des droits de l'antiquité*
RIDC	*Revue internationale de droit comparé*
ROHGE	*Entscheidungen des Reichsoberhandelsgerichts*
s.	section
SA	South African Law Reports
SALJ	*South African Law Journal*
Salkeld	Salkeld's Reports, King's Bench
SAR	Reports of the High Court of the South African Republic
Saund	Saunders's King's Bench Reports
SC	Session Cases
SC (HL)	Session Cases, House of Lords
Sect.	Section
SeuffArch	*Seufferts Archiv für Entscheidungen der obersten Gerichte in den deutschen Staaten*

THRHR	*Tydskrif vir Hedendaagse Romeins-Hollandse Reg*
tit.	title; *titulus; titre*
TPD	South African Law Reports, Transvaal Provincial Division
TR	*Tijdschrift voor rechtsgeschiedenis*
tr.	translated
TS	Reports of the Transvaal Supreme Court
TSAR	*Tydskrif vir die Suid-Afrikaanse Reg*
Ulp.	Ulpian
Vaugh	Vaughan's Common Pleas Reports
vol.	volume
Vor	*Vorbemerkung*
W	Witwatersrand Local Division of the South African Supreme Court
WarnRspr.	*Warneyer, Die Rechtsprechung des Reichsgerichts in Zivilsachen*
W Bl	Sir William Blackstone's King's Bench Reports
WLD	Reports of the Witwatersrand Local Division
WR	Weekly Reports
ZEuP	*Zeitschrift für europäisches Privatrecht*
ZfRV	*Zeitschrift für Rechtsvergleichung*
ZNR	*Zeitschrift für neuere Rechtsgeschichte*
ZSS (GA)	*Zeitschrift der Savigny-Stiftung für Rechtsgeschichte, Germanistische Abteilung*
ZSS (KA)	*Zeitschrift der Savigny-Stiftung für Rechtsgeschichte, Kanonistische Abteilung*
ZSS (RA)	*Zeitschrift der Savigny-Stiftung für Rechtsgeschichte, Romanistische Abteilung*

Introduction

The present set of Clarendon lectures is delivered at the end of one century and will be published at the beginning of the next. Thus, these lectures provide an opportunity to look both backwards and forwards.[1] For the German lawyer interested in private law, the twentieth century has been dominated by the German Civil Code. This Code entered into force nearly exactly 100 years ago, on 1 January 1900. Over the past twenty years, however, we have been witnessing far-reaching changes. Our modern private law is in the process of reacquiring a European character. Since about 1990 scholars in Germany (and, of course, elsewhere) have begun to react to this change of perspective. A European private law scholarship is gradually emerging.[2] It is not too difficult to predict that it will dominate private law in the twenty-first century. Eventually, a European civil code may even replace the existing national codes.[3] Obviously, we stand at an important juncture. It may, therefore, be appropriate to try to take stock. I have, on a previous occasion, argued for the reconstitution of Savigny's Historical School of Law on a European level.[4] Essentially, in these lectures, I would like to ask why this is necessary and suggest what may be done to implement such a programme. Savigny's Historical School flourished in Germany. The implementa-

[1] Such double perspective is not unusual for comparative law; see W. J. Zwalve, *Het Janushoofd der rechtsvergelijking* (1988).

[2] See, for example, the textbooks by Hein Kötz, *Europäisches Privatrecht*, vol. i (1996) and Christian von Bar, *Gemeineuropäisches Deliktsrecht*, vol. i (1996), vol. ii (1999) or journals like *Zeitschrift für europäisches Privatrecht* (since 1993), *European Review of Private Law* (since 1993), or *Europa e diritto privato* (since 1998).

[3] A very forceful argument in favour of a European code of obligations has recently been advanced by Jürgen Basedow, 'Das BGB im künftigen europäischen Privatrecht: Der hybride Kodex', (200) 2000 *AcP* 445 ff.

[4] 'Savigny's Legacy: Legal History, Comparative Law, and the Emergence of a European Legal Science', (1996) 112 *LQR* 576 ff.

tion of the BGB, 100 years ago, may be regarded as its supreme triumph or its ultimate failure. Indisputably, the Code has changed our legal perception. It has led to an emancipation of Roman law from contemporary legal doctrine. This process is sketched in the first lecture. But has it also resulted in an emancipation of contemporary doctrine from Roman law? Has there been, in other words, a qualitative change in our substantive private law as a result of codification? This is the question underlying the second lecture. Lawyers in nineteenth-century Germany were constantly aware, in spite of the bewildering legal diversity with which they were faced, of a fundamental intellectual unity created by a common tradition. The re-creation of such an awareness is of central importance to sustain the Europeanization of private law. The third lecture attempts to demonstrate how this may be achieved. In this sense, then, it may be said that the first lecture is devoted to Roman law (scholarship), the second to contemporary (German) law, and the third to European (private) law: past, present, and future. The focus in the first two lectures on developments in Germany is, hopefully, permissible in view of the BGB's anniversary.

Lecture One—The End of an Era: Transformation of Scholarship in Roman Law

I. THE NATURAL LAW CODIFICATIONS AND ROMAN LAW

1. Effects of Codification in General

The codification of European private law since the close of the eighteenth century is very widely regarded as a major turning point in its development.[1] Obviously, some of the high hopes and expectations entertained at the time of the Enlightenment have not been fulfilled: neither have the codifications made the learned lawyer redundant, nor have they led to a lasting consolidation (or, to put it negatively: ossification) of private law. Still, however, they have significantly contributed towards the national fragmentation of the European legal tradition: after all, they were enacted by the legislature of a specific state and were applicable, therefore, only within the limited territorial area for which that legislature was competent to lay down laws. The first signs of this fragmentation of the civilian tradition had already become visible at the time of the *usus modernus pandectarum* of the seventeeth and eighteenth centuries when the 'institutional' writers had no longer discussed Roman law as such but Roman-Dutch, Roman-Scots, Roman-Hispanic, or Roman-Saxon

[1] See, in general, Franz Wieacker, *A History of Private Law in Europe*, tr. Tony Weir (1995), 257 ff.; Pio Caroni, 'Kodifikation', in *HRG*, vol. ii (1978), cols. 907 ff.; idem, *Saggi sulla storia della codificazione* (1998); Helmut Coing, *Europäisches Privatrecht*, vol. ii (1989), 7 ff.; J. H. A. Lokin and W. J. Zwalve, *Hoofdstukken uit de Europese Codificatiegeschiedenis* (1990), 1 ff.; Reinhard Zimmermann, 'Codification: History and Present Significance of an Idea', (1995) 3 *ERPL* 95 ff.

law.[2] But it had always been clear that ultimately these were merely regional or national variations of an essentially uniform theme: different emanations of a common legal tradition. This was demonstrated, for instance, by the continuing habit of the *peregrinatio academica,* the quotation conventions of the learned literature, and the appointment policies within the law faculties. With the enactment of the codifications there was a change. The awareness of a fundamental intellectual unity was gradually lost, and thus the national isolation of legal practice, legal training, and legal scholarship gained ground which they are only now beginning to surrender.

Moreover the codifications have ended the 'second life' of Roman law during which it was directly applied in practice. Since the days of the 'reception' Roman law had provided the basis for the administration of justice in Western and Central Europe and had become a *ius commune,* or common law. In the process, it had absorbed many elements of Canon law and of the indigenous customary laws: it was no longer the *usus antiquus* but had been transformed into an *usus modernus.*[3] At the same time, however, a string of authors from François Hotman to Hermann Conring and Christian Thomasius had started to shake the authority of Roman law: of a law that had given rise to intricate doctrinal disputes, that was wedded to outdated and impractical subtleties, and that had been enacted by the despotic rulers of another age and country. Also, since Roman law was only applicable *in subsidio,* countless more specific territorial or local laws could govern a particular dispute.[4] The great number and complexity of legal

[2] See, in particular, Klaus Luig, 'The Institutes of National Law in the Seventeenth and Eighteenth Centuries', (1972) 17 *JR* 193 ff.; cf. also, for example, Alan Watson, 'The Impact of Justinian's Institutes on Academic Treatises: The Civil Law', in idem, *Roman and Comparative Law* (1991), 147 ff.

[3] For an overview, see Helmut Coing, *Europäisches Privatrecht,* vol. i (1985), 7 ff.; Manlio Bellomo, *The Common Legal Past of Europe, 1000–1800* (1995), 55 ff.; Reinhard Zimmermann, 'Das römisch-kanonische ius commune als Grundlage europäischer Rechtseinheit', 1992 *JZ* 10 ff.

[4] Cf., e.g., Wolfgang Wiegand, 'Die privatrechtlichen Quellen des Usus modernus', in Dieter Simon (ed.), *Akten des 26. Deutschen Rechtshistorikertages* (1987), 237

sources thus contributed to a widespread feeling of both legal uncertainty and inefficiency as far as the administration of justice was concerned. The codifications of the age of the Law of Reason were supposed to tidy up this messy situation: they were to provide a systematic regulation of the entire private law, ousting all rival sources of law including, in particular, the Roman-Canon *ius commune*. Thus, art. 1 of the Dutch Abrogation Act (*Afschaffingswet*) crisply stated: 'The legal validity of Roman law is and remains abrogated.'

2. France and the Netherlands

This rule, however, suffused by a strange mixture of fear, relief, and elation, remained at first mere theory. In his book *Lex Scripta Abrogata*[5] Hendrik Kooiker has demonstrated that Roman law continued to play a very significant role in the first decades after the enactment of the codifications, in both the Netherlands and France. He even refers to a 'third renaissance' of Roman law. Its practical significance, according to Kooiker, can hardly be overstated. The extraordinary degree of substantial continuity between the tradition of the *ius commune* and the *code civil* led to Roman law becoming an indispensable tool in interpreting the new code, in resolving doctrinal disputes, and in filling gaps in the law. The *code civil* had been intended to establish uniform law, not new law. It brought to an end the prevailing diversity of regional laws and thus ultimately completed the process of 'reception'.[6] The *ius commune* rendered an essential contribution towards the establishment of a 'systhème d'application'; it continued to be regarded as *ratio scripta* and to be applied as such in

ff.; Bellomo (n. 3) 78 ff., 149 ff.; Gottfried Schiemann, 'Usus modernus und Gesetzgebung', in Barbara Dölemeyer and Diethelm Klippel (eds.), *Gesetz und Gesetzgebung in der frühen Neuzeit* (1998), 157 ff.

5 *Lex Scripta Abrogata: De derde renaissance van het Romeinse recht*, part i: *De uitwendige ontwikkeling*, Ars Aequi Libri (1996).

6 The continuity between *ius commune* and the French code is also emphasized by James Gordley, 'Myths of the French Civil Code', (1994) 2 *American JCL* 459 ff.

practice. It was only towards the middle of the nineteenth century that a strictly exegetical approach gained ascendancy.

3. Prussia

Structurally similar was the development in Prussian law, as has been demonstrated particularly clearly by Jörn Eckert.[7] It is widely known that the Prussian Code of 1794 only played a minor part, as far as legal scholarship and legal education were concerned.[8] For many decades it was not taught, interpreted, and applied as such but only in relation to the *ius commune*: it was compared with, and assessed and evaluated from the point of view of, contemporary Roman law. Savigny with his lectures on the Prussian Code provided the authoritative example.[9] Interestingly, however, even in the practice of the Prussian courts the Code in the first years after its enactment appears to have been applied—in marked contrast to the intention of the legislature[10]—like one among many other common law sources. Thus, the judges of the Supreme Court of Appeal tended thoroughly to examine the literature of the *ius commune*, but to refer to the provisions of the Prussian Code only 'comparatively rarely' and merely in order to affirm a result already arrived at by different means.[11] Also in Prussia, therefore, Roman law remained in force as *ratio scripta*: a state of affairs which seems to have been regarded as self-evident by all those involved in the administration of justice. By and large, one may refer to a process of 'pandectification' of Prussian law.

[7] 'Gesetzesbegriff und Rechtsanwendung im späten Naturrecht: Die Spruchpraxis preußischer Gerichte unter dem Allgemeinen Landrecht', (1998) 37 *Der Staat* 571 ff.

[8] Cf. Wieacker (n. 1) 334 f.; Konrad Zweigert and Hein Kötz, *An Introduction to Comparative Law*, tr. Tony Weir (3rd edn., 1998), 138.

[9] Cf. Christian Wollschläger, 'Praktische Theorie: Die Landrechtsvorlesung in Savignys wissenschaftlichem Programm', in Friedrich Carl von Savigny, *Landrechtsvorlesung 1824: Drei Nachschriften*, ed. and introd. Christian Wollschläger (1994), pp. xxiii ff.

[10] Eckert, (1998) 37 *Der Staat* 576 ff.; cf. also Gerhard Dilcher, 'Die janusköpfige Kodifikation', (1994) 2 *ZEuP* 453 ff.

[11] Eckert, (1998) 37 *Der Staat* 586.

4. Austria

A 'pandectification' also occurred in Austrian law.[12] More than forty years after the ABGB had become the source of private law applicable in Austria, Count Thun-Hohenstein introduced a legal curriculum,[13] in which Roman law eclipsed the Austrian code.[14] This reform of legal training coincided, and was inspired by, the efforts of Joseph Unger[15] to refashion Austrian law in the mould of German pandectist scholarship. Since the ABGB, he argued, had essentially merely restated the law applicable at the time of codification, it could only be understood from the point of view of the legal sources prevailing at that stage, i.e. particularly Roman law. Moreover, it had to be carefully examined how far the provisions contained in the code 'could still claim recognition as a matter of legal theory'.[16] Once

[12] Cf., in general, Werner Ogris, *Die Entwicklung der österreichischen Privatrechtswissenschaft im 19. Jahrhundert* (1968); idem, 'Die Wissenschaft des gemeinen römischen Rechts und das österreichische Allgemeine Bürgerliche Gesetzbuch', in Helmut Coing and Walter Wilhelm (eds.), *Wissenschaft und Kodifikation des Privatrechts im 19. Jahrhundert*, vol. i (1974), 153 ff.; Wilhelm Brauneder, 'Privatrechtsfortbildung durch Juristenrecht in Exegetik und Pandektistik in Österreich', (1983) 5 *ZNR* 22 ff.

[13] See, e.g., Gunter Wesener, *Römisches Recht und Naturrecht* (1978) (= *Geschichte der Rechtswissenschaftlichen Fakultät der Universität Graz*, part I), 41 ff.

[14] Paul Koschaker reports, on the basis of his lecture book, that he heard 7 hours' institutions of Roman law, 25 hours' Roman private law (*Pandekten*), 3 hours' Roman legal history and Roman civil procedure, and 2 hours' Roman criminal law, 'all in all, and including 2 practical exercises, 44 hours Roman law, as opposed to which 18 hours on the law of the General Civil Code looked somewhat pitiful—all the more so if account is taken of the fact that this excellent private law code had by that time been the valid law in Austria for 90 years': 'Leopold Wenger: Ein halbes Jahrhundert rechtsgeschichtlicher Romanistik: Ein Rückblick', in *Festschrift für Leopold Wenger*, vol. i (1944), 3. Koschaker studied in the first years of the 20th century, first in Graz, before he went to Ludwig Mitteis in Leipzig.

[15] Joseph Unger, 1828–1913, professor in Prague and Vienna, member of the Upper Chamber of the Reichstag, government minister, president of the Imperial Court; cf. Jan Schröder, in Gerhard Kleinheyer and Jan Schröder (eds.), *Deutsche und europäische Juristen aus neun Jahrhunderten* (4th edn., 1996), 431 ff.; and see Hugo Sinzheimer, *Jüdische Klassiker der deutschen Rechtswissenschaft* (2nd edn., 1953), 83 ff.; Wilhelm Brauneder, in idem (ed.), *Juristen in Österreich 1200–1980* (1987), 177 ff.; Barbara Dölemeyer, in Michael Stolleis (ed.), *Juristen: Ein biographisches Lexikon* (1995), 628 f.

[16] Joseph Unger, *System des österreichischen allgemeinen Privatrechts*, vol. i (1856), p. viii.

again, Roman law, in its contemporary German version, provided the self-evident point of reference for understanding, assessing, and discussing the Austrian codification.[17] Unger's programme[18] decisively shaped Austrian legal science in the second half of the nineteenth century and stimulated a process which may be described as a 'reception'.[19]

II. LEGAL UNITY IN GERMANY: PANDECTIST LEGAL SCHOLARSHIP AND THE CIVIL CODE

1. The 'Third Renaissance of Roman Law' in the Nineteenth Century

This surprising phenomenon of a 'third renaissance of Roman law' on both a theoretical and practical level in the areas of application of all of the great Natural law codifications is in stark contrast to the expectations and intentions of the draftsmen of these codes, and largely even contrary to what they specifically laid down.[20] But it meant that at

[17] Brauneder (n. 15) 182 refers to a turn to the Historical School, 'confined, however, as if that were self-evident to its romanistic branch'.

[18] Carried out in his *System des österreichischen allgemeinen Privatrechts* (System of Austrian General Private Law), 3 vols. (1856–64), a work 'that commenced with the detailed exposition of "general doctrines" as they were characteristic of the pandectist system but still alien to the code itself': Paul Koschaker, *Europa und das römische Recht* (4th edn., 1966), 264. Koschaker also refers to similar contemporary literature in Prussia, Württemberg, and Switzerland. For Switzerland, see Julius G. Lautner, *Zur Bedeutung des römischen Rechts für die europäische Rechtskultur und zu seiner Stellung im Rechtsunterricht* (1976) 158 ff. and, more recently, Pio Caroni, 'Die Schweizer Romanistik im 19. Jahrhundert', (1994) 16 *ZNR* 250 ff.

[19] See Peter Landau, 'Juristen jüdischer Herkunft im Kaiserreich und in der Weimarer Republik', in Helmut Heinrichs, Harald Franzki, Klaus Schmalz, and Michael Stolleis (eds.), *Deutsche Juristen jüdischer Herkunft* (1993), 196. This reception was supported also by the fact that Count Thun-Hohenstein created a number of new chairs for legal history which were predominantly filled by scholars from Germany. Particularly eminent among them, as far as Roman law was concerned, was Gustav Demelius (1831–91, professor in Cracow, Graz, and Vienna); cf. the appreciation by Emil Strohal, (1894) 15 *ZSS* (*RA*) 1 ff.; cf. also Wesener (n. 13) 55 ff.

[20] For Prussia, see Eckert, (1998) 37 *Der Staat* 571 ff.; for France, cf. Loi du 30 ventôse de l'an XII, art. 7: 'A compter du jour où le code sera exécutoire, les lois

least in what was to constitute the German Empire a fundamental intellectual legal unity, in spite of all differences in detail, continued to exist. That unity was forcefully promoted by the Historical School of Law and the pandectist legal scholarship that emerged from it, and it comprised Prussia, Austria, and the German territories of French law.[21] Thus, the contemporary version of Roman law did not only apply in the areas still governed by the *ius commune*;[22] even in the countries of codified law it contributed the underlying legal theory.[23] Thus, it remained perfectly possible for a law professor to be called from Königsberg to Strasbourg, from Gießen to Vienna, or from Heidelberg to Leipzig. Nor were law students, as far as choice and change of universities were concerned, confined to the institutions of the state in which they later wanted to practise.

The German law teachers who met in March 1896 in Eisenach in order to consider the future organization of legal studies in Germany regarded it as curious though understandable

> that in the universities of those German states possessing a codification no prominent place had been assigned to that codification.

romaines, les ordonnances, les coutumes générales ou locales, les statuts, les règlements cesseront d'avoir force de loi générale ou particulière dans les matières qui sont l'objet des dites lois composant le présent code.' On the *effet abrogatoire* of the French codification, see Raymond Salleilles, 'Méthode historique et codification', in *Atti del congresso internazionale di scienze storiche*, vol. ix (1904), 3 ff.; François Gény, *Méthode d'interprétation et sources en droit privé positif* (2nd edn., 1919), i. 230 f., ii. 18; and see now Kooiker (n. 5) 190 ff.

[21] On the latter, cf. the recent contributions by Antonio Grilli, 'Das linksrheinische Partikularrecht und das römische Recht in der Rechtsprechung der Cour d'Appel/Cour Impérial de Trèves nach 1804', in Reiner Schulze (ed.), *Französisches Zivilrecht in Europa während des 19. Jahrhunderts* (1994), 67 ff.; Hans-Jürgen Becker, 'Das rheinische Recht und seine Bedeutung für die Rechtsentwicklung in Europa während des 19. Jahrhunderts', 1985 *JuS* 338 ff.; Reiner Schulze (ed.), *Rheinisches Recht und europäische Rechtsgeschichte* (1998).

[22] In 1890 about 14,416,000 (of a total of 50,000,000) inhabitants of the German Empire lived in areas where mainly the *ius commune* was applicable. See the map edited by Diethelm Klippel, *Deutsche Rechts- und Gerichtskarte* (1996), with an introduction by the editor.

[23] Koschaker (n. 18) 292. Cf. also Reiner Schulze, 'Vergleichende Gesetzesauslegung und Rechtsangleichung', (1997) 38 *ZfRV* 193: 'conceptual basis for the comprehension of all particular laws prevailing in Germany'.

Neither the Prussian Code, nor the law of the *code civil* or that of the *Badisches Landrecht*, nor indeed the law of the Saxonian Civil Code became the focal point for legal training in the universities of the respective states. Just as they were neglected, at first, by legal scholarship, so they only constituted an appendix in the lecture lists of the law faculties. And even where and when the academic elaboration of these laws had reached the level of the modern requirements, there was no change in their position within the curriculum. For since such elaboration had principally consisted in establishing the inner relationship between the codified legal material and the *ius commune*, the importance of a legal training in the *ius commune* was thereby re-emphasized: such training was regarded as suitable to provide a sufficient introduction to the understanding of the codified laws. Thus, the possibility existed that the Prussian, Saxonian or the native of *Baden* could receive his educational background in law at a university in a different state, as long as he acquired, at the end of his studies, some more specific—not necessarily very profound—knowledge of the legal system which, however, he might be required to apply for the rest of his life.[24]

2. The Development in the Twentieth Century (Overview)

The law teachers assembled in Eisenach adopted a recommendation by Emil Strohal[25] to assign an 'essentially different and more prominent' position to the BGB in the legal

[24] Emil Friedberg, *Die künftige Gestaltung des deutschen Rechtsstudiums nach den Beschlüssen der Eisenacher Konferenz* (1896), 7 f. The conference, initiated by the law faculties of Leipzig, Berlin, and Munich, was attended by 65 professors who came from all German law faculties, apart from Strasbourg. An obvious parallel, today, is the legal training offered by the 'national' law schools in the United States; see Axel Flessner, 'Rechtsvereinheitlichung durch Rechtswissenschaft und Juristenausbildung', (1992) 56 *RabelsZ* 246; Melvin Eisenberg, 'Why is American Contract Law so Uniform? National Law in the United States', in Hans-Leo Weyers (ed.), *Europäisches Vertragsrecht* (1997) 23 ff.

[25] 1844–1914. Strohal, an Austrian lawyer, had studied in Graz and Vienna and became professor in Graz, Göttingen (in succession to Jhering), and Leipzig. His main areas of study and research were property law and the law of succession. On the law of succession (according to the BGB) he produced a systematic exposition (1896; 3rd edn,. 1903) and he was also the author of the relevant section in the commentary by Planck. Mitteis referred to him as a 'pioneer in the field of the new private law'; cf. Ludwig Mitteis, 'Emil Strohal 1844–1914', (1915) 65 *JhJb* 1 ff. (quotation on p. 22); and see Herbert Hofmeister, in Brauneder (n. 15) 217 ff.

curriculum than had been allocated to the previous codes of private law.[26] In particular, the lectures on the BGB were intended to teach the private law prevailing in Germany as a systematic entity. The *pièce de résistance* of all German law faculties in the nineteenth century, the course on the system of Roman private law in its pandectist mould (*Pandektenvorlesung*), had thus fallen by the wayside[27] and Roman law had been reduced to a propaedeutic level: it merely constituted a 'pedagogical tool'.[28] The relevant legal training statutes in the various German states followed this line.[29] The scene was thus set for a legal development that differed markedly from that under the Natural law codifications. For the enactment of the German Civil Code did not stimulate a 'third renaissance of Roman law'. References to the *ius commune*, to its sources and legal literature, vanished from the pages of the law reports. Academic legal writers confined their attention, and their intellectual horizon, to the BGB and led German private law scholarship into a national isolation.[30] And legislation in the field of private law also became enamoured 'with the example of the Chinese Wall'.[31] Scholarship in Roman law, in turn, freed from its

[26] Cf. the propositions advanced by Strohal, as printed in Friedberg (n. 24) 13 f.

[27] See resolution IV of the Eisenach conference. According to resolution I, moreover, the course on the Institutes of Roman law was to be replaced by the study of 'General legal theory, particularly the theory of private law'. Matters remained different in Austria and Switzerland for a long time to come: cf. Lautner (n. 18) 57 ff., 158 ff.

[28] Friedberg (n. 24) 10. Cf., in this context, Friedrich Carl von Savigny who attributed to the 'a-historical school' (which he rejected) the intention to regard history only as 'a collection of moral and political examples': 'Ueber den Zweck dieser Zeitschrift', (1815) 1 *Zeitschrift für geschichtliche Rechtswissenschaft* 3.

[29] See the references in Diethelm Klippel, *Juristische Zeitgeschichte: Die Bedeutung der Rechtsgeschichte für die Zivilrechtswissenschaft* (1985), 8 ff. Klippel also provides an overview of the contemporary discussion. See, in particular, the assessments by P. Oertmann, 'Die Bedeutung des Corpus juris nach dem 1. Januar 1900', 1900 *DJZ* 19 ff.; R. Leonhard, 'Erfahrungen mit der Herrschaft des neuen Studienplanes', 1900 *DJZ* 325 ff.; R. Sohm, 'Das Studium des römischen Rechts', 1908 *DJZ* 34 ff.

[30] Cf., e.g., Hermann Isay, *Die Isolierung des deutschen Rechtsdenkens* (1924).

[31] Ernst Rabel in an article of 1913/14; the relevant passage is quoted in Ernst Rabel, 'Aufgabe und Notwendigkeit der Rechtsvergleichung', in idem, *Gesammelte Aufsätze*, vol. iii (1967), 13 f. This is not true, however, for the draftsmen preparing

obligation to serve the needs of modern private law,[32] was in the process thoroughly to historicize its subject.

A process had started which was pointedly described by Ernst Immanuel Bekker as an 'emancipation . . . by thinking apart Roman law and modern law'.[33] Bekker[34] is usually regarded as one of the last great pandectist scholars[35] who, unlike Windscheid, lived to see the new era. But he was also one of the first who started, already in the 1860s, to abandon the methodological tenets of pandectist science.[36] Significantly one of his most important works was entitled *Die Aktionen des Römischen Privatrechts* (The Actions of Roman Private Law) and not, like Bernhard Windscheid's even more celebrated study, *Die Actio des römischen Civilrechts, vom Standpunkte des heutigen Rechts* (The Action of Roman Private Law, from the Point of View of Contemporary Law). Windscheid aimed at modern law and laid the foundations of one of the conceptual pillars of modern private law doctrine: the substantive rather than

the BGB (though they sometimes displayed an anti-French bias; cf. the examples provided in (1994/5) 1 *Columbia Journal of European Law* 87 f.). Generally on comparative law as the basis of 19th-century legislation see Helmut Coing, 'Rechtsvergleichung als Grundlage von Gesetzgebung im 19. Jahrhundert', (1978) 7 *Ius Commune* 168 ff.

32 'Long enough has legal history patiently done the donkey-work for contemporary law; it has been weighed down by the exertions of gathering together the stones which others have used to build palaces. Legal history now revolts against such suppression' (Ernst von Möller, *Die Trennung der Deutschen und der Römischen Rechtsgeschichte* (1905), 68); 'It is high time that the unhappy marriage between legal history and legal doctrine is dissolved' (Hermann U. Kantorowicz, 'Probleme der Strafrechtsvergleichung', (1908) 4 *Monatsschrift für Kriminalpsychologie und Strafrechtsreform* 108).

33 *Die Aktionen des römischen Privatrechts*, vol. i (1871), 2. Cf. the analysis presented by Maximiliane Kriechbaum, *Dogmatik und Rechtsgeschichte bei Ernst Immanuel Bekker* (1984), 30 ff. The catchword of 'thinking apart' (*auseinanderdenken*) has also been picked up by Willem Zwalve, 'Teaching Roman Law in the Netherlands', (1997) 5 *ZEuP* 393 ff.; Zwalve refers, in this context, to a 'severe case of intellectual schizophrenia' (p. 398).

34 Ernst Immanuel Bekker, 1827–1916, professor in Halle, Greifswald, and Heidelberg. On his life and work, see Kriechbaum (n. 33) 1 ff.

35 Klaus Luig, 'Pandektenwissenschaft', in *HRG*, vol. iii, col. 1423; Kleinheyer and Schröder (n. 15) 466.

36 Kriechbaum (n. 33) 277 (who adds: 'as it appears . . . quite independently').

procedural notion of an *Anspruch* (claim);[37] Bekker, on the other hand, specifically did not attempt to transform Roman law into a contemporary Roman law but wrote his book 'unaffected by the overwhelming weight of having to consider how Roman law might still be applied'.[38] Bekker also, incidentally, was both a friend and mentor of Otto Gradenwitz, one of the initiators of the modern interpolationist research.[39]

The development sketched here in its broadest outlines has today led to a situation where Roman law, as part of legal history, is merely one out of several 'foundational subjects'. In most German universities it is perfectly possible as well as permissible to obtain a law degree without having done a single course in legal history. Legal scholarship has become a completely a-historical discipline. The doctrinal literature very largely dispenses with any reference to historical (or comparative) material. And for the courts the sources of the *ius commune* have lost any relevance.[40] Such isolation, as far as both the historical sources and comparative material are concerned, was regarded as 'completely outdated'[41] by Ernst Rabel as early as 1913/14. Yet, it still essentially characterizes our modern private law. How was this possible?

III. HISTORICAL LEGAL SCHOLARSHIP IN THE NINETEENTH CENTURY

1. The Vital Connection between Present and Past

Nineteenth-century German legal scholarship was dominated by the Historical School. Its founding father, Friedrich Carl von Savigny, had outlined the programme of

[37] See Reinhard Zimmermann, 'An Introduction to German Legal Culture', in Werner F. Ebke and Matthew W. Finkin (eds.), *Introduction to German Law* (1996), 31 (with references).

[38] Ernst Landsberg, *Geschichte der deutschen Rechtswissenschaft*, vol. iii/2 (1910), 850.

[39] See infra n. 100.

[40] For an exceptional case, see Berthold Kupisch, 'Eine Moselinsel, Kaiser Napoleon und das römische Recht', 1987 *JZ* 1017 ff.

[41] Rabel (n. 31) 14. Cf. also Josef Partsch, *Vom Beruf des römischen Rechts in der heutigen Universität* (1920), 21 ff.

a 'historical legal scholarship' (*geschichtliche Rechtswissenschaft*).[42] Of course, Savigny was also interested in legal history as such; the *Geschichte des römischen Rechts im Mittelalter* (History of Roman Law in the Middle Ages)[43] in six volumes, his main work as a legal historian, essentially created the modern discipline of legal history—'previously there had only been legal antiquities'.[44] However, the central concern of his programmatic writings, as well as of his celebrated *System des heutigen römischen Rechts* (System of Contemporary Roman Law), was legal scholarship rather than legal history. But it was to be an 'organically progressive'[45] legal scholarship, aware always of the 'vital connection'[46] between present and past. The main task of the modern private lawyer thus consisted in the 'intellectual penetration, adaptation and rejuvenation of the legal material as it has come down to us'.[47] Since there is no 'completely separate and independent human existence . . . every age creates its own legal world, not for itself and arbitrarily, but in indissoluble community with the entire past'.[48] This was a fascinating vision[49] which was to prove extraordinarily influential and significantly affected the

[42] For details, see Joachim Rückert, *Idealismus, Jurisprudenz und Politik bei Savigny* (1984); Horst Heinrich Jakobs, *Die Begründung der geschichtlichen Rechtswissenschaft* (1992); Maximiliane Kriechbaum, 'Römisches Recht und neuere Privatrechtsgeschichte in Savignys Auffassung von Rechtsgeschichte und Rechtswissenschaft', in Reinhard Zimmermann, Rolf Knütel, and Jens Peter Meincke (eds.), *Rechtsgeschichte und Privatrechtsdogmatik* (2000), 41 ff.; cf. also the clear overview provided by Mathias Reimann, 'Nineteenth Century German Legal Science', (1990) 31 *Boston College Law Review* 837 ff. and the classic exposition by Wieacker (n. 1) 279 ff.

[43] 1815–31; 2nd edn., 1834–51 in 7 vols.; it has 'remained a standard work to this day' (Jan Schröder, in Kleinheyer and Schröder (n. 15) 358).

[44] Koschaker (n. 18) 269. On the 'discovery of legal history' in the 19th century, see Wieacker (n. 1) 330 ff.

[45] *Vom Beruf unserer Zeit für Gesetzgebung und Rechtswissenschaft* (1814); cf. the reprint in Hans Hattenhauer (ed.), *Thibaut und Savigny* (1973), 192.

[46] *System des heutigen römischen Rechts*, vol. i (1840), xv.

[47] (1815) 1 *Zeitschrift für geschichtliche Rechtswissenschaft* 6.

[48] Ibid. 3.

[49] '[A] disclosure, a revelation': Bernhard Windscheid, 'Recht und Rechtswissenschaft', in idem, *Gesammelte Reden und Abhandlungen*, ed. Paul Oertmann (1904), 16.

legal development far beyond the boundaries of Germany.[50] Soon, however, a number of problems became apparent which were partly inherent in Savigny's programme itself, or associated with some of its intellectual presuppositions, but which also partly arose from the way in which it was implemented by subsequent pandectist scholarship.

2. The Role of Roman Law

An obvious paradox that has been frequently discussed consisted in the emphasis on Roman law as basis for a contemporary theory of private law. It ill matched the idea of law as being the product of the spirit of the people (*Volksgeist*). The phenomenon of the 'reception' could only be explained in a very tortuous way on that basis.[51] A second problem arose from Savigny's partiality for the pure and undiluted Roman law, corresponding to the educational principles of contemporary humanism and the aesthetic ideas of classicism.[52] It entailed a somewhat disdainful attitude towards the immediately preceding period of the *usus modernus pandectarum* and a negative, and essentially unjust, evaluation of the work of the medieval Commentators whose *mos italicus* had paved the way for the *usus modernus*. This attitude was in fundamental opposition to a programme that was fundamentally based upon the notion of 'organic growth' and insisted on 'the even and dispassionate recognition of the value and individuality of every age'.[53]

Moreover, Savigny strove to 'discover and determine within the entire body of our law what is in reality of Roman origin . . . and to eliminate, within the environs of

[50] Cf., e.g., Alfons Bürge, 'Ausstrahlungen der Historischen Rechtsschule in Frankreich', (1997) 5 *ZEuP* 643 ff.; John W. Cairns, 'The Influence of the German Historical School in Early Nineteenth Century Edinburgh', (1994) 20 *Syracuse Journal of International Law and Commerce* 191 ff.; Mathias Reimann, *Historische Schule und Common Law* (1993).

[51] Cf. Wieacker (n. 1) 309 ff.

[52] Ibid. 290 f.

[53] Savigny (n. 46) pp. xiv f. Cf. also Wieacker (n. 1) 312.

these Roman elements of our legal consciousness, whatever has in fact withered away and merely continues to lead a troublesome shadow existence, as a result of our misunderstanding'.[54] He (as well as his pandectist successors down to Ernst Immanuel Bekker) thus assessed Roman law from the point of view of modern doctrine. There was the danger of a skewed perception of the past: a perception affected by 'considerations of how Roman law might still be applied' (*gemeinrechtliche Anwendbarkeitsrücksichten*). For if the ultimate challenge is the transformation of Roman law into a contemporary Roman law, a certain temptation always exists to read contemporary law into Roman law.[55] By aiming at productive assimilation the scholarship of the Historical School intended to be historical and doctrinal at one and the same time: an enterprise as likely to succeed as 'the mixing up of fire and water'.[56]

3. The Question of Codification

And finally there was, within the Historical School, an ambivalence towards the question of a codification of private law that was never quite resolved. The 'founding manifesto'[57] of the Historical School was Savigny's reply to A. F. J. Thibaut's call to end the intolerable and inconve-

[54] Savigny (n. 46) p. xv.

[55] Cf. also, in this context, Heinrich Mitteis, *Vom Lebenswert der Rechtsgeschichte* (1947), 44.

[56] Koschaker (n. 18) 283 f. The same criticism is raised today against modern attempts to establish a historical scholarship operating on the basis of 'intensive comparative studies which are substantiated historically' and which are 'driven by practical and doctrinal interests' by Tomasz Giaro, 'Europäische Privatrechtsgeschichte: Werkzeug der Rechtsvereinheitlichung oder Produkt der Kategorienvermengung', (1994) 21 *Ius Commune* 1 ff. (the first quotation is taken from Max Kaser, 'Wege und Ziele der deutschen Zivilrechtswissenschaft', in *Europa e il diritto romano: Studi in memoria di Paolo Koschaker*, vol. i (1954), 578; the second comes from Koschaker (n. 18) 346). Zwalve, (1997) 5 *ZEuP* 398, describes this methodological insight as 'a truism that [is] presented as a stroke of genius'.

[57] Bernhard Windscheid, 'Die geschichtliche Schule in der Rechtswissenschaft', in *Gesammelte Reden und Abhandlungen*, ed. Paul Oertmann (1904), 66.

nient diversity of private laws prevailing in Germany by adopting a General German Civil Code, modelled on the French *code civil*.[58] In his famous essay entitled *Vom Beruf unserer Zeit für Gesetzgebung und Rechtswissenschaft* (Of the Vocation of our Time for Legislation and Legal Science) Savigny not only rejected the idea of a codification to be drafted and enacted *hic et nunc*, but criticized the very notion of a codification as 'inorganic', unscientific, arbitrary, and hostile to tradition. At best, it was unnecessary, at worst it would distort and stifle 'organic' legal development.[59]

None the less it was widely accepted, from about the middle of the nineteenth century, that a codification of private law in Germany was about to come and would end the direct application of Roman law. Theodor Mommsen in 1848 voiced the German nation's desire for the creation of a uniform and national law,[60] and Rudolf von Jhering predicted in 1852 that his own generation of lawyers would see the demise of Roman law in its present form.[61] The editorial of the first volume of the *Zeitschrift für Rechtsgeschichte* (Journal of Legal History, 1861),[62] while professing to continue the plan and the aims of Savigny's *Zeitschrift für geschichtliche Rechtswissenschaft* (Journal of Historical Legal Science),[63] gave expression to the prevailing conviction that

[58] A. F. J. Thibaut, *Über die Notwendigkeit eines allgemeinen bürgerlichen Rechts für Deutschland* (1814), easily accessible today in Hattenhauer (n. 45) 61 ff.

[59] Savigny (n. 45) *passim*, e.g. 111, 123 ff., 162 ff.

[60] Theodor Mommsen, 'Die Aufgabe der historischen Rechtswissenschaft', in idem, *Gesammelte Schriften*, vol. iii (1907), 587.

[61] *Geist des römischen Rechts auf den verschiedenen Stufen seiner Entwicklung* (1st edn., 1852), i, 2; cf. also Walter Wilhelm, 'Das Recht im römischen Recht', in *Jherings Erbe*, ed. Franz Wieacker and Christian Wollschläger (1970), 228 ff.; Horst Heinrich Jakobs, *Wissenschaft und Gesetzgebung im bürgerlichen Recht nach der Rechtsquellenlehre des 19. Jahrhunderts* (1983), 76 ff.; Hermann Conrad, 'Der Deutsche Juristentag 1860–1960', in Hermann Conrad, Gerhard Dilcher, and Hans-Joachim Kurland, *Der Deutsche Juristentag 1860–1994* (1997), 23 ff.

[62] For an overview of the history of 'the leading journal in the field of legal history in Germany', see Adalbert Erler, 'Savignyzeitschrift für Rechtsgeschichte', in *HRG*, vol. iv (1990), cols. 1323 ff.; Hans Thieme, 'Hundert Jahre Zeitschrift für Rechtsgeschichte', (1961) 78 *ZSS* (*RA*) pp. xi ff.; Theo Mayer-Maly, 'Rückblick', (1983) 100 *ZSS* (*RA*) 1 ff.

[63] See (1861) 1 *Zeitschrift für Rechtsgeschichte* 1 f.

the historical development of the law could now sufficiently clearly be assessed 'for the results of the historical inquiry to be employed in the legislative process'.[64] And even one of Savigny's most faithful disciples, who had sat at his feet in the University of Berlin and who had never ceased to see in him his own scholarly ideal, Bernhard Windscheid,[65] was among the most influential proponents of a German codification. In a number of public speeches and essays he expressed his support for a code that would leave behind Roman law and at the same time complete its reception.[66]

Of course, it was possible to argue that Savigny had only wanted to dispute the vocation of his own time for legislation: a successful code of private law required a fully worked out doctrinal framework which had in the meantime, and due to the efforts of the Historical School, been established.[67] Paul Koschaker even maintained that the Historical School, a movement of professors, could become practically effective only by means of legislation.[68] But the very idea that the conceptual and doctrinal structure of the law might be elaborated in a sufficiently sophisticated

[64] See (1861) 1 *Zeitschrift für Rechtsgeschichte* 2 f.

[65] Cf., e.g., his address in memory of Savigny, in Windscheid (n. 49) 81 ff. On Windscheid's attitude to Savigny, see Oertmann (in his preface to Windscheid (n. 49) pp. xxvii ff.); Jakobs (n. 61) 101 ff.; Ulrich Falk, *Ein Gelehrter wie Windscheid* (1989), 174 ff.

[66] Cf., in particular, Bernhard Windscheid, 'Das römische Recht in Deutschland' (1858), in idem, *Gesammelte Reden und Abhandlungen*, ed. Paul Oertmann (1904), 46 ff. ('But nevertheless it is something great, if the foundations of a judicial decision are as accessible to the individual citizen as to the judge himself. . . . That such a state may ever be achieved, is a dream. But all ideals are dreams, and mankind should not have fewer ideals for this reason,—and as mankind in general, so also the legislator': 47 f.); or also idem, 'Die geschichtliche Schule' (n. 57) 66 ff. ('and among the German lawyers there are probably relatively few who have not, with all the strength of soul available to them, yearned for the great work of a German code of private law': 70); cf., in this context, also Falk (n. 65) 163 ff. Above all, of course, Windscheid was a member of the (first) commission for the preparation of the BGB.

[67] This was the view of the editors of the *Zeitschrift für Rechtsgeschichte*: see p. 2 of the first volume (1861). Cf. also Windscheid (n. 49) 66 f. ('Are we still historical jurists, still disciples of the Historical school?': 70).

[68] Koschaker (n. 18) 258.

manner to be perpetuated in a codification ran counter to the basic supposition of the Historical School that law develops gradually and organically; the idealization of the present is as a-historical as that of a specific epoch of the past (i.e. of classical Roman law).[69] Otto Lenel was therefore, perhaps, Savigny's truer disciple when he saw in the enactment of the BGB the dawn of a reign of the letter of the statute book. Every codification, he warned, was bound to embody imperfect and immature doctrines; it would always be 'too early'.[70] One of those imperfect doctrines in his own time, in Lenel's view, was Windscheid's 'presupposition doctrine' (*Lehre von der Voraussetzung*) which he attacked in a number of articles.[71] He was able to prevent the inclusion of this doctrine in the BGB but not the BGB itself.

[69] How Windscheid resolved this conflict for himself has been the subject of a detailed examination by Jakobs (n. 61) 101 ff. In his article 'Die geschichtliche Schule in der Rechtswissenschaft' (n. 57) Windscheid says on p. 75 f.: 'We want to have the code and also the legal achievements of the centuries: as genuinely historical jurists we will take care of that. As historical jurists we know that the code will be nothing but a moment in the development, certainly more tangible than the ripple in a stream, but still only the ripple in a stream.' Taking this as a point of departure, Jakobs regards the BGB as a 'code that does not carry the source of the law in itself; that source lies in the scholarship which has created the code. The code, therefore, does not control legal scholarship but is and will be controlled by it, as long as this scholarship is—in the full sense of the word—a historical one' (p. 160). Thus, the BGB 'does not limit legal scholarship in the formation of the [juristic] element of the law' (p. 120).

[70] See Fritz Pringsheim, 'Römisches Recht in Freiburg nach 1900', in *Aus der Geschichte der Rechts- und Staatswissenschaften zu Freiburg i.Br.*, ed. H. J. Wolff (1957), 121 f.

[71] See, in particular, 'Die Lehre von der Voraussetzung (im Hinblick auf den Entwurf eines bürgerlichen Gesetzbuches)', (1889) 74 *AcP* 213 ff.; idem, 'Nochmals die Lehre von der Voraussetzung', (1892) 79 *AcP* 49 ff. Windscheid saw the notion of a 'presupposition' as an 'undeveloped condition': one party wishes the effects of a transaction to be dependent on a certain state of affairs without, however, elevating such a presupposition, by way of express declaration, to the status of a term of the transaction. Such party may refuse to render performance, if his contractual opponent was in a position to gauge, from the circumstances of the transaction, that the presuppostion in fact formed an element of his intention. Windscheid's presupposition doctrine was, essentially, the old *clausula rebus sic stantibus* in a new cloak. For a modern analysis see Falk (n. 65) 193 ff.

IV. HISTORICAL LEGAL SCHOLARSHIP AND LEGAL HISTORY

1. Identification of the 'Pure' Roman Private Law

In spite, or possibly in view, of these problems Savigny's disciples, as far as they embarked on the study of Roman law, were much more interested in the 'certainty, with which we think and adjudicate in law',[72] i.e. in legal doctrine, than in legal history. The Historical School was thus transformed into a Pandectist School.

As far as legal history itself, particularly the study of Roman law, is concerned, this had a number of consequences. (i) It led to a neglect of constitutional law, criminal law, and all the other sources and areas of law which were regarded as irrelevant for modern legal doctrine.[73] (ii) But even in the field of private law the pandectist perspective prevented a clear recognition of the historical realities. On the one hand, of course, scholars were interested in identifying, understanding, and studying the best, i.e. classical, Roman law. On the other hand, however, modern private law doctrine required a firm and reliable basis which could only be provided by the *Corpus Iuris*. These two objects could only be reconciled by presuming the *Corpus Iuris* to contain, essentially in unchanged form, the achievements of classical jurisprudence. 'Pure' and 'unadulterated' Roman law, therefore, meant a law without the deformations and distortions inflicted by *mos gallicus* and *usus modernus*, as it presented itself in the *Corpus Iuris*. A more radical 'purification' by applying the methods of textual criticism to the Justinianic law books was not taken into consideration. This indifference to the study of interpolations was all the more remarkable[74] in view of the fact that the lawyers of the French and Dutch humanism had already embarked on textual criticism and had presented detailed studies and

[72] (1861) 1 *Zeitschrift für Rechtsgeschichte* 2.
[73] Cf., e.g., the statements by Windscheid, 'Das römische Recht' (n. 66) 35 ff.
[74] Koschaker (n. 18) 270.

research agendas.[75] Also, after all, Gaius' *Institutes*, our principal authentic source of information about classical Roman law, had been discovered in 1816 by Barthold Georg Niebuhr: by a scholar, that is, whose *Römische Geschichte* (Roman History) 'made . . . a sensation'[76] on account of its critical use of the sources.

(iii) The focus of academic interest on modern private law doctrine (which in its traditional core areas was based on Roman law) and the emergence of pandectist legal science associated with it was also bound to antagonize the so-called 'Germanists'. They did not feel sufficiently represented in Savigny's *Zeitschrift für geschichtliche Rechtswissenschaft* (Journal of Historical Legal Science) and thus created their own periodical in 1839 in the form of a *Zeitschrift für deutsches Recht und deutsche Rechtswissenschaft* (Journal of German Law and German Legal Science);[77] they organized 'Assemblies of Germanists' (*Germanistenversammlungen*) (they are regarded today as preliminary steps in the process of intellectual and political unification of Germany[78]); in the spirit of contemporary Romanticism they made the 'Germanic cultural component' the object of their research;[79] and they attempted to construct a system and a science of German Private Law:[80] an a-historical enterprise clearly inspired by the outstanding success of the pandectist agenda and described already in 1906 by Paul Laband as a 'peculiar mixture of positive and doctrinarian, antiquated and modern, specific and natural law rules'.[81]

[75] For Roman-Dutch law see, most recently, Govaert C. J. J. van den Bergh, 'Paligenesia in the Dutch Elegant School', (1997) 65 *TR* 71 ff. and the references in Robert Feenstra and Reinhard Zimmermann (eds.), *Das römisch-holländische Recht: Fortschritte des Zivilrechts im 17. und 18. Jahrhundert* (1992), 53.

[76] Wieacker (n. 1) 330.

[77] Ed. August Ludwig Reyscher and Wilhelm Eduard Wilda; on whom, see Joachim Rückert, *August Ludwig Reyschers Leben und Rechtstheorie* (1974); idem, 'Reyscher, August Ludwig', in *HRG*, vol. iv (1990), cols. 966 ff.; B.-R. Kern, 'Wilda, Wilhelm Eduard', in *HRG*, vol. v, (1998), cols. 1415 ff.

[78] Adalbert Erler, 'Germanisten', in *HRG*, vol. i (1971), col. 1583.

[79] Wieacker (n. 1) 319 ff.

[80] Ibid. 320 f.

[81] Paul Laband, 'Die Fortschritte des Rechts', 1906 *DJZ* col. 4. Cf. also H. Mitteis (n. 55) 40: 'qualified, nationally coloured Natural law'.

2. The Neglect of the More Recent History of Private Law

(iv) The separation of a Romanist and a Germanist branch of the Historical School, in turn, had a number of detrimental consequences. Thus, in particular, it contributed to the remarkable neglect of research into the historical development of private law from the Middle Ages until the age of codification. Both Romanists and Germanists tended to concentrate on topics and periods which were undoubtedly within their sphere of competency: the former on pandectist doctrine and later, since the 1880s, on ancient Roman law, the latter on the 'Germanic' law of the pre-reception era. Thus, as far as the Romanists were concerned, there was a yawning gap between Justinian's *Corpus Iuris* and the moment when 'the legal world was recreated by Savigny and his associates'.[82] The early Middle Ages were claimed by the Germanists who tended to overlook the many complex interactions between the Roman 'vulgar' law of late antiquity and the customary laws of the 'Germanic' tribes.[83] As far as the 'reception' and the subsequent legal development is concerned, however, it was obvious that it could not be tackled by either Germanists or Romanists alone.

The necessity of interdisciplinary collaboration was recognized already in 1861, on the occasion of the foundation of the *Journal of Legal History*. It was designed to reunite the *Journal of Historical Legal Science* and its younger Germanist sister, the *Journal of German Law and German Legal Science*. The editors specifically subscribed to the program-

[82] Koschaker (n. 18) 274.

[83] See, e.g., Karl Kroeschell, 'Germanisches Recht als Forschungsproblem', in *Festschrift für Hans Thieme* (1986), 7; the summary in Hans Schlosser, *Grundzüge der neueren Privatrechtsgeschichte* (8th edn., 1996), 6 ff.; and the panoramic discussion by Maurizio Lupoi, *Alle radici del mondo giuridico europeo* (1994). For exemplary studies of individual areas of the law, see Hermann Nehlsen, *Sklavenrecht zwischen Antike und Mittelalter* (1972), and Harald Siems, *Handel und Wucher im Spiegel frühmittelalterlicher Rechtsquellen* (1992). In his *History of Roman Law in the Middle Ages* Savigny had already laid the foundations for the assumption that Roman law had survived the fall of the West Roman Empire: Schröder, in Kleinheyer and Schröder (n. 15) 357.

matic statement under whose auspices Savigny had launched his journal, but they noted one difference: 'the law of the fatherland' had acquired greater significance in comparison with Roman law. Thus, it would also be the task of the new journal to investigate 'the legal relationships, the shape and evaluation of which [was] the free act of the German legal consciousness' and to trace the legal development also through periods which 'had hitherto been skipped'.[84] The *Journal of Legal History* was continued, in 1880, as *Zeitschrift der Savigny-Stiftung für Rechtsgeschichte* (Journal of the Savigny-Foundation for Legal History). The Savigny-Foundation had been set up with a specifically comparative objective in mind: it was supposed to promote scholarly work 'in the field of the law of the various nations . . . particularly studies which discuss Roman law and the various Germanic laws both as such and in their relation to each other'.[85]

The attainment of this objective was not facilitated by the fact that the journal was split into two divisions, a Romanist and a Germanist one; in 1911 a third division, devoted to Canon law, was added. To this day the journal appears in the form of three practically independent yearbooks.[86] Studies devoted to the more recent history of private law have remained, for a long time, very much the exception. For them a fourth division would have been required since the split-up into the three traditional branches of legal history simply does not make sense when it comes to tracing the history of the foundation, the *fiducia*, or the testamentory executor.[87] Strangely, therefore, the *Journal of the*

[84] (1861) 1 *Zeitschrift für Rechtsgeschichte* 4 f. Cf. also Theodor Kipp in his obituary for Emil Seckel, (1924) 44 *ZSS (RA)* p. x ('One usually jumps from pure Roman law to 19th-century pandectist doctrine').

[85] G. Bruns, 'Die Savigny-Stiftung', (1880) 1 *ZSS (RA)* pp. viii f. On the activities of this foundation until 1900, see Heinrich Brunner, 'Die Savigny-Stiftung seit 1880', (1901) 22 *ZSS (RA)* pp. v ff.

[86] For critical comment, cf. also Michael Stolleis, 'Einleitung', in idem (ed.), *Juristische Zeitgeschichte: Ein neues Fach?* (1993), 9; and see Theo Mayer-Maly, 'Resultate, Probleme und Aufgaben der rechtsgeschichtlichen Arbeit im deutschen Sprachraum', (1994) 62 *TR* 58.

[87] As to the latter, see infra pp. 160 ff.

Savigny-Foundation for Legal History perpetuates a division of academic endeavours[88] that was entirely alien to the person in whose name it is still published today: it was inherent in his concept of historical legal scholarship that *all* strands of the tradition had to be taken into account which had contributed to modern law.

That division was defensible, if at all, only as a matter of specialization concerning historical research, particularly as far as classical Roman law was concerned. This was, in fact, its purpose. For Savigny's programme had, in the meantime, been subtly changed: a *Journal of Historical Legal Science* had been turned into a *Journal of Legal History*. The destination of a historical legal science, so it appeared to many, had been achieved: with Windscheid's *Lehrbuch des Pandektenrechts* (Textbook of Pandectist Law) the mastery of private law had been perfected to such an extent as was required by a codification. All that remained to be done was to cast that textbook into statutory provisions. If, however, historical legal science had arrived at its ultimate destination, scholars were now free to turn their attention to legal history: and this time legal history as such, not one controlled by contemporary needs.[89]

V. ROMAN LAW AS LEGAL HISTORY

1. The Reconstruction of the Classical Law Texts

As far as scholarship in Roman law was concerned, the new era commenced with Otto Lenel (1849–1935, professor in

[88] In 1979 a *Zeitschrift für neuere Rechtsgeschichte* (Journal of More Recent History of Law) has started to appear. None of the five editors is a Romanist scholar. This is particularly odd in view of the fact that the establishment, after the Second World War, of the History of Private Law in the Modern Era as a new subject is largely due to the work of three great Romanists: Paul Koschaker, Franz Wieacker, and Helmut Coing.

[89] Cf. also Mayer-Maly, (1983) 100 *ZSS (RA)* 3 who emphasizes that the *Journal of the Savigny-Foundation for Legal History* had never, not even before 1900, been a mouthpiece of pandectist scholarship and that, as a result, 'private law subjects play a relatively modest role in most of its volumes before 1900'.

Kiel, Marburg, Strasbourg, and Freiburg/Br.).[90] In his *Edictum Perpetuum* (1883) he reconstructed the praetorian edict, i.e. the document that had been of central importance for the administration and development of private law in Roman antiquity. He accomplished this, essentially, on the basis of fragments from commentaries by classical jurists on the edict, as contained in the *Digest*.[91] The *Palingenesia Juris Civilis* (1889) was the sustained attempt of restoring the classical law library, as far as this is possible on the basis of the fragments that have come down to us. As Lenel himself observed, both research projects had been implicit in Savigny's programme; and he expressed his astonishment that they had been so much neglected by the Historical School.[92] These two works made Lenel the man 'who was regarded, in the whole world, as the preeminent contemporary scholar in his subject'.[93] But even if 'young academics from all European countries' flocked to his chair in Freiburg,[94] he did not found a 'school'. He did not have 'pupils' in the normal sense of the word, just as he himself had not had an academic teacher who had significantly influenced the direction of his research.[95] *Palingenesia Juris*

[90] On the life and work of Otto Lenel, see Leopold Wenger, (1935) 55 *ZSS (RA)* 55; Sinzheimer (n. 15) 121 ff.; Pringsheim (n. 70) 118 ff.; Okko Behrends, 'Otto Lenel, Positivismus im nationalen Rechtsstaat als Haltung und Methode', introduction to Otto Lenel, *Gesammelte Schriften*, vol. i (1990), pp. xiii ff.; idem, 'Das Werk Otto Lenels und die Kontinuität der romanistischen Fragestellungen: Zugleich ein Beitrag zur grundsätzlichen Überwindung der interpolationistischen Methode', (1991) 19 *Index* 169 ff.; Elmar Bund, in (1985) 14 *NDB* 204 f.

[91] This work originated in a submission to the Bavarian Academy of Letters and Sciences which had promised a prize for the best work on the topic of 'The Formulae of the Edictum Perpetuum (Hadriani): Their Wording and their Context'; the prize was awarded to Lenel in 1882: see Brunner, (1901) 22 *ZSS (RA)* p. vii.

[92] Otto Lenel, in Hans Planitz (ed.), *Die Rechtswissenschaft der Gegenwart in Selbstdarstellungen*, vol. i (1924), 140 (on the reconstruction of the edict, 'the most important achievement in the way of codification since the XII Tables') and 146 ('the idea to extend the work that I had done with regard to the commentaries on the edict to the entire tradition of classical law').

[93] Pringsheim (n. 70) 119.

[94] Ibid.

[95] As a student in Leipzig he had been particularly impressed by Karl Georg von Wächter, who 'won his heart for the law' and in whose lectures on criminal law and the Roman pledge he had 'first become conscious of the relationship between our scholarship and real life': Lenel (n. 90) 134. Significantly, Kleinheyer

Civilis and *Edictum Perpetuum* have remained to this day essential research tools: Lenel's authority was so striking that further palingenetic research appeared to be hardly worth the trouble.[96]

In the course of his studies Lenel was, of course, constantly confronted with problems of textual criticism and he was thus able 'conclusively to establish numerous interpolations that had hitherto been overlooked'.[97] But while Lenel, in the process of re-establishing the original sequence of the classical texts, was bound, more or less incidentally, to hit upon interpolations,[98] others started systematically, both from a stylistic and substantive perspective, to hunt for such changes of the classical texts on the part of the compilers. The pioneers in this respect were Fridolin Eisele (Lenel's colleague in Freiburg for four years, until he made way for Josef Partsch)[99] and Otto Gradenwitz whose book *Interpolationen in den Pandekten* (Interpolations in the Digest, 1887), in his own view, established the methodical foundations of interpolationist research.[100]

and Schröder (n. 15) 517 write on Wächter today: 'Wächter's immense reputation among his contemporaries—E. Landsberg still regards him as "one of the greatest jurists of all time"—cannot be explained alone by his writings.' On Wächter as the first president of the Deutscher Juristentag (German Lawyer's Association) see the recent evaluation by Hans-Jürgen Rabe, 'Der Deutsche Juristentag und sein erster Präsident', 1998 *NJW* 1681 ff.

96 See David Johnston, 'Lenel's Palingenesia Iuris Civilis: Four Questions and an Answer', (1997) 65 *TR* 57 ff. ('Until very recently the flame of palingenetic research on the Digest was in danger of extinction'). But see the contributions by Alan Rodger, quoted by Johnston in n. 3 of his article; Hans Ankum, 'Towards Additions to Lenel's ' "Palingenesia Iuris Civili" ', (1994) 41 *RIDA* 125 ff.

97 Lenel (n. 90) 142.

98 'Like islands from the sea the remanants of classical law emerged from Justinian's Digest': ibid.

99 On Eisele (1837–1920; at first county judge in Hechingen, later professor in Basle and Freiburg) see the obituary by Otto Lenel, (1920) 41 *ZSS (RA)* pp. v ff. and Pringsheim (n. 70) 120 f.

100 Otto Gradenwitz, in Hans Planitz (ed.), *Die Rechtswissenschaft der Gegenwart in Selbstdarstellungen*, vol. iii (1929), 87 (mentioned, in a summary of the academic achievements of his life, in the first place). Gradenwitz (1860–1935) was professor in Königsberg, Strasbourg, and (from 1909) Heidelberg. In Heidelberg he is remembered as a particularly characteristic embodiment of the whimsical features of the German professoriate (Landau (n. 19) 162). Cf. also the obituary by Paul Koschaker, (1936) 56 *ZSS (RA)* pp. ix ff.; Johannes Herrmann, 'Otto Gradenwitz',

Emil Friedberg, the great Canon lawyer,[101] mentioned in an autobiographical sketch[102] that his academic teacher Friedrich Ludwig Keller[103] in Berlin had encouraged him to write a thesis on all interpolations in the *Digest* and their significance. Koschaker relates this anecdote in order to illustrate the total neglect of textual criticism by the Historical School.[104] By 1909 the interpolationist research had reached such dimensions that the editors of the Romanist division of the *Journal of the Savigny-Foundation* called for the preparation of a list of interpolations that had been established:[105] a plan that was carried out, after many years of preparation, by Ernst Levy and Ernst Rabel in their *Index Interpolationum Quae in Iustiniani Digestis Esse Dicuntur* (3 vols., 1929–35).[106]

2. 'Imperial Law and Vulgar Law' and the Consequences

(a) Ludwig Mitteis

Of central importance for the process of historicization of Roman law was also the contribution of Ludwig Mitteis (1859–1921, professor in Prague, Vienna, and, from 1899, Leipzig).[107] It consisted, on the one hand, of his book

in *Semper Apertus: Sechshundert Jahre Ruprecht-Karls-Universität Heidelberg 1386–1986*, vol. iii (1985), 136 ff.; Max Kaser, in (1964) 6 *NDB* 702 f.

[101] Friedberg (1837–1910) prepared the edition of the *Corpus Iuris Canonici* that is still authoritative today; cf., e.g., Hans-Jürgen Becker, in *HRG*, vol. i (1961), col. 1274; Adalbert Erler, in (1961) 5 *NDB*, 443 f.; Christoph Link, 'Emil Friedberg (1837–1910): Kirchenrechtler der historischen Rechtsschule, "Staatskanonist" und Mitstreiter im Kulturkampf', in Heinrichs, Franzki, Schmalz, and Stolleis (n. 19) 283 ff.

[102] 'Autobiographie', 1909 *DJZ* col. 1014.

[103] On whom, see L. Gschwend, in Stolleis (n. 15) 344; Pio Caroni, (1994) 16 *ZNR* 246 ff.

[104] Koschaker (n. 18) 270.

[105] (1909) 30 *ZSS (RA)* pp. v ff. The editors, at that time, were E. I. Bekker and L. Mitteis.

[106] This index suffered from the drawback that 'already on the day of its publication it was outdated': Koschaker (n. 18) 271. Cf. also Max Kaser, 'Ein Jahrhundert Interpolationenforschung an den römischen Rechtsquellen', in idem, *Römische Rechtsquellen und angewandte Juristenmethode* (1986), 145.

[107] On his work and person, see the obituary by Josef Partsch, (1922) 43 *ZSS (RA)* pp. v ff.; Egon Weiss, *Erinnerung an Ludwig Mitteis* (1922); Leopold Wenger, *Ludwig Mitteis und sein Werk* (1923); Gerhard Oberkofler, *Die Vertreter des römischen Rechts mit deutscher Unterrichtssprache an der Karls-Universität Prag* (1991), 37 ff.

Reichsrecht und Volksrecht in den östlichen Provinzen des römischen Kaiserreichs (Imperial Law and Vulgar Law in the Eastern Provinces of the Roman Empire, 1891): written in 'a style enrapturing its reader' and full of the 'temperament and enthusiasm of an inspired teacher',[108] it was even at the time of its publication considered 'by the best in the field as a feat of singular significance'.[109] By focusing on, and analysing, the reality of legal life in the Eastern part of the Roman Empire, it opened up entirely new horizons of historico-comparative research. Mitteis demonstrated that even after the enactment of the *Constitutio Antoniniana* (by means of which all free inhabitants of the Empire were granted Roman citizenship) the indigenous 'vulgar' legal conceptions of, particularly, Hellenistic provenance remained alive. Thus, he shattered the traditional assumption, based on Justinian's *Corpus Iuris Civilis*, of a uniform, and uniformly Roman, legal order in Imperial Rome.[110] At the same time, he painted 'the picture of a first great reception of Roman law that occurred between the third and sixth centuries in the East of the Empire'.[111] Mitteis' research agenda, aiming at the law as it was in fact practised, required the study of sources different from those that had fed the rich stream of pandectist literature: Greek provincial literature, Hellenistic epigraphs, the Syrian-Roman Law Book, but above all the vast masses of Graeco-Egyptian papyri. Mitteis, therefore, also became one of the founders of legal papyrology;[112] his *Grundzüge und Chrestomathie der Papyrusurkunde* (Outlines and

[108] Partsch, (1922) 43 *ZSS (RA)* p. xv.

[109] Ibid., p. xvi. From a modern perspective, cf. Bund (n. 90) 736 f. ('epoch-making').

[110] In Wieacker's words, Mitteis struck questions which have, until this day, 'remained dominant chords of our discipline: Roman Imperial law and the Hellenistic-oriental vulgar laws; the intellectual contribution of Hellenism, in the garb of East Roman legal scholarship, to the transformation of classical law; and, in the background, the ultimate problem of the relationship between the characteristic features of Rome and the Greek intellect which was so much richer and more agile, and also so much more exposed to danger': (1968) 85 *ZSS (RA)* 604.

[111] Partsch, (1922) 43 *ZSS (RA)* p. xv.

[112] Cf., e.g., Max Kaser, *Das römische Privatrecht*, first part (2nd edn., 1971), 9; Franz Wieacker, *Römische Rechtsgeschichte*, first part (1988), 46 f.

Chrestomathy of the Papyrus Document, jointly with the papyrologist Ulrich Wilcken) appeared in 1912.

On the other hand, however, Mitteis's immense effect must also have been attributable to his unusual ability to inspire others for his subject and to encourage and support them in their work, to his vigour and enthusiasm, his example as a scholar, and his strong and humane personality.[113] In his famous Leipzig seminar Mitteis gathered around himself a circle of pupils unequalled as far as both their sheer number and the originality and diversity of their research interests are concerned.

(b) 'In Ludwig Mitteis' School'

Scions of the school of Ludwig Mitteis were, among others: the brilliant[114] *Josef Partsch* (1882–1925, professor in Geneva, Göttingen, Freiburg/Br., Bonn, and Berlin and during his nine years in Freiburg one of the few colleagues to be very close to Otto Lenel, in spite of their differences in age and temperament[115]), who wrote the first great monograph concerning an institution of ancient Greek law (*Griechisches Bürgschaftsrecht* [Greek Law of Suretyship], 1909), and who

113 'How he succeeded in attracting people!': Partsch, (1922) 43 *ZSS (RA)* p. xix. And see Ernst Rabel, 'In der Schule von Ludwig Mitteis', in idem, *Gesammelte Aufsätze*, ed. Hans G. Leser, vol. iii (1967), 376 ff. ('by all of us held in enthusiastic affection').

114 'Partsch . . . in the radiant vigour, the zestful and exuberant nature of his personality, used to spring one hundred ideas on those who spoke to him, of which thirty were absurd, thirty stimulating, twenty important, ten really productive, and ten strokes of genius. It was with a mixture of admiration and concern that one saw the surge of his ideas': Pringsheim (n. 70) 125.

115 On the life and work of Josef Partsch, see the obituary by Otto Lenel, (1925) 45 *ZSS (RA)* pp. v ff.; Pringsheim (n. 70) 122 ff.; Adalbert Erler, in *HRG*, vol. iii (1984), cols. 1525 ff.; Kleinheyer and Schröder (n. 15) 502; and see, for a comprehensive, recent evaluation Rudolf Meyer-Pritzl, 'Der Rechtshistoriker und Pionier der modernen Rechtsvergleichung Josef Partsch (1882–1925)', (1999) 7 *ZEuP* 47. On his relationship with Lenel Pringsheim writes (n. 70) 128: 'Already when Partsch sent Lenel his dissertation he received back the answer: "You are called to carry the torch of scholarship when it will sink from the hands of the older generation". This message came to the young beginner from the heart of a man whose scant criticism almost always remained free of passion and exaggeration. Only Josef Partsch managed, from the beginning here in Freiburg, to transform this critical attitude so completely into a feeling of affection, that no reservation was valid against him.'

later on, as representative of and adviser to the German government in the mixed arbitration tribunals established under the Treaty of Versailles, became 'the man who was to demonstrate, on the international battlefield, what a sword of legal education sharpened by Roman law was worth';[116] *Leopold Wenger* (1874–1953, professor in Graz, Vienna, Heidelberg, Munich, and, again, Vienna),[117] architect and protagonist of the idea of a universal history of antiquity incorporating the history of Roman law[118]—an idea based on the assumption that the legal systems of antiquity had achieved a synthesis in late Roman law—and author of a monumental work on *Die Quellen des römischen Rechts* (The Sources of Roman Law, 1953); *Ernst Rabel* (1874–1955, professor in Leipzig, Basle, Kiel, Göttingen, Munich, and Berlin, founder and first director of the Kaiser-Wilhelm [today: Max-Planck-] Institute for Foreign and International Private Law, 1939 emigrated to the United States),[119] a Romanist of the first rank but even more influential as the pioneer of modern comparative law in Germany (he himself attributed his functional method to the influence of Mitteis),[120] author of the first 'modern monograph of a

[116] Lenel, (1925) 45 *ZSS (RA)* p. xiv.

[117] On the life and work of Leopold Wenger, see the obituary by Max Kaser, (1954) 71 *ZSS (RA)* p. xiii; Wesener (n. 13) 79 ff.; Adalbert Erler, in *HRG*, vol. v (1998), cols. 1262 f.; Kleinheyer and Schröder (n. 15) 519. Cf. also Koschaker, *Festschrift Wenger i* (n. 14) 1 ff.

[118] 'A cultural history of antiquity, seen from the point of view of the lawyer and focusing on the state and the law': Leopold Wenger, *Der heutige Stand der römischen Rechtswissenschaft: Erreichtes und Erstrebtes* (2nd edn., 1927), 5.

[119] On the life and work of Ernst Rabel, see Wolfgang Kunkel, 'Ernst Rabel als Rechtshistoriker', in *Festschrift für Ernst Rabel*, vol. ii (1954), 1 ff.; the obituary by Hans Julius Wolff, (1956) 73 *ZSS (RA)* pp. xi ff.; Hans G. Leser, 'Introduction of the Editor', in Ernst Rabel, *Gesammelte Aufsätze*, ed. Hans G. Leser, vol. i (1965), p. xi ff.; Franz Gamillscheg, 'Ernst Rabel (1874–1955): Rechtsgeschichte und Rechtsvergleichung', in Fritz Loos (ed.), *Rechtswissenschaft in Göttingen: Göttinger Juristen aus 250 Jahrhunderten* (1987), 456 ff.; Gerhard Kegel, 'Ernst Rabel: Werk und Person', (1990) 54 *RabelsZ* 1 ff.; idem, 'Ernst Rabel (1874–1955): Vorkämpfer des Weltkaufrechts', in Heinrichs, Franzki, Schmalz, and Stolleis (n. 19) 571 ff.; Sybille Hofer, in Stolleis (n. 15) 508 f.; Kleinheyer and Schröder (n. 15) 504 f.

[120] Rabel (n. 31) 377 f. Josef Partsch had experienced a very similar extension of his interests from Roman law and the comparative legal history of antiquity to modern comparative law. Meyer-Pritzl, therefore, refers to him as a pioneer of

historical and comparative character'[121] (*Das Recht des Warenkaufs* [The Law of the Sale of Goods], 2 vols., 1936 and 1958) as well as of a standard work of modern scholarship in private international law (*The Conflict of Laws: A Comparative Study*, 4 vols., 1945–58) and one of the early exponents of the idea of a uniform private law; *Paul Koschaker* (1879–1951, professor in Innsbruck, Prague, Frankfurt am Main, Leipzig, Berlin, and Tübingen)[122] who tackled the task of a systematic exploration of the cuneiform laws and in 1911 presented the first pertinent monograph (*Babylonisch-assyrisches Bürgschaftsrecht* [Babylonian-Assyrian Law of Suretyship], 1911), but who also produced *Europa und das römische Recht* (Europe and Roman Law, 1947), 'a work unique in design and execution'[123] which established Roman law as an exponent of European culture; *Hans Peters* (1886–1915)[124] who turned his attention to East Roman school jurisprudence of late antiquity and to its contribution to the formation of the *Corpus Iuris Civilis*;[125] *Fritz Pringsheim* (1882–1967, professor in Göttingen and Freiburg/Br., from 1939 to 1946 in exile in Oxford),[126] whose studies in Greek law culminated in his monograph on *The Greek Law of Sale* (1950), and who was

modern comparative law even before Ernst Rabel and comes to the following conclusion: 'The historical significance of Partsch for the entrenchment of modern comparative scholarship in Germany is great but it is surpassed by the achievements of his successor Ernst Rabel': (1999) 7 *ZEuP* 72. On the cooperation between Partsch and Rabel in the run up to the foundation of the Kaiser-Wilhelm-Institute see Meyer-Pritzl, (1999) 7 *ZEuP* 63 f. Both in Göttingen and in Berlin Rabel succeeded to Partsch's chair.

121 Kleinheyer and Schröder (n. 15) 504.

122 On the life and work of Paul Koschaker, see Leopold Wenger, in *Festschrift Paul Koschaker*, vol. iii (1939), 1 ff.; the obituary by Karl-Heinz Below and Adam Falkenstein, (1951) 68 *ZSS (RA)* pp. ix ff.; Wesener (n. 13) 112 ff.; Gerhard Ries, in (1980) 12 *NDB* 608 f.; Kleinheyer and Schröder (n. 15) 491.

123 Max Kaser in his preface to the 4th edition (1966), p. vii.

124 He became professor in Frankfurt am Main at the age of 28 but was killed one year later in the First World War; cf. the obituary by Ludwig Mitteis, (1915) 36 *ZSS (RA)* pp. vii ff.

125 *Die oströmischen Digestenkommentare und die Entstehung der Digesten* (1913).

126 On the life and work of Fritz Pringsheim, see the obituary by Franz Wieacker, (1968) 85 *ZSS (RA)* 602 ff.; Elmar Bund, 'Fritz Pringsheim (1882–1967): Ein Großer der Romanistik', in Heinrichs, Franzki, Schmalz, and Stolleis (n. 19) 733 ff.

also particularly interested in investigating the influence of the Hellenistic spirit on Roman law in late antiquity; *Eberhard F. Bruck* (1877–1960, professor in Geneva, Breslau, Frankfurt am Main, and Bonn, 1939 emigration to the United States),[127] who saw Roman law as part of general cultural history and who set out to gain a better understanding of legal life by taking account of all the available background information in theology, and cultural and social history; *Hans Lewald*[128] and *Leo Raape*[129] who both predominantly devoted themselves to private international law;[130] *Hans Kreller* (1887–1958, professor in Münster, Tübingen, and Vienna), who was particularly attracted by Roman legal doctrine;[131] *August Simonius* (1885–1957, professor in Basle), legal historian, comparative lawyer, and also interested in modern private law;[132] *Andreas Bertalan Schwarz* (1886–1953, professor in Zurich, Freiburg/Br., and, in exile, in Istanbul), papyrologist and, at the same time, 'one of the few impartial pioneers of a *ius commune*

[127] See the obituary by Werner Flume, (1961) 78 *ZSS (RA)* 550 ff.; Horst Göppinger, *Juristen jüdischer Abstammung im Dritten Reich* (1990), 271 f.; Ernst C. Stiefel and Frank Mecklenburg, *Deutsche Juristen im amerikanischen Exil* (1991), 45; cf. also (1998) 6 *ZEuP* 1057 ff.

[128] Lewald (1883–1963, professor in Lausanne, Frankfurt am Main, Cologne, again Frankfurt am Main, Berlin, and Basle) has become known, above all, through his works *Das deutsche internationale Privatrecht auf Grundlage der Rechtsprechung* (1931) and *Règles générales des conflits des lois* (1941). Both his dissertation and his habilitation, however, were in the field of legal papyrology. On Lewald's life and work, see the obituaries by Wolfgang Kunkel, (1964) 81 *ZSS (RA)* 514 ff. and Alexander N. Makarov (1964) 28 *RabelsZ* 208 ff.; Axel Flessner, 'Hans Lewald', in Bernhard Diestelkamp and Michael Stolleis (eds.), *Juristen an der Universität Frankfurt am Main* (1989), 128 ff.; Karl-Heinz Below, in (1985) 14 *NDB* 411 f.

[129] Raape (1878–1964, professor in Halle and Hamburg) had first been influenced by Ernst Zitelmann but in 1909/10, when he was already professor in Halle, he attended Mitteis' seminar in Leipzig. In 1912, he published a study dealing with Greek pledge law. Cf. the obituary by Hans Julius Wolff, (1965) 82 *ZSS (RA)* 497 f.

[130] The combination of an interest in Roman law and private international law, of course, dates back to Savigny who in vol. viii of his *System of Contemporary Roman Law* laid the modern foundations of the latter area of study. Ernst Zitelmann provides another good example; cf. his autobiography, in Planitz (n. 92) 196 ff.

[131] See the obituary by Max Kaser, (1958) 75 *ZSS (RA)* pp. xv ff.

[132] See the obituary by Johannes G. Fuchs, (1958) 75 *ZSS (RA)* 513 ff.

europaeum';[133] the papyrologist *Rafael Taubenschlag* (1881–1958, professor in Cracow, in 1939 emigration first to France, later to the United States, after the war professor in Warsaw);[134] *Egon Weiß* (1880–1953, professor in Prague, 1938 removed from his office),[135] scholar in ancient Greek law; and *Demetrios Pappoulias* (1878–1932),[136] who emphasized the continuity of Greek legal development from antiquity to the present day and who attempted to explain Greek private law under the auspices of its historical evolution. Moreover, Mitteis was closely associated with *Moritz Wlassak* (1854–1939, professor in Czernowitz, Graz, Breslau, Strasbourg, and Vienna; he brought the historico-critical approach to bear upon the study of Roman civil procedure);[137] Mitteis and Wlassak had both studied under *Adolf Exner* (1841–1894, professor in Zurich and Vienna; Exner in turn was a pupil of *Joseph Unger* who survived him by close to twenty years).[138]

(c) The Generation of the Academic Grandsons

It is remarkable, moreover, how many famous scholars of Roman law of around the middle of this century and how many contemporary professors of Roman law can trace their academic ancestry back to Mitteis. Among them are *Hans Julius Wolff* (through Partsch and Rabel), *Mariano San*

133 Wieacker, (1954) 71 *ZSS (RA)* 591 ff.; the quotation is on p. 605. Apart from legal papyrology, Schwarz was particularly interested in the history of the *ius commune* in conjunction with comparative law. Cf. also Landau (n. 19) 165.

134 See the obituaries by Johannes Herrmann, (1959) 76 *ZSS (RA)* 682 ff. and Henryk Kupiszewski, (1985) 88 *BIDR* 103 ff.; Göppinger (n. 127) 363.

135 On the life and work (in particular: *Das griechische Privatrecht auf rechtsvergleichender Grundlage* [Greek Private Law on a Comparative Basis], vol. i, (1923) of Egon Weiß, see (1953) 70 *ZSS (RA)* 518 ff.; cf. also Landau (n. 19) 163.

136 Chr. Argyriadis, in Stolleis (n. 15) 474 f.

137 See the obituary by Leopold Wenger, (1940) 60 *ZSS (RA)* pp. ix ff.; Wesener (n. 13) 60 ff.

138 On Exner, see Hans Hoyer, 'Adolf Exner', in Brauneder (n. 15) 205 ff.; Oberkofler (n. 107) 29 ff. Both Unger and L. Mitteis have written obituaries; they are referred to by Hoyer, p. 318. Particularly interesting, in the present context, is Exner's inaugural lecture in Zurich on the topic *Die praktischen Aufgaben der romanistischen Wissenschaft in Staaten mit kodifiziertem Privatrecht* (The Practical Task of Roman Law Scholarship in Countries with a Codified Private Law, (1869).

Nicolò and *Artur Steinwenter* (through Wenger), *Julius G. Lautner* (through Koschaker),[139] *Max Kaser* (through Steinwenter and Wenger), *Wilhelm Felgentraeger* (through Pringsheim), *Franz Wieacker* (through Pringsheim and Partsch), *Theo Mayer-Maly* (through Kreller), and (through Rabel) most modern representatives of the disciplines of comparative law and private international law.[140] *Wolff* provided the decisive impulses for modern scholarship in ancient Greek law;[141] *Wieacker* reconstructed, as far as that is possible, the history of the Roman law library from the classical period down to the days of the Justinianic compilers (*Textstufen klassischer Juristen* [Stages in the Textual History of the Writings of Classical Roman Lawyers], 1960), he wrote the standard work on the sources, legal development, legal theory, and legal literature of Roman antiquity (*Römische Rechtsgeschichte* [Roman Legal History], first part, 1988; the work has remained incomplete), and he provided in his *Privatrechtsgeschichte der Neuzeit* (History of Private Law in Europe, 1st edn., 1952; 2nd edn., 1967), the first and, so far, unsurpassed treatise analysing and, at the same time, helping to establish what was then essentially still a new subject;[142] and *Max Kaser* managed to provide a restatement of the entire Roman private law and legal procedure in its development from the archaic down to the post-classical

[139] Lautner (1896–1972) was from 1930 until his retirement in 1967 professor at the University of Zurich. He had studied in Graz and had prepared his habilitation (at the University of Graz) during a one-year sojourn in Leipzig. He was not only a pupil of Koschaker (his habilitation dealt with the Babylonian law of procedure), but also still directly of L. Mitteis. In his posthumous work, quoted above (n. 18), Lautner emphasizes, just like Koschaker, the relevance of Roman law for European legal culture. On Lautner, see the obituary by Max Kaser, (1972) 89 *ZSS (RA)* 518 ff.; Wesener (n. 13) 102 ff.

[140] Among Rabel's assistents and collaborators at his institute in Berlin were Max Rheinstein, Friedrich Keßler, Ernst von Caemmerer, Gerhard Kegel, Wilhelm Wengler, Konrad Duden, Eduard Wahl, Walter Hallstein, Ludwig Raiser, and Arwed Blomeyer.

[141] Gerhard Thür, (1984) 101 *ZSS (RA)* 476 ff.

[142] See, above all, the memorial speech by Joseph Georg Wolf, 'In Memoriam Franz Wieacker', *Göttinger Universitätsreden* 90 (1995), 17 ff. and Okko Behrends, (1995) 112 *ZSS (RA)* pp. xiii ff.; Joachim Rückert, 'Geschichte des Privatrechts als Apologie des Juristen: Franz Wieacker zum Gedächtnis', (1995) 24 *Quaderni Fiorentini* 531 ff.

period that is unmatched in both its sweep and precision and that must be regarded as authoritative for our time.[143]

3. Emil Seckel and his Pupils

The only other scholar whose long-term influence may possibly be compared to that of Ludwig Mitteis is *Emil Seckel*. Seckel (1864–1924, professor in Berlin)[144] is well known today to Roman lawyers by virtue of his revision of H. Heumann's *Handlexikon zu den Quellen des römischen Rechts* (Dictionary on the Sources of Roman Law [1907; today the 10th edn., 1958, is used]). To private law scholarship he contributed 'one of the most brilliant studies of which modern private law doctrine can boast'.[145] Above all, however, and in his own time, he was regarded as the pre-eminent expert in medieval law. He was one of the first to see that 'the *ius commune* of the 19th century, fatally re-approximated to Justinian's law, had been thoroughly worked through' and that, therefore, a particularly important task for contemporary legal historians consisted in exploring 'the history of the *ius commune* in its continuous

[143] See the assessments by Rolf Knütel, 'Max Kaser (21.4.1906–13.1.1997)', (1998) 115 *ZSS (RA)* pp. xv ff.; Felix Wubbe, 'Bei Max Kaser in Münster', (1998) 115 *ZSS (RA)* 2 ff.; Götz Landwehr, 'Max Kaser in Hamburg 1959–1971', (1998) 115 *ZSS (RA)* 10 ff.; Luigi Labruna, 'Allievi stranieri di Max Kaser', (1998) 115 *ZSS (RA)* 22 ff.

It is also interesting to see the extent to which the *Savigny-Zeitschrift, Romanistische Abteilung*, was carried by the 'Mitteis-school'. Ludwig Mitteis was among the editors from vol. 22 (1901) to vol. 42 (1921), after him Josef Partsch from vol. 43 (1922) to vol. 45 (1925), Ernst Rabel from vol. 46 (1926) to vol. 54 (1934), Leopold Wenger from vol. 54 (1934) to vol. 55 (1935) and from vol. 59 (1939) to vol. 64 (1944), Hans Kreller from vol. 54 (1934) to vol. 64 (1944) and Paul Koschaker from vol. 56 (1936) to vol. 64 (1944). After the war, Ludwig Mitteis' son, the Germanist Heinrich Mitteis, undertook the sole editorship of all three divisions of the journal.

[144] On the life and work of Emil Seckel, see the obituary by Erich Genzmer, (1926) 46 *ZSS (RA)* 216 ff.; Gero Dolezalek, in *HRG*, vol. iv, col. 1588 f.; Kleinheyer and Schröder (n. 15) 509 f. The following two sentences are very largely taken from Kleinheyer and Schröder.

[145] Hans Dölle, 'Juristische Entdeckungen', in *Verhandlungen des 42. Deutschen Juristentages*, vol. ii (1959), B 11. The study referred to is Emil Seckel, 'Die Gestaltungsrechte des bürgerlichen Rechts', in *Festgabe der juristischen Gesellschaft zu Berlin für Richard Koch* (1903), 205 ff.

development from Justinian to the BGB'.[146] In view of the great difficulties and the enormous scope of this task Seckel's pupil *Erich Genzmer* proposed the setting up of a research institute[147] which was eventually founded by Genzmer's pupil *Helmut Coing* (Max-Planck-Institute for European Legal History). Through his institute, Coing was able to arrange the publication of a comprehensive reference work on the sources and literature on the history of European private law (*Handbuch der Quellen und Literatur der neueren europäischen Privatrechtsgeschichte* (8 vols., so far incomplete)); and in his treatise on *Europäisches Privatrecht* (European Private Law, 2 vols., 1985, 1989) he gave the first comprehensive overview of the history of private law doctrine. Another of Seckel's prominent pupils, *Fritz Schulz*, concentrated on modern legal doctrine (he 'discovered' the enrichment action based on an encroachment [*Eingriffskondiktion*][148]) and classical Roman law. Schulz (1879–1957, professor in Innsbruck, Kiel, Göttingen, Bonn, and Berlin, from 1939 in exile in Oxford)[149] wrote the first history of Roman legal science and established the hypothesis (subsequently further developed by Wieacker) of pre-Justinianic

[146] Genzmer, (1926) 46 *ZSS (RA)* 244. 'Seckel had absorbed the basic truths of the Historical School but had steered clear of its biases and exaggerations. He knew that Savigny's "misunderstandings of the more recent writers" had in reality been the most valuable achievements of the Medieval jurists and those of the usus modernus' (p. 244); he realized that 'Roman law, Canon law and Germanic law in the Middle Ages are interwoven so thorougly that their study cannot, without detriment, be separated. Thus, the Romanist also became a Canonist and a meticulous expert of Germanic law' (p. 222). 'Seckel was, ultimately, thinking of the formation of a thorough history of the *ius commune* which, indeed, we very urgently require' (Kipp, (1924) 44 *ZSS (RA)* p. x).

[147] See Genzmer, (1926) 46 *ZSS (RA)* 221 f. Genzmer (1893–1970) was professor in Königsberg, Frankfurt am Main, and Hamburg; cf. the biographical account by Helmut Coing, 'Erich Genzmer', in Diestelkamp and Stolleis (n. 128) 200 ff. (p. 205: Genzmer has 'taken the crucial first steps towards founding the Max-Planck-Institute for European Legal History').

[148] 'System der Rechte auf den Eingriffserwerb', (1909) 105 *AcP* 1–488.

[149] On the life and work of Fritz Schulz, see the obituary by Werner Flume, (1958) 75 *ZSS (RA)* 496 ff.; Kleinheyer and Schröder (n. 15) 509. Cf. also Landau (n. 19) 165; Wolfgang Ernst, 'Preface', in Fritz Schulz, *Classical Roman Law* (reprint 1992), 5* ff.

interference with the classical legal writings (in early post-classical West Roman literature). Also a pupil of Seckel was *Ernst Levy* (1881–1968, professor in Frankfurt am Main, Freiburg/Br., and Heidelberg, 1936 emigration to the United States).[150] He, essentially, did for West Roman law what Mitteis had done for the East Roman provinces: he discovered a 'vulgar' law which had evolved in the post-classical period, largely independent of the developments in the East.[151] Thus, he opened up 'a previously unknown world'[152] between Roman law of antiquity and medieval 'Germanic' law, i.e. at the intersection between the areas of scholarship in Roman law and Germanic legal history.[153] Levy's pupil *Wolfgang Kunkel*,[154] examined the *Herkunft und soziale Stellung der römischen Juristen* (Origin and Social Status of Roman Lawyers, 1952; 2nd edn., 1967) and turned his attention to Roman criminal and constitutional law. Both areas had, so far, still been dominated by Theodor Mommsen's work which, in turn, was characterized by the systematic approach of nineteenth-century vintage.[155] In Emil Seckel's case, too, it is remarkable how many contemporary legal historians belong to his academic descendants, among them particularly the pupils of Kunkel, Coing, and Werner Flume.

150 On the life and work of Ernst Levy, see the obituary by Wolfgang Kunkel, (1969) 86 *ZSS (RA)* pp. xiii ff.; Adalbert Erler, in *HRG*, vol. ii (1978), cols. 1877 ff.; Karlheinz Misera and Ralph Backhaus, 'Ernst Levy und das Vulgarrecht', in *Semper Apertus: Sechshundert Jahre Ruprecht-Karls-Universität Heidelberg 1386–1986*, vol. iii (1985), 186 ff.; Dietrich V. Simon, in (1985) 14 *NDB* 403 f.; Dieter Simon, 'Ernst Levy', in Diestelkamp and Stolleis (n. 128) 94 ff.; Kleinheyer and Schröder (n. 15) 494.

151 See, in particular, Ernst Levy, 'Westen und Osten in der nachklassischen Entwicklung des römischen Rechts', (1929) 49 *ZSS (RA)* 230 ff.

152 Landau (n. 19) 164.

153 Thus, e.g., he enabled Max Kaser to write the second volume of his handbook.

154 On the life and work of Wolfgang Kunkel (1902–81, professor in Leipzig, Freiburg/Br., Göttingen, Bonn, Heidelberg, and Munich) see the obituary by Helmut Coing, (1981) 98 *ZSS (RA)* pp. iii ff.; Dieter Nörr, 'Wolfgang Kunkel', in *Gedächtnisschrift für Wolfgang Kunkel* (1984), 9 ff.; Kleinheyer and Schröder (n. 15) 491.

155 See, e.g., Wieacker (n. 1) 332 who refers to 'the fatal effects of legal formalism on this prince of philologists'.

4. Balance Sheet

Even these few intimations provide an impression of how far and in how many respects our perception of the ancient legal world has been enhanced over the past 120 years. Of course, not every new hypothesis has stood the test of time. This is particularly obvious in the area of interpolationist research. Entire volumes of the *Journal of the Savigny-Foundation* were dominated by endless lists of supposedly unclassical phrases and expressions;[156] and several authors turned the rules of Roman law upside down in their desire 'to reconstruct the outlines of classical law in their admirable simplicity and consistency . . . and to wipe out, once and for all, (the) blot(s) on the badge of honour of those great and unrivalled masters'.[157] Today, under the influence mainly of Max Kaser, a much more conservative attitude prevails.[158]

Similar observations may be made as far as other approaches are concerned. Thus, modern scholars tend to stress, once again, Justinian's classicism as a cultural counterbalance to the Hellenization of Roman law in the East;[159] radical theories according to which the *Digest* is based on a

[156] See, in particular, the contributions by Gerhard Beseler in vols. 43 (1922) to 50 (1930).

[157] Franz Haymann, 'Textkritische Studien zum römischen Obligationenrecht, Periculum est Emptoris', (1920) 41 *ZSS (RA)* 48 f. On Haymann, see the obituary by Hermann Nolte, (1950) 67 *ZSS (RA)* 615 ff.; on the specific problem to which the quotation relates, see, most recently, Martin Bauer, *Periculum Emptoris: Eine dogmengeschichtliche Untersuchung zur Gefahrtragung beim Kauf* (1998); and see infra, pp. 119 ff.

[158] Cf., in particular, Max Kaser, 'Zum heutigen Stand der Interpolationenforschung', (1952) 69 *ZSS (RA)* 60 ff.; idem, 'Zur Glaubwürdigkeit der römischen Rechtsquellen', in *Atti del II Congresso Internazionale della Società Italiana per la Storia del Diritto* 1 (1971), 291 ff. and the overview 'Ein Jahrhundert Interpolationenforschung an den römischen Rechtsquellen', in Max Kaser, *Römische Rechtsquellen und angewandte Juristenmethode* (1986), 112 ff.; and see now the analysis by Rolf Knütel, '"Nicht leichter, aber umso reizvoller"', (1998) 115 *ZSS (RA)* 33 ff.; cf. also Franz Wieacker, 'Zur gegenwärtigen Lage der romanistischen Textkritik', in *Atti del II Congresso Internazionale della Società Italiana per la Storia del Diritto* 2 (1971), 1099 ff.; and now also idem (n. 112) 17 ff. Cf. also already Paul Kretschmar, 'Kritik der Interpolationenkritik', (1939) 59 *ZSS (RA)* 102 ff.

[159] Max Kaser, *Das römische Privatrecht*, second part (2nd edn., 1975), 26 f., 32 ff.; Wieacker (n. 1) 50 f.

private compilation before Justinian are generally rejected;[160] Greek philosophy has, according to modern research, influenced Roman law since the days of the Republic already, i.e. at the heyday of Hellenism;[161] Leopold Wenger's conception of a universal history of law in the ancient world has never gained much support;[162] and Wlassak's theories about the *legis actiones* and the formulary procedure as being, essentially, determined by the litigants themselves (theories which he 'defended throughout his career tenaciously and not without exaggerations'[163]) had to give way to a view which places more emphasis on the authority of the judicial magistrate, the *praetor*. The flood of new papyri, too, has in the meantime dried up. Much remains disputed or unclear;[164] none the less, the advance in our knowledge is so significant that it is quite justified to refer to a 'second age of discovery of legal history in antiquity'.[165] And even as far as the history of the *ius commune* is concerned we have now, though with considerable delay, advanced beyond the history of the legal literature and the learned lawyers.[166] The history of private law in modern times (*Privatrechtsgeschichte der Neuzeit*), created as a new discipline in the 1930s, has firmly established itself.[167] Franz

160 See already Mitteis, (1915) 36 *ZSS (RA)* p. x.

161 Wieacker (n. 1) 51 f., 618 ff., 639 ff.; cf. also the overview provided by Martin Josef Schermaier, *Materia: Beiträge zur Frage der Naturphilosophie im klassischen römischen Recht* (1992) 35 ff.

162 Kaser (n. 159) 9 f.; Wieacker (n. 1) 11 f.

163 Max Kaser and Karl Hackl, *Das römische Zivilprozeßrecht* (2nd edn., 1996), 18, cf. also 291 f.; and see Wieacker (n. 1) 52 with further references.

164 On the discussion about vulgar law, provoked by Levy, see Misera and Backhaus (n. 150) 206 ff.; for critical discussion of the concept of a 'vulgarization' of West Roman law see, from the point of view of research into individual topics of private law, Carlo Augusto Cannata, *'Possessio', 'Possessor', 'possidere' nelle fonte giuridiche del basso impero romano* (1962); Wulf Eckart Voß, *Recht und Rhetorik in den Kaisergesetzen der Spätantike* (1983); and see Dietrich V. Simon, *Konstantinisches Kaiserrecht* (1977); Misera and Backhaus (n. 150) 204 ff.

165 Wieacker (n. 1) 332.

166 This is the expression used by Genzmer, (1926) 46 *ZSS (RA)* 247 for 19th-century research.

167 See Diethelm Klippel, 'Entstehung und heutige Aufgabe der "Privatrechtsgeschichte der Neuzeit" ', in *Wege europäischer Rechtsgeschichte: Festschrift für Karl Kroeschell* (1987), 145 ff.

Wieacker provided the authoritative account of the history of private law scholarship, i.e. of the ways in which private lawyers conceived of their subject and how these thought patterns changed over the centuries;[168] and a first sustained attempt has been made, within the parameters set by Wieacker, to sketch the development of private law legal doctrine.[169] Much, however, remains to be done to fill in the details of this picture.[170]

5. Advancement of Legal Training under the Austrian Monarchy

It is, incidentally, remarkable to see how much Austrian scholars have done to advance our knowledge, particularly in the field of the legal history of antiquity: among them, as far as the Mitteis school is concerned, Wenger, Koschaker, Rabel, Lautner, and Steinwenter. Wlassak and Kaser may also be mentioned. Mitteis himself was Austrian, although he exercised his greatest influence as professor in Leipzig after 1899.[171] Specifically important, in this context, was the tradition of the travel scholarships awarded until the fall of the monarchy by the Austrian department of education for 'further study with famous scholars in Germany'. A number of subsequently famous legal historians benefited from these scholarships: Wenger,[172] Koschaker,[173] Wlassak,[174] Weiß,[175] and Steinwenter[176] were among

[168] See supra p. 32. Two years after the publication of Wieacker's *Privatrechtsgeschichte der Neuzeit* the *Forschungen zur neueren Privatrechtsgeschichte* (Studies on the More Recent History of Private Law) were founded (ed. Franz Beyerle and Wolfgang Kunkel, in collaboration with H. Coing, E. Molitor, H. Thieme, and F. Wieacker).

[169] See supra p. 34.

[170] See, e.g., the references in (1996) 112 *LQR* 599 f.

[171] The same is true of Mitteis's faculty colleague, the private law professor Emil Strohal. On Strohal, see the references above n. 25.

[172] (1954) 71 *ZSS (RA)* p. xiv.

[173] Wesener (n. 13) 112; cf. also (1951) 68 *ZSS (RA)* p. ix.

[174] (1940) 60 *ZSS (RA)* p. xi.

[175] (1953) 70 *ZSS (RA)* 518.

[176] Wesener (n. 13) 90. Steinwenter (1888–1959) used his scholarship to study with Leopold Wenger in Munich and subsequently became professor in Graz. For details, see Kaser, (1959) 76 *ZSS (RA)* 670 ff.; Wesener (n. 13) 89 ff.

them[177] and also, for instance, Mariano San Nicolò,[178] Adolf Berger,[179] Gustav Hanausek,[180] and Ernst Schönbauer.[181] If Joseph Unger had set out to 'channel the rich stream of German legal science onto the fallow lands of Austrian jurisprudence',[182] his academic grandson, with his school, was now able to stimulate legal history and comparative law in Germany.

6. Parallel Developments in Germanic Legal History

Remarkable, too, is the fact that the study of German(ic) legal history was similarly historicized.[183] Specifically significant was the inaugural lecture delivered in Freiburg in 1875 by Karl von Amira under the title *Ueber Zweck und Mittel in der germanischen Rechtsgeschichte* (On Means and Purpose in Germanic Legal History). In this lecture Amira deplored the fact that even 'scholars who feel the warmest sympathy for everything that is historical completely smash to pieces the history of German law for the sake of a consistent modern legal doctrine'.[184] He advocated the

[177] Mitteis himself had gone, 'according to the good Austrian tradition', to Leipzig (1922) 43 *ZSS (RA)* p. ix.

[178] (1955) 72 *ZSS (RA)* 494. Mariano San Nicolò (1887–1955) was professor in Prague and Munich (as successor to Leopold Wenger). His main areas of interest were the cuneiform laws; cf. A. Steinwenter and A. Falkenstein, (1955) 72 *ZSS (RA)* 493 ff.; Wesener (n. 13) 116 ff. On his National Socialistic attitude and his anti-semitism, see Maximilian Fuchs, 'Die Prager Rechtsfakultät in Geschichte und Gegenwart (1348–1998)', (1998) 40 *WGO Monatshefte für osteuropäisches Recht* 178.

[179] (1962) 79 *ZSS (RA)* 526. Adolf Berger (1882–1962) hailed from Lemberg where he also started to study. He used his scholarship to go to Berlin. Eventually, he did not follow an academic career, however, but worked in the Polish embassy in Vienna. After the annexation of Austria in 1938, he emigrated, first to France and later to the United States. Berger is known today, above all, as the author of the *Encyclopedic Dictionary of Roman Law* (1953). See the evaluation by Max Kaser, (1962) 79 *ZSS (RA)* 526 ff.

[180] Wesener (n. 13) 99. Hanausek (1855–1927) studied in Vienna (i.a. with Adolf Exner), Berlin, and Göttingen and became professor in Graz; for details, see Wesener (n. 13) 98 ff.

[181] (1967) 84 *ZSS (RA)* 627. Schönbauer (1885–1966) was awarded the scholarship in 1917 and went, as Berger did, to Berlin.

[182] Quotation according to Schröder, in Kleinheyer and Schröder (n. 15) 432.

[183] Cf., e.g., Wieacker (n. 1) 334 ff.

[184] Karl von Amira, *Ueber Zweck und Mittel der germanischen Rechtsgeschichte* (1876), 8.

methodical affiliation of legal history with historical studies in general and the discharge of German legal history from its position as handmaiden of legal doctrine: 'The recounting of what was once law . . . does not only lead to the doctrine that constitutes the law today'.[185] Scholars in German legal history were no longer inclined to adopt the agenda of the Romanists, geared as it was to modern legal doctrine: they, in turn, now set an enlightened methodological example for the Romanists who had also suddenly become interested in the reality of 'what had once been law'.

VI. UNHISTORICAL LEGAL SCHOLARSHIP AND LEGAL HISTORY

1. *Tabula Rasa*

This very pronounced historicization of legal history, the neo-humanistic turn with all its magnificent discoveries, was bought at a cost. For legal scholarship (*Rechtswissenschaft*) ceased to be a historical scholarship. By the time the BGB was adopted and promulgated in the course of the summer of 1896 an unprecedented avalanche of legal literature had started to sweep down on the German legal fraternity.[186] The first textbooks[187] and commentaries[188] appeared as early as 1897, three years before the BGB entered into effect. In 1899 the librarian of the Imperial Court, Georg Maas, published a bibliography of 324 pages

[185] von Amira (n. 184) 61. See also the analysis by Hans Thieme, 'Die germanistische Rechtsgeschichte in Freiburg', in *Aus der Geschichte der Rechts- und Staatswissenschaften zu Freiburg i.Br.*, ed. Hans Julius Wolff (1957), 131 ff. and the contributions to Peter Landau, Hermann Nehlsen, and Mathias Schmoeckel (eds.), *Karl von Amira zum Gedächtnis* (1999).

[186] See Laband, 1906 *DJZ* cols. 2 f. ('abounding literature in the field of private law . . . which has poured down with the suddenness and the violence of a cloudburst').

[187] For details, see Sibylle Hofer, 'Haarspalten, Wortklauben, Silbenstechen? 100 Jahre Lehrbücher zum BGB: Eine Lebensbilanz', 1999 *JuS* 112 ff.

[188] For details, see Heinz Mohnhaupt, 'Die Kommentare zum BGB als Reflex der Rechtsprechung (1897–1914)', in Ulrich Falk and Heinz Mohnhaupt (eds.), *Das Bürgerliche Gesetzbuch und seine Richter: Fallstudien zur Reaktion der Rechtspraxis auf die Kodifikation des deutschen Privatrechts (1896–1914)*, in preparation.

containing about 4,000 titles.[189] Very largely, however, this literature was purely exegetic in character;[190] the words and concepts used in the Code provided the authoritative points of reference. Many authors hardly went beyond paraphrasing the text of the statutory provisions. They waited to see how the Code would be applied in practice;[191] and as the century advanced and the courts handed down an ever increasing number of decisions, they integrated the case law into the new editions of their works. Thus, the letters of the Code were gradually filled with life; but, at least in theory, it was a new and youthful life. Since the Code was supposed to be comprehensive,[192] it provided an autonomous interpretational space. Thus, as Koschaker wrote in 1947, 'the recollection of pandectist scholarship, one of the supreme achievements of the German legal mind, faded remarkably quickly in both doctrine and practice of German private law. Whatever monograph, textbook or commentary written within the past thirty years on the BGB one chooses to open, one will hardly ever find the names of the great pandectists, of Savigny, Puchta, Jhering, Dernburg, Windscheid and others mentioned'.[193] In a way, this is the continental variation of a typically common law maxim: the law of a country is to be found in the last thirty years of its law reports.[194]

Considerable discussion was devoted to the question to what extent the *travaux préparatoires* of the various commissions and individuals involved in the drafting of the Code could be, or would have to be, consulted in order to establish

[189] See Mohnhaupt (n. 188) n. 2.

[190] For early criticism, see Kuhlenbeck (n. 196) p. vii; and see Mohnhaupt (n. 188) sub I.

[191] See the characteristic remarks in (1900) 29 *JW* 4 (under the heading: The Most Recent Private Law Literature).

[192] See, e.g., Heinz Hübner, *Kodifikation und Entscheidungsfreiheit des Richters in der Geschichte des Privatrechts* (1980), 67. For certain qualifications of this view, see Zimmermann (n. 37) 12 ff.

[193] Koschaker (n. 18) 190.

[194] This was the view expressed by 'Proculus Redivivus' in a famous South African controversy: 'South African Law at the Crossroads, or What is Our Common Law', (1965) 82 *SALJ* 24.

the true meaning of a legal rule; or whether they even had authoritative status.[195] (This was a new question insofar as it had never arisen with regard to the *Corpus Iuris Civilis*). Courts and legal writers tended to attribute substantial weight to these materials as is apparent, for instance, from repeated warnings not to become too absorbed with the 'paper trash' left behind by the draftsmen of the Code.[196] As a result, the scope of the 'historical' argument, one of the four elements traditionally used in the process of interpreting the law,[197] was significantly reduced: 'history' was taken to be more or less equivalent to the origin of the specific rule under consideration, as it could be established in the deliberations of its draftsmen. There was little inclination to go back further and to investigate the broader historical context or to explore the law that had prevailed before the BGB.[198] The Code was widely regarded as *the* turning point in German legal history,[199] a boundary between the new and the old law. Few academics, and even fewer practitioners, continued to be aware of the 'vital connection which ties the past to the present'.[200]

[195] See Thomas Honsell, *Historische Argumente im Zivilrecht: Ihr Gebrauch und ihre Wertschätzung im Wandel unseres Jahrhunderts* (1982), 47 ff.

[196] Ludwig Kuhlenbeck, *Von den Pandekten zum Bürgerlichen Gesetzbuch: Eine dogmatische Einführung in das Studium des Bürgerlichen Rechts*, first part (1898), p. vii. Cf. also Thomas Finkenauer, 'Das entstehungsgeschichtliche Argument als Etikettenschwindel: Zwei Beispiele aus der Rechtsprechung des Reichsgerichts zum Bereicherungsrecht', in Falk and Mohnhaupt (n. 188) sub III. 2.

[197] See Karl Larenz and Claus-Wilhelm Canaris, *Methodenlehre der Rechtswissenschaft* (3rd edn., 1995), 149 ff.; on which see Klippel (n. 29) 28 ff. But cf. also Robert Alexy, *Theorie der juristischen Argumentation* (3rd edn, 1996), 294; Robert Alexy and Ralf Dreier, 'Statutory Interpretation in the Federal Republic of Germany', in D. Neil MacCormick and Robert S. Summers (eds.), *Interpreting Statutes: A Comparative Study* (1991), 87 f. drawing a distinction between historical and genetic interpretation. Cf. also (1997) 56 *CLJ* 320.

[198] For the contemporary discussion, see Th. Honsell (n. 195) 60 ff. See, e.g., the critical remark (obviously inspired by Jhering) by Kuhlenbeck (n. 196) IV: 'One has advanced beyond Roman law but appears to be all too inclined . . . to forget about the fact that the path has led through Roman law.'

[199] This was, for instance, the view of one of the most influential early commentators of the BGB, the Imperial Court judge A. Achilles; see Mohnhaupt (n. 188) text to n. 42 with references.

[200] Savigny (n. 46) p. xv.

2. Ptolemaios Philadelphos

Partly responsible for this development were the state and style of the literature in legal history. That literature was no longer likely to be regarded as relevant by a modern private lawyer;[201] usually he did not even notice it. As far as scholarship in Roman law was concerned, Paul Koschaker commented: 'Whoever pages through the German literature on Roman law produced from around 1900 until the outbreak of the First World War, could all but gain the impression that it was more important for the German Romanist to know about the tax laws of Ptolemaios Philadelphos and the court structure in Egypt at the time of Ptolemaios Euergetes than to be familiar with the *Corpus Iuris*'.[202] Whoever was about to set out to explore the niceties of the claims for compensation for improvements under the BGB could hardly hope for much inspiration from that kind of research. And concerning studies in the history of German law, Gustav Radbruch remarked: 'The old Empire decays, as an old castle decays, it is slowly covered by ivy and becomes increasingly picturesque, increasingly poetical with its hollow windows and its cracked turrets, but also increasingly unsuitable to be inhabited; and it is this ideal that the historical school (which may also be called the Romantic one) admires, full of profound emotions'.[203] Obviously the 'predilection for antiquity' had won the day, the very attitude which, as Savigny had emphasized, was completely different from

201 For a clear manifestation of this attitude see, e.g., the preface to Justus Wilhelm Hedemann, *Die Fortschritte des Zivilrechts im 19. Jahrhundert*, first part (1910). On Hedemann, see Heinz Mohnhaupt, 'Justus Wilhelm Hedemann als Rechtshistoriker und Zivilrechtler vor und während der Epoche des Nationalsozialismus', in Michael Stolleis and Dieter Simon (eds.), *Rechtsgeschichte des Nationalsozialismus: Beiträge zur Geschichte einer Disziplin* (1989), 107 ff.

202 Koschaker (n. 18) 303, 310 ('esotericism'). Cf. also Lautner (n. 18) 147 f. and the remarks in (1995) 16 *JLH* 21 ff. Zwalve, (1997) 5 *ZEuP* 398, refers to the 'quest for the tombs of the pre-Adamite kings' and asks: 'how many modern legal historians still are really lawyers at heart?' (p. 399 n. 15).

203 Gustav Radbruch, *Einführung in die Rechtswissenschaft* (1910), 20. The term 'historical school', in this context, obviously does not refer to Savigny's Historical School but to contemporary legal history.

and was not to be confused with a historical perception of the law.[204]

3. A Sense of Crisis

In the curriculum of the law faculties, as has been mentioned,[205] the BGB immediately acquired the central position whereas Roman law was reduced to a propaedeutic role. But it was only a matter of time until it was questioned why a student should be introduced to modern private law through Roman law if he could spend his time equally well, and possibly better, studying modern private law itself.[206] Thus, Roman law gradually vanished from the intellectual horizon of the students of law. For very few of them were ready, voluntarily and 'without any extraneous thoughts . . . to immerse themselves in the contemplation of the grandeur and beauty' of Roman law; and the Roman law professors, no longer high priests of scholarship conjuring up the legal spirit of the nation,[207] were faced with the bitter experience that Bernhard Windscheid's noble vision ('When the authority of the *Corpus Iuris* is cast aside in Germany, then, for the first time, the lecture halls of the teachers of Roman law shall truly fill; and the rising generations shall sit at their feet, to learn . . . what beauty is'[208]) would not come true. The position of legal history within the law faculties was steadily weakened until one started to doubt its rightful place within those faculties.[209] Essentially, it was argued, legal history is a part of general social history and should therefore have its place in the faculties of

[204] Friedrich Carl von Savigny, 'Stimmen für und wider neue Gesetzbücher', (1817) 3 *Zeitschrift für geschichtliche Rechtswissenschaft* 13.

[205] Supra pp. 8 f.

[206] Cf. also Lautner (n. 18) 147 who emphasizes the (legitimate) expectation of law students that what they learn should be useful in a practical sense.

[207] See James Q. Whitman, *The Legacy of Roman Law in the German Romantic Era* (1990), *passim*.

[208] Windscheid, 'Das römische Recht in Deutschland' (n. 66) 48, from where also the quotation in the previous sentence is taken. Cf. also Ernst Zitelmann, in Planitz (n. 92) 193 who saw the 'dawn of a splendid day for Romanists'.

[209] The parallel development in the Netherlands is analysed by Zwalve, (1997) 5 *ZEuP* 393 ff.

history. Its establishment in the law faculties was based on an historical accident. Its methods were distinctly different from those employed in modern doctrinal scholarship;[210] and its results were entirely irrelevant for the practical application of the law.[211]

As a result, among many legal historians a feeling gained ground of a deep-rooted crisis,[212] or even of being threatened.[213] This resulted in ever repeated attempts to 'legitimize' legal history as part of a law curriculum[214] and in permanently smouldering methodological debates.[215] Characteristically, one of the main events of the 22nd German Legal History Conference (*Deutscher Rechtshistorikertag*) was a panel discussion on 'The Tasks of Legal History',[216] the panel discussion on the 23rd German Legal History Conference was devoted to 'The Place of Legal

[210] Dieter Simon, 'Rechtsgeschichte', in Axel Görlitz (ed.), *Handlexikon zur Rechtswissenschaft* (1974), 314 ff.; cf. also, e.g., Dieter Grimm, 'Rechtswissenschaft und Geschichte', in idem (ed.), *Rechtswissenschaft und Sozialwissenschaften*, vol. ii (1976), 9 ff. Cf. also already Windscheid: 'But legal history, if it proceeds from this point of view, is a branch of history rather than law': 'Die Aufgaben der Rechtswissenschaft', in Bernhard Windscheid, *Gesammelte Reden und Abhandlungen*, ed. Paul Oertmann (1904), 101 f. 'This point of view' is 'to trace the development of the law of a people merely for its own sake, without any extraneous thought'. Generally on the history of legal history in Germany after the Second World War, see Regina Ogorek, in Dieter Simon (ed.), *Rechtswissenschaft in der Bonner Republik* (1994), 12 ff., 34 ff.

[211] Dieter Simon, 'Vom Segen historischer Betrachtung für die Rechtsanwendung', (1985) 4 *Rechtshistorisches Journal* 272 ff.; idem, 'Normdurch setzung', (1988) 15 *Ius Commune* 202. For a recent and radical restatement of this view, culminating in the exhortation to 'renounce the inheritance (of Roman law)', see Regina Ogorek, 'Die Erbschaft ausschlagen?', in Pio Caroni and Gerhard Dilcher (eds.), *Norm und Tradition?* (1998), 183 ff. Cf. also the critical comments by Lautner (n. 18) 146. For a modern attempt to re-establish a connection between (a fully historicized) legal history and modern legal doctrine, see, in particular, Dietmar Klippel's concept of a *juristische Zeitgeschichte* (contemporary legal history), supra n. 29.

[212] Arising also from the fact that for some time 'the flood of new information had swallowed any contemplation on the purpose of the work': H. Mitteis (n. 55) 50.

[213] See Lautner (n. 18) 137 ff.; Klippel (n. 29) 1 ff. with references.

[214] See, again, Klippel (n. 29) 16 ff. with many references.

[215] Klippel (n. 29) 13 ff. and the discussion by Ogorek (n. 210) 23 ff., 34 ff. Cf. also already Wieacker (n. 1) 336 ff.

[216] See the report by Thomas Honsell, (1979) 96 *ZSS (RA)* 493 ff., 500 f.

History in the Modern Law Curriculum',[217] and the 24th German Legal History Conference saw a lively debate on the role of the historical argument in the theory and practice of modern law.[218] Equally characteristic is the response given by a leading comparative lawyer[219] when he was faced with the anxious question 'What Does Comparative Law Expect of Legal History?': he referred to a dictum by Radbruch according to which 'disciplines which have reason to examine their own methodology are ailing disciplines'.[220]

VII. FROM CONTEMPORARY ROMAN LAW TO ROMAN LAW

1. Digest Lemon and Lotus Flower

Where do we have to seek the reasons for the study of Roman law acquiring an exclusively historical character and superseding pandectist scholarship so radically and conclusively? Not, at any rate, in the fact of codification as such, for the change of perspective started before the BGB came into effect and it did not happen in the same, or a similar, manner under the codifications preceding the BGB. A number of factors coincided. Thus, there was the 'immeasurable'[221] wealth of sources (business documents and documents emanating from legal proceedings, administrative files, inscriptions, etc.) discovered, deciphered, and published in the course of the nineteenth and early twentieth centuries: the *Codex Hammurabi* was found in 1902, the Gortyn law code in 1884, and the great discoveries of papyri had already begun towards the end of the 1870s.[222]

217 See the report by Georg Klingenberg, (1982) 99 *ZSS (RA)* 575 ff., 578 ff.

218 See the report by Ralph Backhaus, (1983) 100 *ZSS (RA)* 795 ff., 800 f.

219 Hein Kötz, ' "Was erwartet die Rechtsvergleichung von der Rechtsgeschichte?" ', 1992 *JZ* 20.

220 Gustav Radbruch, *Einführung in die Rechtswissenschaft* (12th edn., 1969), 253.

221 Wieacker (n. 1) 46; Lautner (n. 18) 97.

222 These are merely three important examples; on the papyri cf., e.g., Leopold Wenger, *Die Quellen des römischen Rechts* (1953), 78 ff., 86 ff. On the other hand, of course, it is hardly accidental that these sources were discovered during this period.

The evaluation of these new sources was bound to be a fascinating task for legal historians: it offered the promise to break new ground.

It had thus become possible to advance far beyond the standard canon of legal sources dominated by the texts of the *Corpus Iuris*. These texts had by now been scrutinized ever more closely, under doctrinal auspices, for many decades: a process which ultimately resulted in a certain weariness, or even boredom and satiety. These feelings are apparent from many contemporary statements.[223] Typical for the mood prevailing among the younger generation of scholars, born in the second half of the nineteenth century, is a comment by Otto Gradenwitz: he expressed his delight in having in the person of Ludwig Mitteis such an eminently talented colleague 'who cheerfully distributed a fresh fruit, a lotus flower, while the rest of us were busy extracting from the squeezed-out old Digest lemon, by finding different pressure points, a few more drops of liquid'.[224] There appears to have been an idea that the end of an epoch had been reached. About every famous jurist of the nineteenth century had set out his views (usually by way of writing a monograph) on the nature of the concept of possession,[225] the sheer quantity of literature that had been produced since 1827[226] on the distinction between (simple) solidarity and correality was surpassed only by its absolute barrenness, and many other examples could be mentioned where ever more refined discussions had given rise to 'doctrinal hot-house plants, . . . to bastards of logic and

[223] See, e.g., Ernst Immanual Bekker, 'Aus den Grenzmarken der geschichtlichen Rechtswissenschaft', (1885) 6 *ZSS (RA)* 87.

[224] Gradenwitz (n. 100) 31.

[225] See the literature referred to in Bernhard Windscheid and Theodor Kipp, *Lehrbuch des Pandektenrechts* (9th edn., 1906), Vor § 148 n. * (pp. 732–4).

[226] The year when F. L. Keller, *Ueber Litis Contestation und Urtheil nach classischem römischen Recht*, appeared; cf. also Georg Julius Ribbentrop, *Zur Lehre von den Correal-Obligationen* (1831). The subsequent literature is compiled in Windscheid and Kipp (n. 225) § 292 n. *. Windscheid and Kipp quote a comment from 1829 according to which there was hardly another principal problem in Roman law on which the literature is so scarce, and they add: 'A good many [lawyers] will probably wish to turn back the time to that happy state.'

erudition with law, to unsound lecture-room jurisprudence'.[227] The time had come to cut the Gordian knot by means of a decision by the legislature. The services of the legal historian were no longer required, he could now turn his attention to the lotus flowers.

2. Beyond Roman Law by Means of Roman Law

These were the famous excesses of pandectist scholarship. But in many other areas the same pandectists, consciously or unconsciously, had heeded Jhering's famous call to venture beyond Roman law by means of Roman law.[228] They tried to strip Roman law of everything specifically Roman, or contingent, and to turn it into a kind of Natural law. They thus made it ready for codification (thereby in fact following the example of the Natural lawyers whose work they generally so strongly rejected). Paradoxically, therefore, the very high level of their achievements contributed to the process of historicizing Roman law. The codification was based on the most advanced and refined pandectist learning and thus it did not require, contrary to all previous codifications, a legal theory beyond itself that would have represented a higher level of reflection and to which it would have had to be intellectually related.[229] At the same time, Roman law was bound to appear to contemporary lawyers as something historically contingent which could be left to legal historians. The enormous success of private law legal science during the nineteenth

[227] Rudolf von Jhering, *Geist des römischen Rechts auf den verschiedenen Stufen seiner Entwicklung* (9th edn. [reprint], part II/2, 1968), 324.

[228] Rudolf von Jhering, *Geist des römischen Rechts auf den verschiedenen Stufen seiner Entwicklung* (3rd edn., vol. i, 1873), 14. Cf. also Bernhard Windscheid, 'Das römische Recht in Deutschland' (n. 66) 46 who refers to a purification of Roman law by means of Roman law and continues: 'If this work has been completed, Roman law is, at one and the same time, overcome and truly acquired'; for comment, see Wilhelm (n. 61) 228 ff. As a result, Roman law in some respects was less 'Roman' than the Natural law codifications. See the remarks in Reinhard Zimmermann, 'The Civil Law in European Codes', in David L. Carey Miller and Reinhard Zimmermann (eds.), *The Civilian Tradition and Scots Law: Aberdeen Quincentenary Essays* (1997), 283 ff.

[229] But see Jakobs (n. 61) *passim*; see, e.g., the quotations, supra n. 23.

century thus led to a disjunction from its own basis.[230] And it is hardly surprising if the opinion soon gained ground that the world of private law consisted exclusively of the BGB. A modern textbook author like Konrad Cosack specifically refused to discuss, and develop, the law historically;[231] such a way of proceeding was likely to distort either the old or the contemporary law. The challenge of 'thinking apart' Roman law and contemporary law and thereby 'emancipating' the one from the other, as issued by Bekker,[232] could hardly have found a more unequivocal response.[233]

3. The True Lawyer

Closely associated is another aspect. Nineteenth-century pandectist legal scholarship culminated in Windscheid's three-volume treatise. Since it was based on the sources of Roman law it appeared antiquated and 'scholastic' to those who wanted to emancipate contemporary law from legal history.[234] But it was also, decidedly, not a work of legal history. Thus, it contains a fairly extensive exposition[235] of the presupposition doctrine as it had been developed by Windscheid himself.[236] As early as 1856 this doctrine was seen as an attempt 'courageously to rise above the tyranny of Roman law'.[237] Windscheid himself considered the

230 Cf. also Koschaker (n. 18) 293: 'Thus, the thread of life of pandectism seemed to have been cut, and its continued presence in the curriculum appeared to be apt only to lead to meaningless repetitions or misunderstandings.'

231 Konrad Cosack, in Planitz (n. 92) 16 ('I simply do not believe that contemporary law has emerged from the old law, but I regard it as something new, created by the needs of the present day and the arbitrary power of the legislature').

232 Supra p. 10.

233 See, in this context, also Zwalve, (1997) 5 *ZEuP* 399, who points out that the close relationship 'between Roman law and classical antiquity, as emphasized by the civilians themselves, has proved almost fatal to the civilian profession'.

234 See, e.g., Cosack (n. 231) 6 ('Above all I studied Windscheid's textbook page for page, and line for line, without inner sympathy and somewhat uncheerfully, but strongly conscious of the fact that it would once be necessary to join battle specifically with Windscheid'), 15 ('legal scholasticism').

235 Windscheid and Kipp (n. 225) §§ 97–100.

236 Cf. supra p. 17.

237 J. E. Kuntze, *Der Wendepunkt der Rechtswissenschaft* (1856), 20 in connection with p. 18.

sources which appeared to recognize the doctrine in fact though not in name as 'building material for the edifice' which he intended to construct and he freely admitted that there were other sources contradicting his view.[238] Obviously, the presupposition doctrine was in accordance neither with classical Roman law nor with the law of the *Corpus Iuris*. This was pointed out by the Imperial Court (*Reichsgericht*): it refused to apply a doctrine for which there was 'no foundation in the sources at all'.[239] Even for the Imperial Court, however, historical authenticity was not the decisive point: central to the Court's rejection of the doctrine was the fear that legal certainty would otherwise be gravely jeopardized.[240] How, then, was it possible, asked Otto Lenel,[241] that 'a scholar such as Windscheid could hit upon a theory, so blatantly untenable' from the point of view of the Roman sources? Because he had proved, when he created (or 'constructed') it, to be 'a true lawyer' (*wahrer Jurist*). For the true lawyer is 'a man about whom stand ranged the concepts of his law, like marble statues, sharp and cold, and yet familiar figures, awaiting only the wave of his hand to set themselves in motion and accomplish their work; [a man] who knows how, at one and the same time, to serve his concepts and how to rise above them in conscious freedom'.[242] To rise above his concepts in conscious freedom: a true *legal historian* could

[238] Bernhard Windscheid, *Die Lehre des römischen Rechts von der Voraussetzung* (1850), 10, 207.

[239] RGZ 24, 169 (170).

[240] See the analysis by Falk (n. 65) 193 ff.

[241] Lenel, (1889) 74 *AcP* 226. This quotation provides the point of departure for Falk's book on Windscheid (n. 65).

[242] Windscheid, 'Das römische Recht' (n. 66) 48 f.; in the same lecture, Windscheid had invited those 'who are today called to cultivate Roman law', on the one hand, to hand over 'the proud possession intact and, as far as their abilities permit, more beautifully adorned to the next generations', on the other hand, however, 'to free the German people from the rule of the letter of Roman law'. Legal history, according to Windscheid, is only of value 'for the specific purposes of legal scholarship' insofar as it 'contributes something to the comprehension of the law that is to be applied' ('Die Aufgaben der Rechtswissenschaft', in *Gesammelte Reden und Abhandlungen*, ed. Paul Oertmann (1904), 109).

hardly identify himself with statements such as this. Nor would he easily have likened the colourful mixture of case decisions, legal opinions and rules, commentary, disputes, and excerpts from textbooks and monographs contained in the *Digest* to 'marble statues, sharp and cold'. Thus, it was hardly accidental that a scholar such as Otto Lenel became one of the harshest critics of the presupposition doctrine.[243]

4. From Scholarly Positivism to Statutory Positivism

Particularly important for the process of disjunction between private law and legal history was the positivism prevailing since about the 1830s. The nineteenth-century pandectists related it to the system, concepts, and legal doctrine based on the *Corpus Iuris*.[244] The system of contemporary Roman law was supposed to be comprehensive in that it had to be possible to find a logically consistent solution even for problems not specifically dealt with in the sources. Obviously, these notions were bound to be transferred to the BGB. The scholarly positivism was turned into a statutory positivism.[245] Statutory positivism identifies the law with the entire body of statutory provisions, as long as they have been properly enacted. These provisions constitute exclusive reasons to act. Nobody is allowed to argue that there may be better reasons prescribing a different action.[246] For the positivistic judge within a codified system this means that the 'old' law prevailing before the enactment of the code has to be ignored even if it appears to offer a more appropriate solution. Hence, for instance, the widespread reduction of the historical argument to an exploration of the preparatory 'paper trash'.[247] That Roman law

243 See the references supra n. 71.

244 See, above all, Wieacker (n. 1) 341 ff. On the doctrine of legal sources in 19th-century Germany see Peter Landau, 'Die Rechtsquellenlehre in der deutschen Rechtswissenschaft des 19. Jahrhunderts', (1993) 19 *Rättshistoriska Studier* 69 ff.

245 Wieacker (n. 1) 363 ff.

246 See Joseph Raz, *Practical Reason and Norms* (1975), 35 ff., 58 ff.; John Finnis, *Natural Law and Natural Rights* (1980), 233 f., 255.

247 See supra n. 196.

had been conclusively superseded and abolished appears to have been so self-evident that a specific rule along the lines of art. 1 of the Dutch 'Abrogation Act' appeared unnecessary.[248]

[248] See, e.g., Friedrich Endemann, *Einführung in das Studium des Bürgerlichen Gesetzbuchs* (3rd edn., first part, 1897), 45, 51; Eduard Heilfron, *Lehrbuch des Bürgerlichen Rechts* (4th edn., first part, 1908), 41.

Lecture Two—The Transition from Civil Law to Civil Code in Germany: Dawn of a New Era?

I. THE GERMAN CIVIL CODE: A PRISON CELL FOR LEGAL SCHOLARSHIP?

When the BGB entered into effect, on the first day of the new century, it was regarded as a triumph of German legal scholarship.[1] What German arms had achieved on the battlefields of France—political unity—had now also been peacefully accomplished in the area of private law:[2] 'One People. One Empire. One Law', to quote the headline of a special front page in the German Lawyers' Journal (*Deutsche Juristenzeitung*).[3] For the first time, there was a

[1] Also abroad. See, e.g., the charming piece by F. W. Maitland, 'The Making of the German Civil Code', as printed in H. A. L. Fisher (ed.), *The Collected Papers of Frederic William Maitland*, vol. iii (1911), 474 ff. For an assessment from a modern point of view see, e.g., Mathias Schmoeckel, '100 Jahre BGB: Erbe und Aufgabe', 1996 *NJW* 1697 ff.; Rolf Stürner, 'Der hundertste Geburtstag des BGB: Nationale Kodifikation im Greisenalter?', 1996 *JZ* 741 ff.; Uwe Diederichsen, '1. Januar 1900: Der Tag, an dem der deutsche Bürger sein Recht bekam', in Ulrich Mölk (ed.), *Europäische Jahrhundertwende* (1999), 161 ff.; and the contributions in the special volume of *Staudinger's Kommentar zum Bürgerlichen Gesetzbuch* entitled *100 Jahre BGB—100 Jahre Staudinger*, ed. Michael Martinek and Patrick L. Sellier (1999).

[2] Ernst Zitelmann, 'Zur Begrüßung des neuen Gesetzbuches', 1900 *DJZ* 2.

[3] The other leading practitioners' law journal, called *Juristische Wochenschrift* (Weekly Law Journal), opened its first issue in January 1900 with the sentence: 'The new century puts into effect the greatest feat of which German legal life can boast.' Cf. also Ernst Zitelmann, *Die Gefahren des Bürgerlichen Gesetzbuches für die Rechtswissenschaft* (1896), 4. Windscheid, too, had longed for a code that would be 'a German law for the German people', 'a cathedral of national splendour': 'Das römische Recht in Deutschland', in idem, *Gesammelte Reden und Abhandlungen*, ed. Paul Oertmann (1904), 48.

code of private law for Germany at large, for the first time the energies of scholars and practitioners alike could focus on one and the same authoritative text, and for the first time justice had wrapped itself—as Ernst von Wildenbruch put it in a poem devoted to the occasion[4]—in an indigenous garment. The days of the rule of Roman law were over; the German national spirit had ultimately carried the day. And just as pandectist scholarship was no longer required as a general theory of the law, it was also no longer necessary as a symbol of German legal unity.

But not everybody greeted the new Code with feelings of joy, elation, and national pride. Ever since the First Draft had been published in 1888, there had been sustained and widespread criticism.[5] The draft was condemned as being too abstract and pedantic, it was denounced as a pandectist textbook cast in statutory form and thus as being too un-German; it was attacked as being out of touch with the realities of life and as lacking even a drop of socialist oil. It was a text drafted by and designed for the expert lawyer, not a layman's legal primer. While some of this criticism was heeded by a Second Commission set up in 1890, the Code itself retained most of the basic features for which the First Draft had been criticized. Eventually one had to resign oneself to the fact that too much had been expected of the Code.[6]

At the same time there was considerable anxiety, in the years before 1900, a feeling of uneasiness and fear of how the enactment of the Code might affect the administration of justice.[7] It was realized by many that in view of the peculiar nature of the Roman sources lawyers had enjoyed much leeway. The *Digest*, after all, is no systematic code or textbook but a gigantic torso of Roman legal materials. Its over-

[4] 'Das deutsche Recht', 1900 *DJZ* 1.

[5] See Franz Wieacker, *A History of Private Law in Europe*, tr. Tony Weir (1995), 371 ff.

[6] See, e.g., the discussion in Sternberg, *Einführung in die Rechtswissenschaft*, vol. i (2nd edn., 1927), 133 ff.

[7] See Thomas Honsell, *Historische Argumente im Zivilrecht* (1982), 22 ff. with references.

all character is casuistic. Much of it reflects the position at the various stages of Roman legal history; and it is full of contradictions and controversies. The very complexity and richness of these sources had left ample room for doctrinal development and innovation,[8] and the pandectist scholars had thus been able to attribute authoritative character to their propositions. They were the high priests of legal scholarship.[9] The new Code, so it was feared, would leave no room for any productive scholarship and it would turn the judge into a mere 'subsumption machine' (*Subsumtionsautomat*).[10] Being comprehensive, systematic, precise, and highly technical, it constituted a 'prison cell' for legal scholarship.[11] There was great concern about an impending cult of literalism.[12] These anxieties led a number of authors to claim the status merely of a 'restatement' for the BGB;[13] they stimulated renewed attempts to search for criteria of justice beyond the positive law;[14] and they contributed substantially to the rise of the Free-law movement (*Freirechtsschule*).[15]

How, then, did the courts react to the new Code? It is widely known today that Germany, in the words of John Dawson, experienced a 'case-law revolution'.[16] A whole range of legal rules and institutions is recognized today of which there is no trace in the provisions of the Code. In

[8] That point is emphasized, for instance, in my article 'Roman Law and European Legal Unity', in Arthur Hartkamp, Martijn Hesselink, et al. (eds.), *Towards a European Civil Code* (2nd edn., 1998), 21 ff.

[9] Supra p. 44 (n. 207).

[10] On the notion of the judge as being a 'subsumption machine' see the references in Regina Ogorek's analysis *Richterkönig oder Subsumtionsautomat? Zur Justiztheorie im 19. Jahrhundert* (1986), 1 ff.

[11] Hans Wüstendörfer, 'Die deutsche Rechtswissenschaft am Wendepunkt', (1913) 110 *AcP* 224.

[12] See, e.g., Zitelmann (n. 3) 14.

[13] See, e.g., R. Sohm, 'Das Studium des römischen Rechts', 1908 *DJZ* 39 and the references in Th. Honsell (n. 7) 24.

[14] See Wieacker (n. 5) 586 ff.; Hans Schlosser, *Grundzüge der neueren Privatrechtsgeschichte* (8th edn., 1996), 245 ff.; Th. Honsell (n. 7) 25.

[15] On which, see Wieacker (n. 5) 579 ff.; Schlosser (n. 14) 243 f. Cf. also Rainer Schröder, 'Die deutsche Methodendiskussion um die Jahrhundertwende: Wissenschaftstheoretische Präzisierungsversuche oder Antworten auf den Funktionswandel von Recht und Justiz, (1988) 19 *Rechtstheorie* 323 ff.

[16] John P. Dawson, *The Oracles of the Law* (1968), 432 ff.

certain cases the courts have even, effectively, overruled provisions of the Code.[17] But did this constitute a 'revolution'? Did the courts overturn the established legal order? And did this happen suddenly and only from about the 1920s onwards? It is widely believed today that the first two decades under the BGB were marked by an exaggerated statutory positivism displayed, particularly, by the Imperial Court:[18] a kind of German 'école de l'exégèse' engaging in a 'legal game of chess'.[19] We will consider these questions by looking in some detail at one specific area of German law and then, more briefly, at a number of developments in other areas.[20] The focus of our attention, therefore, now shifts from Roman law to contemporary private law. Roman law, in the words of Ernst Immanuel Bekker,[21] had been 'thought apart' from modern law and had thus emancipated itself. Could the same be said of modern law?

II. THE REACTION OF THE IMPERIAL COURT TO THE CODIFICATION OF PRIVATE LAW: DELICT

The German law of delict has experienced, as Ernst von Caemmerer famously put it, a number of profound changes

[17] See the overview in Reinhard Zimmermann, 'An Introduction to German Legal Culture', in Werner F. Ebke and Matthew W. Finkin (eds.), *Introduction to German Law* (1996), 16 ff.

[18] Wieacker (n. 5) 409 (in the German original—*Privatrechtsgeschichte der Neuzeit* (2nd edn., 1967) 514—Wieacker's statement is not confined to 'doctrinal scholarship'); Schlosser (n. 14) 167. Cf. also already Paul Oertmann, *Interesse und Begriff in der Rechtswissenschaft* (1931), 8.

[19] Josef Partsch, *Vom Beruf des römischen Rechts in der heutigen Universität* (1920), 39.

[20] The analysis is based on a number of contributions to a research project initiated by Ulrich Falk and Heinz Mohnhaupt of the Max-Planck-Institute for European Legal History in Frankfurt. They were presented at a symposium held from 16 to 18 March 1999 in Frankfurt and will be published in the course of the year 2000 under the title *Das Bürgerliche Gesetzbuch und seine Richter: Fallstudien zur Reaktion der Rechtspraxis auf die Kodifikation des deutschen Privatrechts (1896–1914)*. Dr Falk and Dr Mohnhaupt have kindly made available to me (with the permission of the authors) the contributions to this project referred to in subsequent footnotes. The discussion on the law of delict is based on my own contribution; the assistance of Dirk A. Verse, Regensburg, is gratefully acknowledged.

[21] Supra p. 10.

('Wandlungen des Deliktsrechts').[22] We will confine our attention to three particularly prominent ones: the range of objects of legal protection, as set out in § 823 I BGB; the rise of *Verkehrssicherungspflichten*; and liability for others.

1. The Rights and Interests Protected

(*a*) *Introduction*

The draftsmen of the BGB had the choice between several regimes of delictual liability existing side by side during the nineteenth century.[23] On the one hand, there was French law with its famous generalized approach based on the teaching of the Natural lawyers (art. 1382 *code civil*). Many codifications of the 'Romanistic legal family' had followed this model, among them the Dutch BW and the Italian *codice civile*. The Austrian Code contained a provision of similar generality (§ 1295 ABGB). At the same time, however, it included a number of special provisions for specific types of delicts (§§ 1325–32 ABGB). Even more restricted, as a result of a finely differentiated casuistry, was the significance of the general provision of the Prussian Code.[24] The nineteenth century *ius commune*, on the other hand, was based on the Roman law of specific delicts. Of central importance, of course, was the *actio legis Aquiliae* which had, originally, been confined to damage to property but had come to be extended, in the course of time, to cover infringements of bodily integrity.[25]

[22] Ernst von Caemmerer, 'Wandlungen des Deliktsrechts', in *Hundert Jahre deutsches Rechtsleben: Festschrift zum hundertjährigen Bestehen des Deutschen Juristentages 1860–1960*, vol. ii (1960), 49 ff. (= *Gesammelte Schriften*, vol. i (1968), 452 ff.) (references in the following footnotes refer to the latter publication).

[23] See, e.g., the overview provided by Helmut Coing, *Europäisches Privatrecht*, vol. ii (1989), 516 ff.

[24] See, in particular, Thomas Kiefer, *Die Aquilische Haftung im 'Allgemeinen Landrecht für die Preußischen Staaten' von 1794* (1989).

[25] On Aquilian liability in Roman law and on its development in the subsequent *ius commune*, see Reinhard Zimmermann, *The Law of Obligations: Roman Foundations of the Civilian Tradition* (paperback edn., 1996), 953 ff., 998 ff. Under the influence of pandectist doctrine, the Prussian Code was also brought in line as far as possible with Aquilian liability by way of interpretation: see Kiefer (n. 24) 165 ff., 189 ff., 224 ff.

The drafting of §§ 823 ff. BGB was a complex process.[26] Essentially, however, it was the First Commission that established the system of three core provisions as we find it today in §§ 823 I, 823 II, and 826 BGB[27] and as it had been prefigured in pandectist textbooks like the one by Windscheid.[28] Only in the course of the deliberations of the Second Commission was there a sustained argument in favour of a general provision along the lines of the Natural law codifications; it was eventually rejected by a narrow margin of 10 : 8 votes.

§ 823 I BGB,[29] which may be regarded as the modern equivalent of the *lex Aquilia,* lists a certain number of specific rights and interests the infringement of which gives rise to delictual liability. New in this list, compared to the nineteenth-century Aquilian liability, was the right of 'freedom' of a person.[30] Equally new was the clause 'or other right of another' following on from the word 'ownership'. The draftsmen did not, apparently, attach much significance to it. It is hardly mentioned in the various published materials.[31] It was, presumably, intended to cover absolute rights similar to ownership, such as immaterial property rights. At the same time it was clearly not supposed to

[26] It has been thoroughly analysed by Hans-Peter Benöhr, 'Die Redaktion der Paragraphen 823 und 826 BGB', in Reinhard Zimmermann, Rolf Knütel, and Jens Peter Meincke (eds.), *Rechtsgeschichte und Privatrechtsdogmatik* (2000), 449 ff.

[27] See, e.g., 'Motive', in Benno Mugdan, *Die gesammten Materialien zum Bürgerlichen Gesetzbuch für das Deutsche Reich,* vol. ii (1899), 405: it is unlawful 'to act against an absolute statutory prohibition', 'to infringe someone else's absolute right', and 'to commit an act contrary to the *boni mores*'.

[28] Bernhard Windscheid and Theodor Kipp, *Lehrbuch des Pandektenrechts* (9th edn., 1906), §§ 101, 257, 326. The continuity with the *ius commune* is emphasized, particularly, by Benöhr (n. 26) 501 ff., 528 f.

[29] 'A person who wilfully or negligently injures the life, body, health, freedom, property, or other right of another contrary to law is bound to compensate him for any damage arising therefrom': English translation according to B. S. Markesinis, *The German Law of Torts: A Comparative Introduction* (3rd edn., 1994), 12. On pp. 12 ff. also an English translation of all the other delict provisions in the BGB can be found.

[30] For details, see Benöhr (n. 26) 511.

[31] See 'Protokolle', in Mugdan (n. 27) 1078; and cf. Karl Schäfer, in *Staudinger, Kommentar zum Bürgerlichen Gesetzbuch* (12th edn., 1986), § 823 nn. 72 f.; Benöhr (n. 26) 512.

incorporate a person's capacity for work, his sense of decency, and his honour. Proposals to include these objects of legal protection in the text of § 823 I BGB were specifically rejected.[32]

If § 823 I BGB thus forms part of the tradition of Aquilian liability, as it had developed over the centuries and been applied by the Imperial Court until 1900, it would come as a surprise if 1 January 1900 constituted a turning point in the history of the German law of delict. There was in fact no such turning point. What we find, however, even in the early years of the BGB, is a noticeable tendency by the Imperial Court to extend the range of protection.

The central question after 1900 was how to interpret the notion of the 'other right of another'. The following issues may be distinguished.

(b) The Patrimony As Such

From very early on the Imperial Court made clear that the patrimony as such could not be regarded as another right in terms of § 823 I BGB.

> RGZ 51, 92, judgment of 15 March 1902 (I. Division): The plaintiff had successfully rescinded a contract, concluded with the defendant, on account of a mistake which the defendant had grossly negligently induced in him. Trusting in the validity of the contract he had incurred expenses which he now attempted to claim as damages in terms of § 823 I BGB. The Imperial Court curtly dismissed this argument. The plaintiff had merely suffered 'an injury to the patrimony in general, not a patrimonial loss resulting from the infringement of an object of legal protection. Only in the latter situation does § 823 grant a claim for damages. Apart from fault in the form of *culpa* or *dolus*, the unlawful infringement of property or another right is required for such claim. A rule in terms of which a person would generally be liable for any patrimonial loss that he had negligently caused is alien to the Civil Code.'

[32] See, e.g. 'Kommissionsbericht', in Mugdan (n. 27) 1297.

This result was soon confirmed in a decision concerning a negligent misstatement case.

> RGZ 52, 365, judgment of 27 October 1902 (VI. Division): The plaintiff intended to grant H. a loan to be secured by way of a mortgage. He therefore demanded from H. a notarial certificate concerning all encumbrances affecting the piece of property with respect to which the mortgage was to be created. H. asked a notary, the defendant, who negligently stated the other encumbrances of better rank to be lower than they actually were. Relying on this information, the plaintiff granted the loan which H. was subsequently unable to repay. When the piece of property was sold by public auction, he did not obtain satisfaction as a result of these other encumbrances of better rank. The Imperial Court confirmed the decision by the Appeal Court which had refused to grant a claim based on § 823 I BGB against the notary.

The Court, however, managed to assist the plaintiff in a different manner. It maintained that between plaintiff and defendant an implied contract had been concluded to supply the information required. Thus, the notary was liable for damages for breach of contract. Here we can see the origins of a development that was to characterize the modern German law of obligations: circumventing the limitations of the law of delict by a robust expansion of contractual liability.[33]

In a number of decisions the Imperial Court reiterated that the patrimony as such does not enjoy protection in terms of § 823 I BGB.[34] For the Court this was an entirely

[33] On the remarkable expansion of contract law in negligent misstatement cases, see Werner Lorenz, 'Das Problem der Haftung für primäre Vermögensschäden bei der Erteilung einer unrichtigen Auskunft', in *Festschrift für Karl Larenz* (1973), 575 ff.; Siegbert Lammel, 'Zur Auskunftshaftung', (1979) 179 *AcP* 337 ff.; Hein Kötz, *Deliktsrecht* (7th edn., 1996), nn. 673 ff.; most recently: Heinrich Honsell, 'Die Haftung für Gutachten und Auskunft unter besonderer Berücksichtigung von Drittinteressen', in *Festschrift für Dieter Medicus* (1999), 211 ff.

[34] See, e.g., RGZ 59, 49 (51), judgment of 4 Oct. 1904 (III. Division); RGZ 63, 53 (54), judgment of 12 Mar. 1906 (VI. Division); RGZ 64, 344 (345), judgment of 22 Oct. 1906 (VI. Division); RGZ 65, 292 (294), judgment of 14 Mar. 1907 (VI. Division); RGZ 76, 35 (48), judgment of 13 Feb. 1911 (VI. Division).

familiar principle, for it had been repeatedly enunciated in decisions based on the *ius commune* prevailing prior to the enactment of the BGB.[35] These earlier decisions were no longer referred to after 1900. But in view of the fact that the Code had so obviously rejected delictual compensation for pure economic loss there was hardly any need for an impressive array of arguments and precedents.

(c) *Claims Arising under the Law of Obligations*

The Imperial Court also decided, soon after the enactment of the Code, that claims arising under the law of obligations could not be regarded as 'other rights of another' under § 823 I BGB. The leading decision, handed down on 29 April 1904,[36] referred in the first place to the wording of the rule: if the draftsmen had wanted to extend delictual protection to claims, they would expressly have said so. Any such

[35] RGZ 9, 158 (163 ff.), judgment of 10 Feb. 1883 (I. Division) is usually regarded as the leading case; it was confirmed in RGZ 22, 133 (134), judgment of 19 Dec. 1888 (I. Division) and in RGZ 22, 208 (209), judgment of 3 Dec. 1888 (VI. Division). The Court, however, was very liberal in accepting an infringement of the right of a person who had been granted a real right in the object concerned and it was conscious of going beyond what had been recognized by 'the older Roman law'; cf. RGZ 22, 208 (209 f.), RGZ 47, 249 (250), judgment of 29 Nov. 1900 (VI. Division). The question was left open in two decisions of the III. Division: RGZ 26, 204 (207), judgment of 17 Oct. 1890 and RG SeuffArch 49, 14, judgment of 7 Mar. 1893. See Ruth Bilstein, *Das deliktische Schadensersatzrecht der Lex Aquilia in der Rechtsprechung des Reichsgerichts* (1994), 28 ff. Before the establishment of the Imperial Court there had been occasional attempts by the superior courts to advance beyond the confines of Aquilian liability and to grant protection in cases of negligently caused purely patrimonial loss: see Hans Hermann Seiler, 'Römisches deliktisches Schadensersatzrecht in der obergerichtlichen Rechtsprechung des 19. Jahrhunderts', in *Festschrift für Hermann Lange* (1992), 256 ff. This more liberal attitude followed the tradition of the more recent *ius commune*: see Horst Kaufmann, *Rezeption und Usus modernus der Actio Legis Aquiliae* (1958), 46 ff., 62 ff.; Law of Obligations (n. 25) 1023 ff.; Jan Schröder, 'Die zivilrechtliche Haftung für schuldhafte Schadenszufügungen im deutschen Usus modernus', in *La responsabilità civile da atto illecito nella prospettiva storico-comparatistica* (1995), 147 ff. An unclear phrase at the end of Inst. IV, 3, 16 had played a considerable role in this process of extension of the range of application of delictual liability. Nineteenth-century pandectist scholarship had, very widely, turned against the *usus modernus legis Aquiliae* and had rejected a claim for damages in cases of negligently inflicted purely patrimonial loss; cf., e.g., Windscheid and Kipp (n. 28) 451, 455; Johann Christian Hasse, *Die Culpa des römischen Rechts* (2nd edn., 1838), 26 f.

[36] RGZ 57, 353 (VI. Division).

extension would also not be in tune with the nature of a debtor–creditor relationship (*Schuldverhältnis*). The obligation created a tie merely between debtor and creditor and the creditor's claim was therefore of a relative nature: it was directed not against the world at large but merely against a specific debtor. Third parties could safely ignore it. Finally, the Court also referred to a remark in the *travaux préparatoires* supporting its view.[37]

Once again, the principle that a mere right to claim does not enjoy delictual protection had also been recognized in the case law prior to 1900.[38] Thus, in its decision of 1883 the Imperial Court had refused to grant delictual protection to a person who merely had a contractual claim to the object that had been damaged.[39]

(*d*) *Possession*

One exception to this principle soon came to be recognized, however. It related to claims on account of which a person is entitled to possession of the object that is damaged.

> RGZ 59, 326, judgment of 28 December 1904 (V. Division): The defendant ran a restaurant in a house that he had rented. In the house next door the plaintiff operated a wholesale business in petroleum. The defendant alleged that petroleum had soaked through the partition wall and had created a fire-risk. As a result, he was indeed prevented by police order from continuing to operate the restaurant. Out of court, the defendant had claimed damages from the plaintiff and the plaintiff now asked for a declaratory judgment that he did not have to pay any such damages.

The Imperial Court accepted that 'the right of the lessee which had been put into effect by the granting of direct possession' was 'another right of another' in terms of § 823 I BGB. With the transfer of possession the lessee's right had 'outgrown' the law of obligations. There were no longer

[37] 'Motive', in Mugdan (n. 27) 406.

[38] The position had been different under the *usus modernus*; among authors on Prussian law the question was controversial. See Benöhr (n. 26) 510.

[39] RGZ 9, 158 (already referred to supra n. 35).

only relative rights and duties between lessor and lessee. Everybody had to respect the lessee's right that had become clearly discernible on account of the transfer of possession; this right could therefore now be counted among the absolute rights. Ultimately, however, the decision of the Imperial Court went against the lessee since it turned out that the petroleum had seeped through the wall already prior to the conclusion of the contract of lease. Thus, there had been no infringement of the *lessee's* right.

Interestingly, in this case the Imperial Court did not refer to the *travaux préparatoires*. This may have been due to the fact that they contradicted the Court's view. In the course of the deliberations of the Second Commission, a proposal to grant delictual protection to the right of possession by extending the list of absolute rights in § 823 I BGB had been specifically rejected. Protection in terms of §§ 858, 823 II BGB was regarded as sufficient.[40]

The Imperial Court subsequently confirmed its position[41] which, in this case, cannot be traced back to an older line of cases. Thus, for instance, in a decision of 1883[42] the Court had emphasized that D. 9, 2, 27, 14 (a lessee was granted the Aquilian action on account of damage done to crops growing on the leased land) had to be regarded as an 'exceptional case' that could not be generalized. But this view had not been uncontested in nineteenth-century scholarship.[43] If delictual protection was now granted this can hardly be regarded as an abrupt innovation.

(e) The Right to an Established and Operating Business

Another extension of delictual protection also already occurred during the early years of the BGB: recognition of

[40] 'Protokolle', in Mugdan (n. 27) 1077. A different view had been adopted earlier; 'Motive', in Benno Mugdan, *Die gesammten Materialien zum Bürgerlichen Gesetzbuch für das Deutsche Reich*, vol. iii (1899), 110. Cf. also the discussion by Benöhr (n. 26) 509 f.

[41] Cf., e.g., RGZ 91, 60 (65 f.), judgment of 25 Oct. 1917 (VI. Division).

[42] RGZ 9, 158 (163), judgment of 10 Feb. 1883; also referred to above n. 35.

[43] See, e.g., Heinrich Dernburg, *Pandekten*, vol. ii (7th edn., 1903), § 131, n. 15 and text to it; cf. also Friedhelm Keppmann, *Die neuere dogmengeschichtliche Entwicklung der objektiven Tatbestände der §§ 823, 826 BGB* (1959), 62 ff.

the right to an established and operating business (*Recht am eingerichteten und ausgeübten Gewerbebetrieb*). It was first accepted as constituting 'another' right in a decision of 6 March 1902,[44] but the decision that was to become fundamentally important for the subsequent development dates from 1904.

> RGZ 58, 24, judgment of 27 February 1904 (I. Division):[45] On the basis of a design that had been wrongly registered in the official register of designs the defendant had obtained an injunction restraining the plaintiff from producing carpets made of jute pile. Since the plaintiff had, indeed, for some time suspended his production, he now claimed compensation for the loss incurred.

The Appeal Court had refused to apply § 823 I BGB and had consequently turned to § 826. Here it would have been required that the defendant had known the design to have been wrongly registered. The Imperial Court, in turn, applied § 823 I BGB and thus established a liability for negligence. Admittedly, of course, there had been no damage to property: the injunction, after all, did not interfere with the right of ownership in the production facilities. But the plaintiff could rely on his right to an established and operating business. Of decisive importance, for the Imperial Court, was the fact that protection was not merely sought for the exercise of a businessman's free will: his will had already found an 'embodiment' in the production facilities and other objects established in his plant. There was thus a 'firm foundation' for the acceptance of a subjective right in this business. This right had been unlawfully infringed by the defendant since the design asserted by him had not in fact existed.

[44] RG IV 393/01, judgment of 6 Mar. 1902, as quoted in RGZ 58, 24 (29). Previously, the right to an established and operating business had been recognized in RGZ 51, 369, judgment of 29 May 1902 (VI. Division) (boycott of a doctor by an association of doctors), and RGZ 56, 271 (275 f.), judgment of 14 Dec. 1902 (VI. Division) (boycott of a bookseller); in both cases, however, the claim for damages had ultimately been rejected.

[45] A translation of this case can be found in Markesinis (n. 29) 334 ff.

The scope of the right to an established and operating business, however, was narrowly confined. Thus, it was held in 1907 that misleading descriptions of a product do not constitute an infringement of a rival company's right.[46] The rival company was affected only in an 'expectation of profit' which did not enjoy protection.[47] In 1910 the Imperial Court[48] coined the influential formula that there had to be a 'direct' interference with the business, an interference 'aimed against the existence of that business as such'. This was not the case, for instance, if a businessman tried to sidestep the rules on granting rebates adopted by an association of businessmen.

As a result of this restrictive formula we find the Imperial Court in a number of cases accepting the right to an established and operating business in principle but often refusing to grant protection.[49] Protection was granted mainly in situations where one competitor caused damage to another by asserting a patent or similar right without being entitled to it.[50] A boycott, strike, or lockout was not usually brought under § 823 I BGB though this was not for lack of a direct interference but because the boycott, strike, or lockout was, as a rule, held not to have been unlawful.[51] An infringement of the right to an established and operating business was accepted, however, in a case involving a specifically severe form of boycott: a restaurant had for many weeks been besieged and potential guests had been violently prevented from entering it.

It was only later, from the 1930s onwards, that the

[46] RGZ 65, 210, judgment of 22 Feb. 1907 (II. Division).

[47] See also RGZ 73, 253 (256 f.), judgment of 8 Apr. 1910 (II. Division); RGZ 77, 217 (218 f.), judgment of 28 Sept. 1911 (VI. Division).

[48] RGZ 73, 107 (112), judgment of 3 Feb. 1910 (VI. Division).

[49] Cf. also von Caemmerer (n. 22) 494.

[50] Apart from the leading case RGZ 58, 24, see RG 1905 *JW* 430, no. 9, judgment of 27 May 1905 (I. Division); RG 1915 *JW* 327, no. 4, judgment of 26 Jan. 1915 (II. Division); RG 1917 *JW* 712, no. 9, judgment of 2 Jan. 1917. For further references concerning the later case law, see von Caemmerer (n. 22) 494 n. 146.

[51] See, e.g., RGZ 64, 52, judgment of 12 July 1906 (VI. Division). In RGZ 64, 155, judgment of 4 Oct. 1906 (VI. Division) (boycott of a doctor) the requirement of an established and operating *business* was seen not to be satisfied.

Imperial Court gradually abandoned the requirement of an interference aimed against the existence of the business as such.[52] Whether this has brought about a decisive transformation of the system of the German law of delict, the introduction of a generalized form of delictual liability,[53] is open to doubt: the criterion of a 'direct' interference was retained and the Federal Supreme Court came to emphasize the 'subsidiarity' of the right to an established and operating business. For the period at present under consideration, at any rate, the recognition of that right constitutes a cautious extension of § 823 I BGB, relevant only for a very limited range of cases.

Moreover, we are not dealing here with a completely new development of the year 1902. Even prior to 1900 the Imperial Court had granted a claim for damages in cases of an interference with a business. The leading case RGZ 58, 24 (29) indeed referred to the relevant judgments handed down before the enactment of the BGB, particularly to RGZ 28, 238 (247–249).[54] This decision, however, had been based on the provisions of the Prussian and Saxonian codes (§ 8 I 6 ALR; § 116 Saxonian BGB); strictly speaking, therefore, they had little precedential value for the interpretation of the BGB which did not have a similarly general provision of delictual liability.[55] Other decisions had in fact, if not in name, granted protection to an established and operating business.[56]

(f) Protection of the Personality[57]

The draftsmen of the BGB had refused, in spite of protests among legal writers, to extend § 823 I BGB to the protection

[52] See Schäfer, in *Staudinger* (n. 31) § 823 n. 152.

[53] This is the view of von Caemmerer (n. 22) 492.

[54] Judgment of 25 June 1890 (I. Division) (damages resulting from the boycott of a bookseller).

[55] RGZ 56, 271 (273 f.), judgment of 14 Dec. 1902 (VI. Division), dealing with the same type of case, expressly acknowledged that.

[56] RGZ 22, 208 and RGZ 47, 249, both mentioned supra n. 35.

[57] The term 'personality' is chosen here, in line with the standard comparative literature, for lack of a better English term; see Konrad Zweigert and Hein Kötz, *An Introduction to Comparative Law*, tr. Tony Weir (3rd edn., 1998), 685 ff. ('right of personality'); Markesinis (n. 29) 63 ff. ('right to one's personality').

of a person's personality. The right of honour had first been mentioned next to 'freedom' in the First Draft but was subsequently eliminated from the list of objects of legal protection. The provisions contained in the Criminal Code[58] and two specific rules protecting the endangering of credit and the inducement to cohabit[59] were regarded as sufficient. Apart from that, the right to the use of a name was protected by § 12 BGB and the right to a person's image by a special act.[60] A general right to a person's personality appears to have been alien to the statutory conception of delictual liability.

This was, at any rate, the view of the Imperial Court which it never abandoned. The first relevant judgment dates from 1902:

> RGZ 51, 369, judgment of 29 May 1902 (VI. Division): The defendant had called on all the other companies in his line of business not to employ any of the employees that were on strike in his own company. Some of the employees concerned demanded the retraction of this call to boycott and compensation for the economic loss which they had suffered. They relied, i.a., on § 823 I BGB arguing that their personal right to determine how to use their capacity for work as well as their honour had been infringed.

The Imperial Court rejected their action. The recognition, in terms of § 823 I BGB, of personality rights (like the right to determine how to use one's capacity for work) would render the limitations of this rule 'completely uncertain'. As far the right of honour is concerned, the *travaux préparatoires* left 'no doubt' that it was not to be counted among the rights and interests protected by § 823 I BGB.

This decision was confirmed in a number of similar cases[61] and also in cases in the area of copyright law. RGZ

[58] §§ 185 StGB.

[59] §§ 824 and 825 BGB.

[60] *Gesetz betreffend das Urheberrecht an Werken der bildenden Künste und der Photographie* of 9 Jan. 1907.

[61] RGZ 56, 271 (275), judgment of 14 Dec. 1902 (VI. Division); RGZ 64, 155 (156), judgment of 4 Oct. 1906 (VI. Division).

69, 401[62] concerned the posthumous publication of letters by Friedrich Nietzsche, without the consent of his heir. The Court reiterated that a general right of personality was 'alien to the law prevailing today'. Relief was, however, afforded by the copyright law since the letters had to be regarded 'as an individual creation of the mind, as the emanation of the intellectual activity of an individual'.[63] Ordinary letters which merely related personal news or discussed business matters would not have been covered by this formula; this had already expressly been stated, prior to 1900, by the Imperial Court in a case concerning the letters of Richard Wagner.[64]

Even if the Imperial Court never recognized a general right to the protection of a person's personality, it still tried to grant protection, as far as possible, on the basis of existing legal rules. The law relating to copyright has already been mentioned. In other cases the Court resorted to § 826 BGB. RGZ 57, 418[65] provides an example: § 826 BGB was used to protect an employee against lockout and against incriminations by the employer's association. An extensive interpretation of § 826 BGB was undertaken by RGZ 72, 175.[66] A doctor had wrongfully and grossly negligently declared the plaintiff to be of unsound mind. The plaintiff's family had, therefore, started proceedings to have the plaintiff placed under guardianship, and the plaintiff had incurred expenses as a result of these proceedings. His lawsuit against the doctor was successful, since the Imperial Court decided to grant damages on the basis of § 826 BGB. If a doctor is asked to check the mental health of another person, so it was argued, he has to be aware of the grave responsibility that he thereby undertakes, and he also

[62] Judgment of 7 Nov. 1908 (I. Division).

[63] A similar result was reached in RGZ 79, 397, judgment of 8 June 1912 (I. Division) (overpainting a picture as an infringement of the copyright of the painter). Again, the Court does not recognize a general right of personality but proceeds to grant protection on the basis of the infringement of the copyright.

[64] RGZ 41, 43 (49), judgment of 28 Feb. 1898 (I. Division).

[65] Judgment of 17 Mar. 1904 (VI. Division).

[66] Judgment of 15 Nov. 1909 (VI. Division).

has to bear in mind the severe consequences for that other person resulting from his pronouncement. If that pronouncement is based on insufficient evidence, the negligence involved also implies an infringement of the *boni mores*.[67]

From the 1920s onwards the Imperial Court also granted some measure of protection by interpreting extensively the provisions concerning the use of a person's name and image.[68] These decisions tied in with the cautiously extensive line followed by the Court in the first two decades of the century. This line, in turn, can be traced back into the nineteenth century. A general right of personality had also not been recognized.[69] But towards the end of the century the Imperial Court had started to fill this gap, at least in individual cases and by doctrinal detours.[70]

2. *Verkehrssicherungspflichten*

The BGB does not distinguish between liability for commission and omission. Both are, in principle, put on an equal footing. But it has always been recognized, and is taken for granted under the BGB, that there cannot be liability for

[67] The requirements of § 826 BGB have been similarly watered down in many subsequent decisions and contexts; see, with regard to liability for providing mistaken information, Kötz (n. 33) nn. 669 ff. RGZ 72, 175 thus set a pattern.

[68] See the references in von Caemmerer (n. 22) 515.

[69] After the decline of the *actio iniuriarum* in the first part of the 19th century (see *Law of Obligations* (n. 25) 1085 ff.) the last three decades of the century saw the development of a doctrine of 'personality rights' (by Carl Neuner, Karl Gareis, Josef Kohler, and Otto von Gierke; see Coing (n. 23) 296 ff.; Dieter Leuze, *Die Entwicklung des Persönlichkeitsrechts im 19. Jahrhundert* (1962) and the literature referred to in *Law of Obligations* (n. 25) 1083 n. 256) which did not, however, leave any traces in the BGB.

[70] See the famous decision RGZ 45, 170, judgment of 28 Dec. 1899. Photographers had broken into Otto von Bismarck's death chamber and had made flashlight photographs of his corpse. The Imperial Court ordered the photographers to hand over the negatives of the photographs; the decision, characterized by its 'somewhat tortuous reasoning' (Kötz (n. 33) n. 86), was based on the *condictio ob iniustam causam*. The legislature reacted by enacting the law mentioned supra n. 60. For a summary of the developments leading up to recognition of a general right to one's personality in 1954 (BGHZ 13, 334 ff.), see Markesinis (n. 29) 63 ff. with copious references to further literature.

'mere' omissions. An omission can only be relevant, for the purposes of the law of delict, if there has been a duty to act.[71] Such duty to act can flow, in particular, from a previous action, or it may be based on statute or contract.[72] Very soon the Imperial Court went beyond these traditional sources for duties to act by resorting to the notion of a 'duty to ensure the safety of one's neighbour' (*Verkehrssicherungspflicht*).[73]

> RGZ 52, 373, judgment of 30 October 1902, VI. Division: The plaintiff asked the Prussian state to compensate him for the loss which he had suffered as a result of a rotten tree falling onto his property. The tree had grown on a public piece of property.

The Imperial Court emphasized, at the outset, that an

[71] Windscheid had wanted a specific rule to this effect in the Code; see Benöhr (n. 26) 518.

[72] The requirements for delictual liability for omissions had been disputed since the Middle Ages. This was due, above all, to the lack of precise statements in the sources of Roman law. The only thing that appeared to be clear was that *occidere* or *corrumpere per commissionem* and *per omissionem* were not put on a par. Such equation, on the other hand, was exactly what the Natural lawyers and the authors of the later *ius commune* advocated: liability was now imposed for 'culpam omnem, sive in faciendo, sive in non faciendo' (in the words of Hugo Grotius). Nineteenth-century pandectists, again, adopted a restrictive approach; they took D. 7, 1, 13, 2 as their cue and emphasized the exceptional character of liability for omissions. Whether a duty to act can be based on a previous action (see Windscheid and Kipp (n. 28) § 455, 2) remained disputed. Von Kübel who was in charge of the preparatory draft of the law of obligations took the view that this restrictive attitude did not meet contemporary requirements. Generally on the development of liability for omissions, see *Law of Obligations* (n. 25) 1029 f., 1043 ff.; especially for the 19th century, see Detlef Kleindiek, *Deliktshaftung und juristische Person* (1997), 56 ff.; Seiler (n. 35) 255; on von Kübel, in this context, see Benöhr (n. 26) 518 and Kleindiek, 98.

[73] An alternative term is *Verkehrspflicht*. On the terminology, see Hans-Joachim Mertens, in *Münchener Kommentar zum BGB* vol. v (3rd edn., 1997), § 823 nn. 203 ff. on the one hand and Kötz (n. 33) nn. 232 ff. on the other. Fundamentally important is the work of Christian von Bar, *Verkehrspflichten* (1980). The term Verkehrssicherungspflichten was declared untranslatable by F. H. Lawson and B. S. Markesinis, *Tortious Liability for Unintentional Harm in the Common Law and the Civil Law*, vol. i (1982), 78. In his *German Law of Torts* (n. 29) 75 Markesinis says that the term is 'not easy to translate'. He summarizes its meaning in the following way: 'whoever by his activity or through his property establishes in everyday life a source of potential danger which is likely to affect the interests and rights of others, is obliged to ensure their protection against the risks thus created by him.'

unlawful act in terms of § 823 I BGB may also be committed by omission. What was doubtful, however, was whether the defendant could be said to have been under a legal duty to prevent the tree from causing harm to others. The BGB did not provide an express answer. The question had to be answered in the negative if one were to follow the authority of Roman and contemporary Roman law. In Roman law it would have been necessary to have been granted, or at least to have demanded to be granted, a *cautio damni infecti* in order to claim compensation for the loss caused by the defective state of a piece of property; the *actio legis Aquiliae* had not been available for this kind of loss. The BGB had not, however, maintained this point of view, as was apparent from § 836 BGB (liability for the collapse of a building).[74] This provision was not to be understood as excluding the application of § 823 I BGB to cases concerning the collapse of objects other than buildings, particularly the fall of a tree. § 836 BGB, in the view of the Court, was merely one specific emanation of a general principle which was contrary to Roman law, namely 'that today everybody has to be responsible for any loss caused by objects of his, insofar as he had to prevent such damage considering the reasonable interests of the other party'.[75]

Only four months later this decision was confirmed by

> RGZ 54, 53, judgment of 23 February 1903, VI. Division: The plaintiff had fallen on a flight of steps, available for public use, which had become slippery with snow. He claimed damages from the city who owned that flight of steps.

[74] 'If, by the collapse of a building or other structure attached to a piece of land, or by the detachment of parts of the building or structure, a person is killed or injured, or the health of a person is affected, or a thing is damaged, and if the collapse or the detachment was caused by defective construction or inadequate maintenance, the possessor of the land is bound to compensate the injured party for any damage arising therefrom. The duty to make compensation does not arise if the possessor has exercised the requisite care for the purpose of averting danger' (§ 836 I BGB).

[75] RGZ 52, 373 (379). As far as the argument based on § 836 BGB is concerned, see the detailed analysis by Kleindiek (n. 72) 85 ff., particularly 91 ff.

The Appeal Court had rejected the claim; a legal duty, on the part of the defendant, to grit those steps could not be established. The Imperial Court objected to this reasoning and referred to the principle enunciated in RGZ 52, 373. That principle soon became firmly ensconced.[76]

It is remarkable that RGZ 54, 53 did not only rely on RGZ 52, 373 but also on a line of decisions based on Aquilian liability, as it had prevailed prior to codification. These decisions had recognized the responsibility of an owner for the condition of his property, as far as it was available for public use.[77] RGZ 54, 53 did not, therefore, represent a new beginning but merely continued an older tradition.[78]

None the less, the case law establishing the foundations of the concept of *Verkehrssicherungspflicht* is widely regarded today as a bold piece of judicial development of the law that had never been contemplated by the draftsmen of the Code.[79] In view of the continuity between legal practice prior to, and after, the enactment of the Code this view appears to be mistaken. There is nothing to suggest that the BGB had been intended to fall behind the level of protection granted under the *ius commune*.[80]

3. Liability for Others

(*a*) *Introduction*

As far as liability for others is concerned, the draftsmen of the BGB had rejected (as being alien to traditional 'German' notions of justice and fairness)[81] the rule prevailing in

[76] See RGZ 58, 333, judgment of 24 June 1904 (III. Division) (the plaintiff's fall occurred on a slippery path leading back from a restaurant to the road); RGZ 62, 31 (33), judgment of 9 Nov. 1905 (VI. Division) (injury resulting from the decayed floor covering of a bridge); RGZ 68, 358 (365) (III. Division), judgment of 24 Apr. 1908 (damage resulting from some tows having been insufficiently fastened in the Kiel Canal).

[77] See the references in Bilstein (n. 35) 43 ff.; Kleindiek (n. 72) 63 ff.

[78] Kleindiek (n. 72) 85.

[79] Reference is made to a 'contradiction' between § 823 I BGB as conceived by the legislature and by the judiciary; see, e.g., Mertens, in *Münchener Kommentar* (n. 73) § 823 nn. 2 ff.

[80] The prevailing view is refuted on the basis of a detailed analysis by Kleindiek (n. 72) 34 ff., 112 ff.; cf. also Bilstein (n. 35) 48 ff., 117 f.

[81] See *Law of Obligations* (n. 25) 1125.

French law according to which a person is responsible for the harm caused by the act of persons 'for whom he is answerable' (such as his employees).[82] Relying on the *ius commune*,[83] they tied liability under § 831 I BGB to the requirement that the employer himself (or, in the case of juristic persons, the duly appointed representative, § 31 BGB) had been at fault in the selection, instruction, or supervision of his employee.[84] The practical impact of this rule is somewhat diminished as a result of a reversal of the onus of proof: the employer has to establish that no fault was attributable to him. Nevertheless, even while the BGB was in the process of being prepared, the regime established in § 831 I BGB was subject to criticism,[85] and today it is very widely regarded as ill conceived and inappropriate.[86] Over the years the courts have found various ways to circumvent the rule. Some of them can be traced back to decisions in the first years after the enactment of the Code.

(*b*) *Extension of Contractual Liability*

At an early stage the Imperial Court started to evade the restrictive requirements laid down in § 831 I BGB by extending the range of contractual liability to cases which one should normally have considered to fall within the proper domain of the law of delict. The most famous example is the linoleum case from 1911.

82 Art. 1184 *code civil*.

83 The interpretation of D. 19, 2, 25, 7 (concerning the transportation of a column) played a role in this regard. See Reinhard Zimmermann, 'The Civil Law in European Codes', in David L. Carey Miller and Reinhard Zimmermann (eds.), *The Civilian Tradition and Scots Law: Aberdeen Quincentenary Essays* (1997), 272 f. with references. On the fault principle within the BGB in general, see Hans-Peter Benöhr, 'Die Entscheidung des BGB für das Verschuldensprinzip', (1978) 46 *TR* 1 ff. The restrictive attitude towards liability for others in 19th-century Germany has parallels in other legal systems. On the common employment doctrine of English law, see Hartmut Wicke, *Respondeat Superior: Haftung für Verrichtungsgehilfen im römischen, römisch-holländischen und südafrikanischen Recht* (2000), § 4 V 9.

84 On the origin of § 831 BGB, see Hans Hermann Seiler, 'Die deliktische Gehilfenhaftung in historischer Sicht', 1967 *JZ* 525 ff.

85 See 'Protokolle', in Mugdan (n. 27) 1092 ff.

86 See, e.g., Kötz (n. 33) nn. 287 ff. For a modern comparative discussion, see Zweigert and Kötz (n. 57) 629 ff.; Markesinis (n. 29) 676 ff.

RGZ 78, 239, judgment of 7 December 1911, VI. Division:[87] The plaintiff had entered a department store in order to buy a linoleum floor-cover. While she was inspecting various samples she was injured by linoleum rolls which had been carelessly handled by an employee of the department store. The intended contract of sale was not concluded. The plaintiff claimed damages from the person in charge of the department store.

According to the Imperial Court 'a legal relationship preparatory to the contract of sale' had come into existence when the parties had entered into contractual negotiations.[88] This legal relationship was 'similar to a contract in character' and had given rise to obligations insofar as both parties had been under a duty to observe due diligence for the health and property of each other when presenting and inspecting the carpets.

Thus, in effect, the Imperial Court incorporated liability for *culpa in contrahendo*[89] into the field of contractual liability. This opened the way for the application of § 278 BGB: the person operating the department store could be held responsible for the fault of his employee 'to the same extent as for his own fault', i.e., without the additional fault requirement of § 831 I BGB. There can be no doubt that in the linoleum case the Imperial Court left behind the sphere of application previously allotted to the *culpa in contrahendo* doctrine[90] and, indeed, the Imperial Court bluntly stated that the real reason for extending the range of contractual liability was the elimination, in the present case, of § 831 I BGB.

It would be repugnant to the general sense of justice if in cases where the employee in the course of displaying or laying out goods for exhibition, sampling, trial, or the like, carelessly injures a prospective purchaser, the proprietor of the business—with whom the prospector wished to make the purchase—should be

[87] An English translation of this case can be found in Markesinis (n. 29) 774 ff.

[88] It was based, according to the Imperial Court, on an offer to be shown the carpets and on the acceptance of this offer.

[89] The term is not mentioned in the decision.

[90] Cf. infra pp. 88 ff.

answerable only under § 831 BGB rather than unconditionally, so that the injured person should, if the proprietor succeeds in exonerating himself, be referred to the usually impecunious employee.[91]

In the published report of the linoleum case another point, sadly, remains unexplored. Apart from the customer herself her child had also been hit by the linoleum rolls. There is no reference to a possible claim for damages by that child. Such claim would have required the boundaries of contract law to be pushed even further. It would have necessitated recognition of a contract with protective effect vis-à-vis third parties. This development was not, however, long in coming.

> RGZ 91, 21, judgment of 5 October 1917, III. Division:[92] The plaintiff, a civil servant working for the railways, was transferred and moved, with his family, into a new dwelling supplied to him by his employer, the State. Soon afterwards his daughter, the co-plaintiff, contracted tuberculosis. The disease resulted from the fact that the flat had not been disinfected, even though the previous inhabitant had suffered from a pulmonary disease and had thus infected the flat with tuberculosis bacilli. That the disinfection had been omitted was the fault of a railway doctor, employed by the defendant. He had treated the previous inhabitant and should have arranged for the disinfection of the flat.

The defendant had been able to exonerate himself as far as the selection, instruction, and supervision of the railway doctor was concerned. Thus, the plaintiff had no delictual claims against the state. The Appeal Court had also refused to countenance a contractual claim of the daughter in view of the fact that a contractual relationship had only been established with her father. The Imperial Court took a different view.

[91] RGZ 78, 239 (240 f.).

[92] For an English translation of this case, see Markesinis (n. 29) 794 ff.

Unless very peculiar circumstances indicate a different conclusion, the tenant of the family dwelling who concludes a contract of lease must be taken, as the landlord must know, to intend to obtain the maximum protection for the members of his household and to acquire for them the same rights in relation to the safety of the premises as he himself enjoys against the landlord . . . If the landlord's contractual duties are not extended in this manner, injured dependants would be restricted to claims in delict and would not have the benefit afforded to the tenant by §§ 278, 538 BGB . . . To give such different rights to the tenant and to his dependants is offensive to proper legal sentiment.[93]

This decision demonstrates, as the linoleum case also does, that the Court was quite prepared to apply the law in a very free and flexible manner in order to extend the contractual liability rules. The reasoning process was openly determined by the result the Court intended to reach. The course mapped out in RGZ 91, 21 was soon continued,[94] even if the term generally used today (contract with protective effect vis-à-vis third parties) was introduced only by the Federal Supreme Court.[95]

(c) *Extensive Interpretation of § 31 BGB*

Another path that could be used to circumvent the unsuitable rule concerning liability for others consisted in an extensive interpretation of § 31 BGB. In terms of this provision, a juristic person is liable, without any possibility of exoneration, for any damage which a member of the board 'or other duly appointed representative' may, in carrying out his duty, inflict on a third party. The first—albeit somewhat hesistant—steps towards extending this provision were also already undertaken by the Imperial Court in the first years after the enactment of the Code.[96]

The original meaning of the reference to 'other duly

[93] RGZ 91, 21 (24).

[94] See the review of previous case law in RGZ 127, 218 (222 ff.), judgment of 10 Feb. 1930 (the gas-meter case). For background analysis, see the articles by Jörg Neuner and Sibylle Hofer, quoted infra n. 197. On the concept of contracts with protective effect vis-à-vis third parties, see infra pp. 95 ff.

[95] See BGH, 1959 *NJW* 1676, judgment of 30 June 1959 (following Karl Larenz).

[96] See the detailed analysis by Kleindiek (n. 72) 314 ff., 340 ff.

appointed representative[s]' was the inclusion of the special representatives mentioned in § 30 BGB within the liability rule of § 31 BGB.[97] Thus, the possibility of appointing a special representative had to be provided for in the memorandum of association. The Imperial Court at first, indeed, insisted on such provision in the memorandum of association or, in the case of juristic persons under public law, on an equivalent statute establishing the legal person.[98] Soon, however, a tendency gained ground to relax this requirement. Thus, in RGZ 62, 31[99] a district architect was regarded as a 'duly appointed representative' of the district, even though his position was not dealt with by statute. It was held to be sufficient that the office of a district architect had been established on the basis of a resolution of the district council. RGZ 70, 118 (119 f.)[100] emphasized, in a similar case, that the agreement of incorporation (or equivalent statute) did not have to provide expressly for a representative. His appointment merely had to have 'its legal basis' in the agreement of incorporation (or equivalent statute). The architect of a municipality was therefore taken to be a representative in terms of § 31 BGB if the municipality was authorized by the municipal laws to create the office of a municipal architect.[101]

This extension did not change the fact that the application of § 31 BGB was still dependent on the way in which the agreement of incorporation (or equivalent statute) had been drafted. This could lead to unsatisfactory and arbitrary results. The Imperial Court therefore went a step further, converting, under certain circumstances, the *possibility* to appoint a representative into a *duty* to do so.[102] In RGZ 89, 186 (187 f.)[103] the plaintiff twisted his ankle when

[97] See Günter Weick, in *Staudinger, Kommentar zum Bürgerlichen Gesetzbuch* (13th edn., 1995), § 31 n. 24.

[98] RGZ 53, 276 (279 f.), judgment of 15 Jan. 1903 (VI. Division).

[99] Judgment of 9 Nov. 1905 (VI. Division).

[100] Judgment of 14 Dec. 1908 (VI. Division).

[101] For a similarly liberal interpretation, see RGZ 79, 101 (107 f.), judgment of 18 Mar. 1912 (VI. Division). A more restrictive view was taken in RGZ 74, 21 (23), judgment of 2 June 1910 (VI. Division).

[102] Weick, in *Staudinger* (n. 97) § 31 n. 29.

[103] Judgment of 27 Nov. 1916 (VI. Division).

his foot got stuck in a hole in the pavement. The Court was of the opinion that the municipality was liable to the plaintiff even if it could exonerate itself (in terms of § 831 I BGB) with regard to all its officials responsible for road safety. For the municipality had to be organized in a manner that there was always a 'duly appointed representative' in charge. No municipality could be allowed to get away with a situation where responsibility in road safety matters merely lay with officials for which the escape route of exoneration was available.

The liability regime devised by the draftsmen of the Code was definitively abandoned in RGZ 91, 1 (3).[104] Here the head of the branch office of a business corporation was taken to be a 'duly appointed representative', even though the memorandum of association had merely permitted the establishment of a branch office. The restrictive requirement contained in § 31 BGB had, for all practical purposes, been discarded.[105] It was sufficient that the representative, for a certain range of business activities, enjoyed an independent position and that this range of business activities had found some form of expression in the memorandum of association. This liberal extension of § 31 BGB necessarily entailed a restriction of the scope of application of § 831 I BGB.

4. Summary

If one attempts to summarize what has been said so far, the following picture emerges. It can no longer be maintained—not, at least, as far as the law of delict is concerned—that the practice of the Imperial Court during the early years under the BGB was characterized by positivistic narrowness in the application of the Code. In the first two decades the foundations were laid for what von Caemmerer has termed the transformation of the German law of delict. *First*, the range of 'other rights of another' in

[104] Judgment of 8 Oct. 1917 (VI. Division).
[105] Kleindiek (n. 72) 346.

terms of § 823 I BGB was extended at an early stage. The judges adhered to the principle established by the Code that the patrimony as such did not enjoy protection. But they soon began to relax the rigour of this principle by recognizing (lawful) possession and the right to an established and operating business as 'other rights of another'. *Secondly*, even in 1902 already the Imperial Court effectively relied on the concept of *Verkehrssicherungspflicht* which was not mentioned in the Code. And *thirdly* the Court soon began to circumvent the unsatisfactory provision on delictual liability for others, both by greatly extending the range of contractual liability and by an extensive interpretation of § 31 BGB which was no longer reconcilable with the intentions of the draftsmen of the Code.

Of course, there were also areas where the Imperial Court fairly strictly adhered to the intentions of the draftsmen as they had found expression in the Code. This is true, in particular, for the protection of a person's personality. But one can hardly regard this as an extraordinarily positivistic approach. The relevant provisions of the Code were so clear, in this respect, that recognition of a general right to the protection of a person's individual sphere of life would have constituted an unprecedented and impermissible rebellion against the law. Moreover, the judges of the Imperial Court were sympathetic to the evaluations on which the approach adopted in the Code was based. These evaluations reflected a contemporary morality that was widely shared. None the less, even here we have seen that the Court found ways and means to effect marginal corrections where some form of personality protection seemed to be called for.

Interestingly, where the Imperial Court transformed the law of delict, we usually find a continuity reaching back to the law prevailing prior to the enactment of the Code. The right to an established and operating business provides a telling example for it had been recognized by the Imperial Court before 1900. Delictual protection of possession had also been advocated before 1900, though it had not yet been accepted by the Imperial Court. The case law on *Verkehrssicherungspflichten* organically built upon precedents established under nineteenth-century Aquilian liability. Only the attempts to circumvent the restrictions with which liability for others was fettered may be described as bold innovations. They were, however, inspired by a widespread dissatisfaction with the rule of § 831 I BGB. It was a rule outmoded even in 1900 and out of tune with the liability regimes in other European countries.

III. THE REACTION OF THE IMPERIAL COURT TO THE CODIFICATION OF PRIVATE LAW: OTHER AREAS

We have, so far, only examined one specific (though important) area of the law of obligations. But the observations made, so far, are confirmed if we turn our attention to other areas, too. A brief glance at a few examples will have to suffice.

1. *Clausula Rebus Sic Stantibus*[106]

The *clausula rebus sic stantibus* is an implied condition according to which a contract is binding only as long and as far as matters remain the same as they were at the time of conclusion of the contract. It had had its heyday in the late Middle Ages and had also become part and parcel of the *usus modernus* and the systematic blueprints of the Natural lawyers.[107] The Prussian and Austrian codes, however, displayed great reserve. The *code civil* no longer recognized the *clausula*. Nineteenth-century legal science

[106] Klaus Luig, 'Die Kontinuität allgemeiner Rechtsgrundsätze: Das Beispiel der clausula rebus sic stantibus', in Zimmermann, Knütel, and Meincke (n. 26) 171 ff.

[107] On the history of the *clausula rebus sic stantibus*, see *Law of Obligations* (n. 25) 579 ff.; Ralf Köbler, *Die 'clausula rebus sic stantibus' als allgemeiner Rechtsgrundsatz* (1991); Michael Rummel, *Die 'clausula rebus sic stantibus': Eine dogmengeschichtliche Untersuchung unter Berücksichtigung der Zeit von der Rezeption im 14. Jahrhundert bis zum jüngeren Usus modernus in der ersten Hälfte des 18. Jahrhunderts* (1991); Klaus Luig, 'Dogmengeschichte des Privatrechts als rechtswissenschaftliche Grundlagenforschung', (1993) 20 *Ius Commune* 193 ff.

was predominantly hostile to this 'hackneyed little phrase';[108] it did not suit the spirit of a time when freedom of contract, economic liberalism, and certainty of law reigned supreme. As long as the performance of a contractual promise had not become impossible it had to be rendered. Thus, it is not surprising that the BGB refused to accept a general rule dealing with the problem of changed circumstances.[109]

On the other hand, however, the BGB was enacted at a time when the social and economic conditions underpinning the liberalism of nineteenth-century vintage had begun to change. Imperceptibly, at first, the decline of freedom of contract had started and 'classical' contract doctrine, even as early as 1900, was challenged by the new developments.[110] Bernhard Windscheid was sufficiently far-sighted to realize that the considerations on which the *clausula* was based could not simply be rejected out of hand. Thrown out by the door, he famously predicted,[111] they will always re-enter through the window. The legal system obviously has to find a balance between equity and *rigor iuris*. Interestingly, even the BGB took account of a change of circumstances in a number of specific situations.[112] Even more interestingly, the Imperial Court immediately started

[108] *Sprüchelchen*: A. D. Weber, *Systematische Entwicklung der Lehre von der natürlichen Verbindlichkeit* (1784), as quoted by Luig (n. 106) 176.

[109] For the views of the draftsmen of the Code, see Luig (n. 106) 177 ff.

[110] See, e.g., Hellmut Georg Isele, 'Ein halbes Jahrhundert deutsches Bürgerliches Gesetzbuch', (1949) 150 *AcP* 4 ff.; Franz Wieacker, *Industriegesellschaft und Privatrechtsordnung* (1974). For England, P. S. Atiyah, *The Rise and Fall of Freedom of Contract* (1979), 571 ff., also shows 'the decline and fall of freedom of contract' to have started around 1870.

[111] 'Die Voraussetzung', (1892) 78 *AcP* 197. Windscheid's *dictum* referred to his own substitute for the *clausula rebus sic stantibus*, the *Voraussetzungslehre* ('presupposition' doctrine), which the draftsmen of the BGB, like the *clausula*, refused to adopt. On the presupposition doctrine, see supra pp. 17, 49 f.

[112] See, e.g., § 321 BGB ('If a person is obliged by a reciprocal contract to perform his part first, he may, if after the conclusion of the contract a significant deterioration in the financial position of the other party occurs whereby the claim for the counter-performance is endangered, refuse to perform his part until the counter-performance is made or security is given for it'), § 610 BGB ('A person who promises to make a loan may, in case of doubt, revoke his promise if the financial circumstances of the other party significantly deteriorate, so that the claim for

to explore ways and means how the range of situations might be extended.

Of course, it was recognized that the BGB had rejected the *clausula*; nevertheless, 'it had to be examined whether in an individual case the parties might not have intended to grant one or the other of them a right to withdraw from the contract on account of a change of circumstances'.[113] This was in 1902. In 1905 such right of withdrawal was granted first in an individual case (on the basis of an extensive interpretation of the exceptional situations where the BGB had given effect to a change of circumstances [§§ 321, 610 BGB] and of considerations of good faith)[114] and then even with regard to an entire class of contracts (contracts of insurance).[115] The latter case, incidentally, contained the startling pronouncement that the 'general rules of private law cannot be considered as the proper point of departure for the decision to be taken';[116] the Court based its ruling on the 'nature of the contract'. In a decision of 1906 the Imperial Court rejected Windscheid's presupposition doctrine,[117] thus itself presupposing that in principle it was entitled to consider, and possibly even accept, a doctrine not contained in the BGB.[118] But the *clausula* was on the advance. It asserted itself in a growing range of cases, be it on the basis of a tacit agreement by the parties, be it on the basis of good faith, an analogous application of §§ 321 and 610 BGB, the purpose and content of the contract, or the nature of the (type of) contract concerned.[119]

The transition from an ever increasing number of excep-

repayment is endangered'), § 779 BGB ('A contract whereby the dispute or the uncertainty of the parties concerning a legal relationship is ended by way of mutual concession [compromise] is invalid if the state of affairs regarded as essential according to the terms of the contract do not correspond with the actual facts, and if the dispute or the uncertainty would not have arisen if the state of affairs had been known').

[113] RGZ 50, 255 (258); this is based on a statement contained in 'Motive', in Mugdan (n. 27) 109. In the case under consideration, the Imperial Court was able to achieve a satisfactory result by granting a claim for damages based on § 326 BGB (*mora debitoris*).

[114] RG, 1905 *JW* 168.

[115] RGZ 60, 56 (62 f.).

[116] RGZ 60, 56 (58).

[117] RGZ 62, 267 (267 f.).

[118] Luig (n. 106) 180 f.

[119] See the references ibid. 181 ff.

tions to a new principle occurred in 1920 when the Imperial Court asserted that the performance of a contractual obligation could no longer be demanded, if as a result of a complete change of circumstances it had become entirely different from the one originally contemplated and intended by the parties. The plaintiff's claim was regarded as 'justified from the point of view of the *clausula rebus sic stantibus*' which had now 'openly manifested itself' in the Code.[120] This decision was hardly a sensation:[121] in a long line of cases the Imperial Court had prised open a window in the doctrinal edifice of German private law through which the *clausula* was able to make its re-entry.[122]

2. *Exceptio Doli Generalis*[123]

(*a*) *The Background*

Unlike the *clausula rebus sic stantibus*, the *exceptio doli* (defence of fraud, or bad faith), was of Roman origin.[124] It had become part of the *ius commune* though, of course, it had lost all the procedural associations originally connected with the *exceptio doli* of classical Roman law. Essentially, it

120 RGZ 100, 129 (132).

121 This is the view expressed by Uwe Wesel, *Geschichte des Rechts* (1997), 447.

122 See Luig (n. 106) 174, 184. Cf. also RGZ 103, 329 (331 f.) where the Imperial Court blended the *clausula* with Paul Oertmann's notion of the basis of the transaction (see Paul Oertmann, *Die Geschäftsgrundlage: Ein neuer Rechtsbegriff* (1921). The doctrine of *Wegfall der Geschäftsgrundlage* (collapse of the underlying basis of the transaction) that has arisen from this basis is usually related to the corrective function of § 242 BGB (the famous 'good faith' provision); and though it is still today discussed, for the sake of convenience, under this doctrinal umbrella, it has effectively become a sophisticated doctrine in its own right. For discussions in English, see Werner Lorenz, 'Contract Modification as a Result of Change of Circumstances', in Jack Beatson and Daniel Friedmann (eds.), *Good Faith and Fault in Contract Law* (1995), 357 ff.; Werner F. Ebke and Bettina Steinhauer, 'The Doctrine of Good Faith in German Contract Law', in Beatson and Friedmann, 180 ff.; and see the references in Simon Whittaker and Reinhard Zimmermann, 'Good Faith in European Contract Law: Surveying the Landscape', in Reinhard Zimmermann and Simon Whittaker (eds.), *Good Faith in European Contract Law* (2000), 25 f. and the German report to case 25 in the same volume, 557 f.

123 Hans-Peter Haferkamp, 'Die Exceptio Doli generalis in der Rechtsprechung des Reichsgerichts von 1914', in Falk and Mohnhaupt (n. 20) in preparation.

124 For details, see *Law of Obligations* (n. 25) 662 ff.; Whittaker and Zimmermann (n. 122) 16 ff.

was the label commonly used for the notion of *bona fides* suffusing contemporary as much as Roman contract law.[125] By raising the *exceptio doli*, the defendant asserted the notion of good faith, under the auspices of which contractual disputes had to be decided.[126] Obviously, it gave the judge considerable leeway and, in particular, it provided him with the opportunity to take account of substantive notions of justice. This was the main reason why the opinion of legal writers vacillated considerably. Savigny and his followers in the first half of the nineteenth century had been well disposed towards it, and under their influence it had been brought to bear on Prussian law and on the new law relating to bills of exchange.[127] From about the 1870s, however, more and more writers expressed misgivings about the practical application of the *exceptio doli generalis*.[128] The modern judge, it was argued, was no longer in the position of a Roman *praetor*. He was subject to the law and could not simply act *iuris civilis adiuvandi, supplendi,* or *corrigendi causa*. The *exceptio doli* was thus only available in cases where it had specifically been recognized in Roman law. When the BGB was drafted, the tide had began to turn again. Dernburg[129] and Regelsberger[130] were among those who argued that 'the productive force' (Dernburg) of the *exceptio doli generalis* had not been extinguished and that it was still required as a vital mechanism for the implementation of substantive justice.[131] Once again, we see that by the end of the century classical contract doctrine was past its zenith.

The position adopted by the BGB is not quite clear. On

[125] See, in particular, Martin Schermaier, 'Bona Fides in Roman Contract Law', in Zimmermann and Whittaker (n. 122) 63 ff.

[126] See, e.g. Windscheid and Kipp (n. 28) § 47 n. 7: in actual practice the *exceptio doli* is usually tantamount to a recourse to the idea of good faith except that the matter is seen, naturally enough, from the point of view of the defendant.

[127] See Haferkamp (n. 123) sub I and III. 2 (a).

[128] Filippo Ranieri, 'Bonne Foi et exercice du droit dans la tradition du civil law', 1998 *RIDC* 1064 f.; Haferkamp (n. 123) sub III. 2 (a).

[129] Heinrich Dernburg, *Pandekten* (6th edn., 1900), § 138, 4 in fine.

[130] Ferdinand Regelsberger, *Pandekten*, vol. i (1893), 686.

[131] According to Regelsberger, (1902) 44 *Kritische Vierteljahresschrift für Gesetzgebung und Rechtswissenschaft* 434, the *exceptio doli* was required to combat, i.a., the excesses of the 'terrorism of private autonomy'.

the one hand, acceptance of the *exceptio doli* into the code was repeatedly rejected.[132] On the other hand, it was argued that such acceptance was unnecessary in view of a number of provisions already contained in the draft code which could be seen as manifestations of the *exceptio doli generalis*.[133] In fact, however, these provisions (§§ 226,[134] 242, and 826[135] BGB) were all rather narrow. This is true, particularly, of § 242 BGB which merely relates to the manner in which performance must be rendered.[136] Determination of the content of a contract is regulated in § 157[137] BGB and is regarded as a matter of interpretation. Nevertheless, the continued existence of the *exceptio doli generalis* was widely accepted in the first textbooks, commentaries, and lectures on the new Code, be it on the basis of §§ 157, 226, and 242 BGB or simply as a result of 'the grace of God'.[138] The *exceptio doli generalis* was widely welcomed as an antidote against the literalist and narrow

[132] See, e.g., Horst Heinrich Jakobs and Werner Schubert, *Materialien zur Entstehungsgeschichte des BGB, Allgemeiner Teil*, vol. ii (1978), 171.

[133] See, e.g., the statement on behalf of the government in the course of the second reading of the BGB in the Reichstag, in Mugdan (n. 27) 1311.

[134] 'The exercise of a right is unlawful, if its purpose can only be to cause damage to another.' On the historical background to this rule (*aemulatio*), see Bruno Huwiler, 'Aequitas und bona fides als Faktoren der Rechtsverwirklichung', in Bruno Schmidlin (ed.), *Vers un droit privé européen commun? Skizzen zum gemeineuropäischen Privatrecht* (1994), 57 ff. and Antonio Gambaro, 'Abuse of Right in Civil Law Tradition', in Alfredo Mordechai Rabello (ed.), *Aequitas and Equity: Equity in Civil Law and Mixed Jurisdictions* (1997), 632 ff. In view of the wide interpretation given to § 242 BGB, the rule does not have much practical significance ('largely redundant': Helmut Heinrichs, in *Palandt, Bürgerliches Gesetzbuch* (58th edn., 1999), § 226 n. 1).

[135] 'A person who wilfully causes damage to another in a manner *contra bonos mores* is bound to compensate the other for the damage.' For commentary in English, see Markesinis (n. 29) 894 ff.; cf. also supra p. 68.

[136] 'The debtor is bound to perform according to the requirements of good faith, ordinary usage being taken into consideration.'

[137] 'Contracts shall be interpreted according to the requirements of good faith, giving consideration to common usage.'

[138] See, e.g., Wendt, 'Die exceptio doli generalis im heutigen Recht oder Treu und Glauben im Recht der Schuldverhältnisse', (1906) 100 *AcP* 1 ff.; Paul Oertmann, *Das Recht der Schuldverhältnisse* (vol. ii of a commentary to the German Civil Code edited by Biermann, von Blume, and others) (2nd edn., 1906), § 242, 4; and see the detailed references in Haferkamp (n. 123) sub IV. 1 (particularly n. 113).

approach which, it was feared,[139] might prevail under the new Code. When these fears turned out to have been unfounded, the critical voices gained ground again.[140] Soon the discussion became overshadowed by the great methodological debates unleashed by the free law movement.[141] The focus of attention now shifted to the application of § 242 BGB, the provision that had begun to emerge as the heir apparent of the *exceptio doli generalis*. Strong language was used. The good faith provision was seen, on the one hand, as 'the source of the baneful plague gnawing in a most sinister manner at the inner core of our legal culture';[142] on the other hand, it was celebrated as the 'queen of rules'[143] which could be used to unhinge the established legal world.[144]

(*b*) *The Courts*

And the courts? It is highly instructive to see how little they were perturbed, or affected, by these discussions, or indeed by the introduction of the Civil Code. The application of the principle of good faith and of the *exceptio doli* in German legal practice has remained constant, as Ranieri puts it very pointedly,[145] from the days of the *usus modernus pandectarum* to the case law of the Federal Supreme Court. This is confirmed, for the period around the turn of the century, by another recent study.[146] From 1880 to 1914 there was a steady stream of decisions by the Imperial Court—carrying on, in this respect, the tradition established by the Imperial

[139] See, e.g., Jakobs and Schubert (n. 132) 1171.

[140] A good example is Konrad Schneider, *Treu und Glauben im Recht der Schuldverhältnisse*, 1902; and see the references in Haferkamp (n. 123) sub V.

[141] For an overview of the various positions, see Wieacker (n. 5) 363 ff., 453 ff.; Peter Raisch, *Juristische Methoden* (1995), 107 ff.

[142] Rudolf Henle, *Treu und Glauben im Rechtsverkehr* (1912), 3.

[143] See the (critical) discussion by Justus Wilhelm Hedemann, *Die Flucht in die Generalklauseln: Eine Gefahr für Recht und Staat* (1933), 10 f.

[144] Generally on the application and theoretical perception of § 242 BGB, see (in English) Ebke and Steinhauer (n. 122) 171 ff.; Whittaker and Zimmermann (n. 122) 22 ff.

[145] 1998 *RIDC* 1081.

[146] Haferkamp (n. 123) sub III. 1 and 2 (b), IV. 2 and VI.

Supreme Commercial Court (*Reichsoberhandelsgericht*)[147]—evaluating the conduct of the parties from the point of view of good faith and thus imposing an objective standard of honest, loyal, and considerate behaviour. This was done without much ado. Before the enactment of the Code, the Court regarded the existence of the *exceptio doli generalis* (for which it used a number of different terms, both Latin and German) as self-evident and it tended, at least at first, to avoid any sweeping statements but based its reasoning on the facts of the individual case.[148]

In the 1890s, and obviously encouraged by the favourable mood towards the *exceptio doli generalis*, the Court became somewhat more adventurous and openly prescriptive in its process of reasoning.[149] The first relevant decision under the BGB referred to the *exceptio doli* (*Einrede der Arglist*) as if nothing had changed.[150] Then the one or other provision of the Code came to be added in brackets.[151] A little later the first attempt was made to demonstrate that the general principle had been retained by the BGB; no less than eight provisions of the Code were lined up to prove that proposition.[152] From about 1909 onwards, the Court merely stated that the *exceptio doli generalis* was recognized and had been applied repeatedly. 'Merely'[153] its doctrinal foundation remained disputed. The Court thus succeeded in maintaining a middle course: neither was it regarded as sufficient if the plaintiff merely acted inequitably nor was judicial intervention confined to the extreme case where the only purpose of exercising a right had been to cause damage to another. The *exceptio doli generalis* remained a malleable tool to mitigate the rigours of the law.

[147] On the importance of that Court (founded in 1869) for the process of unification of German law, see Herbert Kronke, 'Rechtsvergleichung und Rechtsvereinheitlichung in der Rechtsprechung des Reichsoberhandelsgerichts', (1997) 5 *ZEuP* 735 ff.

[148] See the references provided by Haferkamp (n. 123) sub III. 2 (b).

[149] Haferkamp (n. 123) sub IV. 2.

[150] RG, in Werner Schubert (ed.), *Sammlung sämtlicher Erkenntnisse des Reichsgerichts* (1992 ff.), 1902, 47 n. 76.

[151] See, e.g., RG, 1903 *JW* 432.

[152] RGZ 58, 425 (429).

[153] RGZ 71, 435.

3. *Culpa in Contrahendo*[154]

(*a*) *The Doctrine Devised by Jhering*

Culpa in contrahendo (fault in the formation of contract) was probably Rudolph von Jhering's most celebrated legal 'discovery'.[155] It was a product of the then prevailing method of conceptual 'construction'. Jhering himself at one place in his article acknowledged that 'a most violent effort'[156] was required to squeeze the Roman sources into the doctrinal framework devised by him. Characteristically, it was only towards the end of his study that he turned to Prussian law. Here he found 'a very surprising confirmation of my ideas'[157] in § 284 I 5 prALR which read: 'What is right with regard to the degree of fault for which [a debtor] is responsible when performing his contractual obligation is also applicable if one of the contracting parties has neglected the duties incumbent on him in concluding the contract.' This provision was based on Natural law theory.[158] Jhering's *culpa in contrahendo*[159] was more narrowly conceived in two respects. (i) It only related to cases where one of the contracting parties carries out his obligations under what he presumes to be a valid contract whereas that contract has, in reality, not been concluded or turns out to be void; cases, in other words, where reliance is placed on the mere semblance of a contract. Thus, somewhat paradoxically, contractual diligence is owed in a situation where there was no contract. (ii) Liability was confined to the 'negative interest'.[160]

[154] Tomasz Giaro, 'Culpa in contrahendo: Eine Geschichte der Wiederentdeckungen', in Falk and Mohnhaupt (n. 20) in preparation.

[155] Rudolph von Jhering, 'Culpa in contrahendo, oder Schadensersatz bei nichtigen oder nicht zur Perfektion gelangten Verträgen', (1861) 4 *JhJb* 1 ff.; cf. Hans Dölle, 'Juristische Entdeckungen', in *Verhandlungen des 42. Deutschen Juristentages*, vol. ii (1959), pp. B 1 ff.

[156] (1861) 4 *JhJb* 92.

[157] (1861) 4 *JhJb* 44, 50 f.

[158] See Byoung Jo Choe, *Culpa in contrahendo bei Rudolph von Jhering* (1988), 203 ff.

[159] On which see Dieter Medicus, 'Zur Entdeckungsgeschichte der Culpa in Contrahendo', in *Festgabe für Max Kaser* (1986), 169 ff.; Giaro (n. 154) sub I.

[160] See, e.g., *Law of Obligations* (n. 25) 243 f.

(*b*) *The Position of the BGB*

The Imperial Court accepted *culpa in contrahendo* in this narrow version.[161] So did the BGB. But the Code did not contain a general provision endorsing Jhering's doctrine; it dealt with the individual situations pinpointed by him in a number of special provisions.[162] These provisions could be regarded as emanations of the idea of *culpa in contrahendo*, even though in some of them the requirement of fault had been dropped[163] (Jhering himself had seen the somewhat fictitious nature of a fault requirement[164] and had subsequently pleaded for an 'objective' type of liability).[165] It was easy enough for the Imperial Court—in tune with prevailing doctrine—to accept the new situation: by applying the provisions of the new Code, the Court could effectively continue along the path mapped out under the *ius commune*. A doctrine of *culpa in contrahendo* was no longer required, since a generalized liability for fault committed in the process of contracting was conceivable only if the requirements for delictual liability had been met (i.e., in particular, infringement of one of the objects of legal protection listed in § 823 I BGB).[166]

(*c*) *The Emergence of the Modern Liability for* Culpa in Contrahendo

But this is not the whole truth. Before 1900, the more broadly conceived *culpa in contrahendo* à la Natural law had, of course, been applied (though not under that name) in cases decided according to Prussian law. Apart from that, however, it had also led a crypto-existence under the *ius commune*. Thus, the liability of a banker for bad advice concerning the purchase and sale of negotiable instruments

161 See Giaro (n. 154) sub II.

162 §§ 122, 179 II, 307, 309 BGB. In one important type of case (offer and acceptance) the BGB, by adopting a new approach to the conclusion of a contract by means of offer and acceptance, avoided the problem of a claim for damages altogether. For details, see Medicus (n. 159) 175 ff.; Giaro (n. 154) sub III.

163 §§ 122, 179 II BGB.

164 See Medicus (n. 159) 171 f.

165 Rudolph von Jhering, *Das Schuldmoment im römischen Privatrecht* (1867), 38.

166 See the references in Giaro (n. 154) sub IV.

had been based, by the Imperial Court, on a long-standing business relationship or on the fact that the advice given and the information provided had to be regarded as forming an 'integral part' of the (subsequent!) transaction.[167] Here we have a liability for fault in the pre-contractual sphere in cases where a contract is subsequently concluded, and it appears disguised as a contractual liability. This type of reasoning was continued, and became increasingly more prominent, after the enactment of the BGB. *Culpa in contrahendo* continued to be redefined as *culpa in solvendo* in banking cases.[168] Innkeepers were held liable for injuries sustained by their guests because they had tacitly guaranteed that the rooms in which the latter ate their meals did not contain a source of potential danger for their life and limb and property.[169] Conclusion of the contract involving such guarantee was seen to have occurred already when the guest entered the inn, i.e. before he sat down and ordered his meal.[170] Liability was imposed in a variety of other situations on the basis of fictitious agreements accompanying the main agreement, or preliminary to it,[171] and contractual duties were taken to exist before the conclusion and after the completion of the contract.[172] In other cases the scope of pre-contractual liability was extended by a very liberal interpretation given to the requirement of 'fraud' contained in § 463 BGB: a seller was seen to have 'fraudulently concealed a defect' if he had not disclosed that he was uncertain about whether the object of the sale was defective, as a result of dry rot.[173]

At the beginning of the second decade of the twentieth century the Imperial Court started to move more decisively

[167] RGZ 19, 97 ff (100 f.); RGZ 27, 118 (121 f.); RGZ 42, 125 ff. (131 f.); cf. also Gabriele Freudling, *Die Schadensersatzansprüche des Käufers im Gewährleistungsrecht des 19. und 20. Jahrhunderts* (1987), 34 ff.

[168] Cf., e.g., RG, 1903 *JW* 151 ff.; RG, 1905 *JW* 502 f.

[169] RG, 1905 Gruch 617 ff.

[170] RG, 1911 *JW* 360.

[171] Cf., e.g., RGZ 65, 17 (18 f.); RGZ 73, 148 ff. (150).

[172] See the cases involving accidents by railway passengers before boarding, or after getting off, the train RGZ 55, 335 ff. (336 f.); RG, 1904 *JW* 358; RG, 1904 *JW* 484; RG, 1908 WarnRspr 208.

[173] RG, 1905 *JW* 79.

in the direction of recognition of contractual liability in the pre-contractual situation: of a doctrine of *culpa in contrahendo*, in other words, which had hardly more than the name in common with the theory devised by Jhering. The first landmark was the linoleum case that has been mentioned above.[174] In spite of the contractual cloak in which the Imperial Court still attempted to envelop the negotiations,[175] the Court now squarely focused on the negotiating process; a contract of sale, after all, had not subsequently been concluded in this case since the plaintiff had become 'seriously disturbed by the fall'. Nor had there been the semblance of a contract (as in the cases discussed by Jhering). Another landmark decision followed soon afterwards. In RG *JW* 1912, 743 one party to a contract had negligently failed to draw the other party's attention to certain circumstances which, as he should have known, were of major importance for the implementation of what the latter wished to achieve under the contract. *Culpa in contrahendo* à la Jhering, it was now argued, related to invalid contracts and it had been specifically regulated by the BGB. For cases of a valid contract the BGB did not contain a regulation. But it had also not rejected liability. There was, in the opinion of the Court, 'no sufficient reason' to differentiate between duties of disclosure existing before and after conclusion of the contract. The negotiations leading up to a contract and the contract itself had to be seen 'as a whole'. Good faith and the requirements of honest business dealings called for the imposition of liability even in cases of pre-contractual failure to disclose.

For another few years, the Imperial Court continued to proceed in piecemeal fashion until, in 1918, the various

[174] RGZ 78, 239; cf. supra pp. 74 f.

[175] 'The plaintiff had asked for a piece of linoleum to be laid out for inspection and purchase. W had acceded to her request in order to make a sale. The proposal and its acceptance had for their purpose the conclusion of a sale, and therefore the production of a legal transaction. That was no mere factual proceeding . . . but a legal relationship came into existence between the parties in preparation for a purchase; it bore a character similar to a contract and produced legal obligations' (RGZ 78, 239 (240), translation taken from Markesinis (n. 29) 775).

threads of liability and clusters of cases were brought home under one doctrinal umbrella.[176] 'Liability for fault in the conclusion of a contract' is the programmatic headnote of RGZ 95, 58. The original idea, according to which there was no doctrine of *culpa in contrahendo* under the BGB, had been turned on its head.[177]

4. 'Positive' Breach of Contract[178]

(a) The Claim for Damages

Breach of contract is one of the problem areas of the German law of obligations.[179] Here we find a body of rules that has been developed around a highly artificial concept of impossibility devised by Friedrich Mommsen, and inspired, largely, by the Roman rules applicable to obligations *certam rem dare*.[180] As early as 1902 the commercial lawyer Hermann Staub discovered a 'huge gap' in the system of remedies provided in the Code.[181] While the Code, he argued, had clearly and satisfactorily dealt with the cases where a debtor fails to perform what he has promised under the contract (delay, impossibility of performance) there was no general provision covering cases of a deficient performance. A claim for damages based on 'positive malperformance' (*positive Vertragsverletzung*) was required to fill the gap. Over the years, Staub's theory has

176 See RGZ 93, 163 and RGZ 95, 58.

177 For the further development, see Giaro (n. 154) sub 8 and 9.

178 Hans Peter Glöckner, 'Die positive Vertragsverletzung', in Falk and Mohnhaupt (n. 20) in preparation; Klaus Luig, 'Die "Privilegierung" des Verkäufers', in *Mélanges en l'honneur de Carlo Augusto Cannata* (1999), 317 ff.

179 See, from a comparative point of view, Zweigert and Kötz (n. 57) 486 ff.; Reinhard Zimmermann, 'Konturen eines Europäischen Vertragsrechts', 1995 *JZ* 480 ff.

180 See *Law of Obligations* (n. 25) 806 ff. On breach of contract in pandectist legal theory and in the codes prevailing in 19th-century Germany, cf. also Susanne Würthwein, *Zur Schadensersatzpflicht wegen Vertragsverletzungen im gemeinen Recht des 19. Jahrhunderts* (1990); Michael Kotulla, 'Die historischen Voraussetzungen für die Entstehung des Rechtsinstituts der "positiven Forderungsverletzung" im 19. Jahrhundert', (1991) 108 *ZSS (GA)* 358 ff.; cf. also, as far as the law of sale is concerned, the work by Freudling, quoted supra n. 167, *passim*.

181 Hermann Staub, 'Die positiven Vertragsverletzungen und ihre Rechtsfolgen', in *Festschrift für den 26. Deutschen Juristentag* (1902), 29 ff.

become firmly entrenched; 'positive malperformance' is generally recognized today as a fundamentally important— though uncodified—part of German contract law.[182]

Interestingly, however, the first relevant case under the BGB was decided by the Imperial Supreme Court before Staub's study had appeared.[183] A purchaser had suffered damages as a result of the delivery of damp rye. Without much ado, the Court proceeded to grant a claim for damages based on the following requirements: breach of contractual obligation, fault, damage, and causation. This claim was based on § 276 I 1 BGB:[184] a somewhat unconvincing doctrinal peg in view of the fact that this rule is not intended to *impose* liability but merely to *define* the (normal) standard of a debtor's liability. The real reason for the Court to grant a claim was that it was eminently sensible to do so and that, moreover, the Court had always done so under the *ius commune* as well as under the other legal systems applicable in Germany before 1900.[185] It was as inconceivable for the Court as it was for Staub that there should be no general fault-based claim for deficient performance in twentieth-century German law. In countless decisions the Imperial Court continued to rely on § 276 I 1 BGB; only the Federal Supreme Court started to base the claim for damages on the doctrine of 'positive malperformance'.[186]

182 See. e.g., Max Vollkommer, in Othmar Jauernig (ed.), *Bürgerliches Gesetzbuch* (9th edn., 1999), § 276, V; Dieter Medicus, *Schuldrecht, Allgemeiner Teil* (11th edn., 1999), nn. 411 ff.

183 RGZ 52, 18, judgment of 13 June 1902.

184 'A debtor is responsible, unless otherwise provided, for wilful conduct and negligence. A person who does not exercise the care required in ordinary intercourse, acts negligently.'

185 See Würthwein (n. 180) 210 ff.; Gabriele Freudling, 'Die Schadensersatzansprüche des Käufers bei Schlechterfüllung in der Gerichtspraxis während der Entstehungszeit und der Zeit nach Inkrafttreten des Bürgerlichen Gesetzbuchs', (1998) 198 *AcP* 599 ff.; for a detailed examination of 19th-century legal practice, see now Hans Peter Glöckner, *Positive Vertragsverletzung: Die Geburt eines Rechtsinstituts*, unpublished habilitation thesis (1999), sub III. 2 (Prussia), 3 (*code civil*), 4 (Saxonia), 5 (*ius commune*).

186 The doctrine was, by then, predominantly founded on a general analogy to §§ 280, 286, 325, and 326 BGB; today, a doctrinal basis in the BGB is regarded as dispensable since *positive Forderungsverletzung* is widely held to constitute *Gewohnheitsrecht* (customary law).

(b) The Right to Withdraw from the Contract

There was, however, an additional twist to Staub's theory.[187] The claim for damages in cases of deficient performance was not new; Staub merely wanted to provide it with a proper doctrinal foundation under the Code. But he also argued that, under certain circumstances, the aggrieved party should have the right to withdraw from the contract.[188] This was new. Until the end of the nineteenth century, contract doctrine under the German *ius commune* had preserved the general rule of Roman law excluding any right of unilateral withdrawal from a contract.[189] The General German Commercial Code of 1861 had broken with this doctrine in cases of *mora debitoris* (delay on the part of the debtor).[190] The draftsmen of the BGB followed suit and transplanted this successful innovation from commercial into the world of general private law.[191] But it was only in cases of *mora debitoris* and supervening impossibility that the aggrieved party was granted a right to withdraw from the contract. Extension of this right to cases of deficient performance had certainly not been envisaged by the draftsmen of the Code;[192] this was the point where Staub's doctrine entailed a change in the law. In spite of its allegedly positivistic attitude, the Imperial Court immediately implemented that change, this time expressly referring to Staub's article and endorsing his concept of 'positive malperformance'.[193]

Once again, therefore, we see, how little the development of the law was affected by the Code. The Court, on the one hand, continued to grant a claim for damages in cases of deficient performance in spite of the fact that this claim did not find a specific endorsement in the Code. On the other

[187] See Glöckner (n. 178) sub II.5.

[188] Staub (n. 181) 44 ff.

[189] *Law of Obligations* (n. 25) 800 ff.

[190] Artt. 354 ff. ADHGB. On the background and origin of these rules, see Karl Otto Scherner, *Rücktrittsrecht wegen Nichterfüllung* (1965), 157 ff.

[191] For details, see Hans G. Leser, *Der Rücktritt vom Vertrag* (1975), 16 ff., 26 ff.

[192] Apart, of course, from the *actio redhibitoria* that remained available in cases of latent defects in an object sold; see §§ 459, 462 BGB.

[193] RGZ 54, 98, judgment of 6 Mar. 1903.

hand, it was prepared boldly to extend the range of sanctions available in these types of cases. The Court thus actively continued a line of development which had started in the commercial law of the latter half of the nineteenth century, and within which the BGB was hardly more than an episode. It is likely, moreover, that the judges of the II. Division of the Imperial Court,[194] when they handed down the decision in RGZ 54, 98, were very much aware of the general provision of art. 1184 *code civil* ('La condition résolutoire est toujours sous-entendue dans les contrats synallagmatiques, pour le cas où l'une des deux parties ne satisfera point à son engagement')[195] which they had hitherto had to apply. Staub's theory was most welcome in this situation to prevent them from having to take what would have appeared to them as a retrogressive step.[196]

5. Third Party Loss[197]

(*a*) *Contracts with Protective Effects vis-à-vis Third Parties*

Recovery of third party loss has already been touched upon in the course of our discussion of the law of delict.[198] Generally speaking, a contractual party may only claim

[194] Both RGZ 52, 18 and RGZ 54, 98 were decisions of the II. Division of the Imperial Court. That Division had previously been responsible for appeals involving French law (hence it was dubbed the 'Rhenish' Division; for the background, see Zimmermann (n. 83) 287 f. with references); and it remained responsible for such appeals as long as they were still coming in for the first few years after codification. See, in this context, Ernst Hubert Remelé, 'Bemerkungen zu der Frage der positiven Vertragsverletzungen', (1912) 26 *Recht* 569 ff. (572). Hans Peter Glöckner (n. 178) has drawn attention to these intellectual connections.

[195] (The resolutive condition is always tacitly incorporated in bilateral contracts for the case where one of the two parties does not honour his obligation.) On the history and background of this provision, see Scherner (n. 190) 135 ff.; Reinhard Zimmermann, ' "Heard Melodies are sweet, but those unheard are sweeter . . .": Condicio tacita, implied Condition und die Fortbildung des europäischen Vertragsrechts', (1993) 193 *AcP* 165 with further references.

[196] The further development of the doctrine of 'positive malperformance' in the case law of the Imperial Court and other superior courts is traced by Glöckner, both in his article (n. 178) and in his book (n. 185).

[197] Jörg Neuner, 'Die Entwicklung der Haftung für Drittschäden', in Falk and Mohnhaupt (n. 20) in preparation; Sibylle Hofer, 'Drittschutz und Zeitgeist: Ein Beitrag zur privatrechtlichen Zeitgeschichte', (2000) 117 *ZSS (GA)* in preparation.

[198] Supra pp. 75 f.

damages that he himself has suffered.[199] Of course, two parties may conclude a contract for the benefit of a third party (§ 328 I BGB): the third party, under these circumstances, has the right directly to demand performance to himself. Does this also mean that the third party may claim damages for failure to perform, or to perform properly? This question was answered in the affirmative by two Regional Appeal Courts[200] and, since 1915, also by the Imperial Court.[201] But in 1917 the Imperial Court went a significant step further.[202] Even though the daughter of the tenant had not become a party to the contract of lease and had also not, apparently, acquired a right to claim performance, she was still granted a claim for the loss that she had suffered as a result of the defendant's failure to disinfect the family flat. The decision, as we have seen, was based on the desire to prevent the daughter's claim from foundering on the shallow sands of § 831 BGB. It was the origin of a device that came to be termed, much later, a 'contract with protective effects vis-à-vis third parties' (*Vertrag mit Schutzwirkung zugunsten Dritter*): third parties may be brought under the protective umbrella of a contract so as to enable them to claim damages for breach of one of the contract's secondary obligations.[203]

The proper legal foundation for this doctrine has remained unclear for a long time; whereas the Federal Supreme Court has repeatedly maintained that it constitutes

[199] *Dogma des Gläubigerinteresses* (principle of the creditor's interest); see, e.g., Dieter Medicus, *Bürgerliches Recht* (18th edn., 1999), n. 834.

[200] HansOLG Hamburg, 1907 *Recht* no. 3469; OLG Colmar, 1914 *Recht* no. 327.

[201] RG, 1915 WarnRspr no. 203; RGZ 87, 64 ff.; both decisions 'triggered a chain reaction of further cases': Neuner (n. 197) sub II. 5; see also Anna Ziegltrum, *Der Vertrag mit Schutzwirkung für Dritte* (1992), 14 ff.

[202] RGZ 91, 21; see supra pp. 75 f.

[203] See, in general, Hein Kötz, *European Contract Law*, tr. Tony Weir, vol. i (1997), pp. 252 ff.; Werner Lorenz, 'Contract Beneficiaries in German Law', in B. S. Markesinis (ed.), *The Gradual Convergence: Foreign Ideas, Foreign Influences, and English Law on the Eve of the 21st Century* (1994), 65 ff.; most recently, see Walter Bayer, *Der Vertrag zugunsten Dritter* (1995), 182 ff.; Johannes Köndgen, 'Einbeziehung Dritter in den Vertrag', in *Karlsruher Forum* (1998), 3 ff. (supplement to the journal *Versicherungsrecht*); Jörg Neuner, 'Der Schutz und die Haftung Dritter nach vertraglichen Grundsätzen', 1999 *JZ* 126 ff.

an example of supplementative interpretation,[204] it is mostly regarded, today, as a case of judicial development of the law based on § 242 BGB.[205] The Imperial Supreme Court usually referred to § 328 BGB. But an agreement to bring a third party under the protective umbrella of, for example, a contract of lease or transportation is usually a somewhat fictitious construct, and the search for such agreement was, sometimes quite openly, guided by policy considerations.[206] The same applies to cases where the Imperial Court operated with a (genuine) contract in favour of a third party that had been tacitly concluded.[207] The dividing line between these two constructions often, however, remained unclear.

(*b*) *Theory of Transferred Loss*

Drittschadensliquidation (often translated as theory of transferred loss[208]) constitutes another exception to the general rule that a party may only claim the damage suffered by himself. But whereas the contract with protective effects vis-à-vis third parties is a device in terms of which *the third party* is granted a right to claim (his own) damages, the theory of *Drittschadensliquidation* allows *a party to a contract*, in a number of reasonably well-defined, exceptional situations, to claim for damages suffered by a third party.[209] The common denominator of these situations is that the law wants to prevent the debtor from benefiting from a shift of loss that must be regarded, as far as the debtor is concerned, as fortuitous. Cases of *Drittschadensliquidation* were recognized already in a long line of nineteenth-century cases;[210]

204 Cf., e.g., BGHZ 56, 269 (273); Heinrichs, in *Palandt* (n. 134) § 328 n. 14.

205 Vollkommer in Jauernig (n. 182) § 328 n. 21; Peter Gottwald, in *Münchener Kommentar zum Bürgerlichen Gesetzbuch*, vol. ii (3rd edn., 1994), § 328 n. 80.

206 See Neuner (n. 197) sub III. 1; cf. also already Joachim Gernhuber, 'Drittwirkungen im Schuldverhältnis kraft Leistungsnähe', in *Festschrift für Arthur Nikisch* (1958), 249 ff.

207 See, e.g., RGZ 127, 218 (222 ff.).

208 Markesinis (n. 29) 56.

209 The distinction between the two devices is explained by Medicus (n. 199) nn. 840 f.

210 OAG Lübeck, (1857) 11 SeuffArch no. 36; OAG Wolfenbüttel, (1861) 14 SeuffArch no. 23; ROHGE 11, 256; ROHGE 17, 78; ROHGE 22, 248; RGZ 12, 108; RGZ 27, 118; RGZ 40, 187. See Neuner (n. 197) sub III. 2.

a number of Roman sources were even invoked in support of this idea.[211] The courts did not provide a clear doctrinal framework; increasingly they merely referred to the previous case law. The introduction of the BGB did not change this position, for we are dealing here with one of those cases where the draftsmen of the Code regarded it as inappropriate to provide a regulation. The problem had not as yet found a definitive doctrinal form and was, therefore, not quite ripe for codification. Even without an express provision the courts could be expected to find the right result, as they had done so far.[212] This is indeed what the Imperial Court did; it simply continued to develop the law along the lines established under the *ius commune*.[213] The typical 'groups of cases' (*Fallgruppen*) thus established still today provide the substantive core of the doctrine.[214]

IV. A SENSE OF CONTINUITY

1. The Code, the Courts, and the Law Prior to Codification

All in all, we get an overwhelming sense of continuity of development.[215] The BGB itself was based on the results of

[211] See Ingo Reichard, *Die Frage des Drittschadensersatzes im klassischen römischen Recht* (1993), 1 ff. Reichard, however, carries on to show (pp. 34 ff., 131 ff.) that the Roman lawyers did not recognize this device.

[212] 'Protokolle', in Mugdan (n. 27) ii. 518.

[213] See, e.g., RGZ 58, 39; RGZ 62, 331; RGZ 93, 39.

[214] See, e.g., Arndt Teichmann, in Jauernig (n. 182) Vor §§ 249–53 nn. 19 ff.; Wolfgang Grunsky, in *Münchener Kommentar zum Bürgerlichen Gesetzbuch*, vol. ii (3rd edn., 1994), Vor § 249 nn. 119 ff.

[215] Cf. also Mathias Schmoeckel, 'Zur Entwicklung des Vertretungsrechts: Von der Vertragsfreiheit zu typisierten Verkehrspflichten', in Falk and Mohnhaupt (n. 20) in preparation (Schmoeckel deals with the law of agency and comes to the following conclusions (sub IV. 1): the Imperial Court 'to a large extent picked up the thread of its case law from the time before 1900'; on the other hand, however, it decisively 'reshaped' the statutory regime and had mapped out, by 1914, the essential contours of the law of agency as it is applied today); Tilman Repgen, 'Das Vermieterpfandrecht im Kaiserreich', in Falk and Mohnhaupt (n. 20) in preparation (on the lessor's right of pledge over the things brought onto the premises by the lessee; he concludes (sub IV) that there was a continuous development as far as both substantive content and method were concerned and that the Code did not bring about a disruption of this continuity); Andreas Thier, 'Zwischen actio

a nineteenth-century scholarship that had been inspired by Savigny's Historical School. Being the fruit of great legal thought, it was characterized by its intellectual maturity, outstanding craftsmanship, and an admirable sense of *legislative* self-restraint.[216] It left considerable room for further development by courts and legal writers. If, then, the BGB may indeed be regarded, largely, as a restatement of contemporary legal doctrine,[217] it was both right and natural for the Imperial Court to pick up the thread of its pre-1900 precedents and to interpret the Code in terms of the law which the latter attempted to restate. But the great achievement of the Court even in the early years of the century was that it continued to do what it had done under the old legal regime: to specify, supplement, and modify the law, i.e. to develop it in accordance with the perceived needs of changed times. Of course, it did not openly rebel against the law. But the Court made full use of the tools available for developing the law *intra* and even *praeter legem*.[218] Among these tools, of course, were doctrinal

negatoria und Aufopferungsanspruch: Nachbarliche Nutzungskonflikte in der Rechtsprechung des 19. und 20. Jahrhunderts', in Falk and Mohnhaupt (n. 20) in preparation (on the legal relationship and the liability between neighbours: from about 1882 there was a new line of development, initiated by the Imperial Court, which developed its own momentum and was not much affected by the Code); Ulrich Falk, 'Zur Sittenwidrigkeit von Testamenten', in Falk and Mohnhaupt (n. 20) in preparation (on testaments that were held to be *contra bonos mores*: 'The disruption created by the Code was, if one looks more closely, rather insignificant in many areas. The continuities, both open and latent, with the case law and doctrine of the later *ius commune* were often more marked'; sub III. 5); Filippo Ranieri, 'Kaufrechtliche Gewährleistung und Irrtumsproblematik: Kontinuität und Diskontinuität in der Judikatur des Reichsgerichts nach 1900', in Falk and Mohnhaupt (n. 20) in preparation (on the relationship between the remedies for latent defects and mistake; Ranieri demonstrates that a decision of the Imperial Court from 1905—RGZ 61, 171—decisively determined the course of the law for the remainder of the century and that the V. Division of the Imperial Court picked up the thread of its own case law from the period before the enactment of the Code). Cf. also Christoph Seiler, *Vom allgemeinen Landrecht zum Bürgerlichen Gesetzbuch* (1996).

216 See Zimmermann (n. 17) 14 f. with further references.

217 See supra p. 55 (n. 13); cf. also p. 17 (n. 69).

218 Cf. also, e.g., Klaus Luig, 'Richter secundum, praeter or contra BGB? Das Beispiel der Sicherungsübereignung', in Falk and Mohnhaupt (n. 20) in preparation.

crutches like implied terms or fictitious contracts: crutches which had been used before, by the Imperial Court as well as by courts in other countries.[219] Of course, the pressure for change picked up the older the Code became. But it is surprising to see for how many of our modern legal doctrines, developed in response to this pressure, the Imperial Court laid the foundations within the first two decades of its existence. 'Positivistic narrowness' is not the right label for this attitude.

If, then, the BGB merely constitutes a transitional stage within an ongoing tradition,[220] it is entirely unnatural to regard 1 January 1900 as a kind of cut-off point separating past and present. In the first place, the BGB itself has become a historical document. It is a text enacted at a time that was vastly different from ours. It has become enveloped by thick layers of case law and by a large range of sophisticated legal doctrines with often only scant support in its wording. Thus, the BGB has to be studied not only as an authoritative but also as an historically conditioned document. It is based on evaluations which may be different from ours. Courts and legal writers have had to find answers to entirely new and unforeseen legal problems; they have had to adjust the law to changed social and economic conditions and to bring it into line, after 1949, with the value system contained in the Basic Law (*Grundgesetz*). But they had to do so by applying, or developing, the Code and on the basis of the thinking patterns inherited from the past. They did not arbitrarily and autonomously fashion the new legal world; they did so 'in

[219] I have attempted to demonstrate the usefulness and versatility of the notion of an implied condition, or *conditio tacita*, in English and continental contract law in (1993) 193 *AcP* 121–73.

[220] Cf. also, e.g., Theo Mayer-Maly, 'Die Wiederkehr von Rechtsfiguren', 1971 *JZ* 3; Helmut Coing, in *Staudinger, Kommentar zum Bürgerlichen Gesetzbuch*, vol. i (12th edn., 1978), n. 113; Joachim Rückert, 'Savignys Einfluß auf die Jurisprudenz in Deutschland nach 1900', in Heinz Mohnhaupt (ed.), *Rechtsgeschichte in den beiden deutschen Staaten* (1991), p. 44; Rolf Knütel, 'Römisches Recht und deutsches bürgerliches Recht', in Walther Ludwig (ed.), *Die Antike in der europäischen Gegenwart* (1993), 64; idem, 'Rechtseinheit in Europa und römisches Recht', (1994) 2 *ZEuP* 265.

indissoluble community with the past'.[221] They were still part of an 'ongoing' tradition.[222] We, too, therefore will only be able to understand our present legal condition by adopting a historical perspective. But, and this is the second point, the past which still determines our modern legal condition did not begin with the BGB. Many 'modern' developments originated prior to the enactment of the Code and were hardly affected by that event. Often, however, the continuities reach back much further. Both the BGB and the case law after its enactment are firmly anchored in the *ius commune* which in turn is based on Roman law. 'Comprehension of the vital connection that ties the present to the past':[223] any such endeavour will therefore have to start with Roman law.

2. A Synthesis of What has been 'Thought Apart'?

Interestingly, this is a point which was particularly forcefully emphasized by the pioneers of the new direction of historical scholarship in Roman law. Contrary to a number of modern legal historians, they did not regard legal history and historical legal scholarship, or interest in Roman law proper and its pandectist version, as mutually exclusive.[224] 'Without its impractical foundations', Emil Seckel wrote,[225] 'the practical private law cannot be understood.' And he continued in terms strongly reminiscent of Savigny: 'The natural connection that ties the present to the past cannot

[221] See supra p. 12 (n. 48).

[222] See, in this context, Harold J. Berman, *Law and Revolution: The Formation of the Western Legal Tradition* (1983), 9 (and *passim*).

[223] Supra p. 12 (n. 46).

[224] For the modern controversy on this point in German and Italian scholarship see the contributions to Pio Caroni and Gerhard Dilcher (eds.), *Norm und Tradition: Welche Geschichtlichkeit für die Rechtsgeschichte?* (1998); and see the contributions to the 32nd German legal history conference by Mathias Reimann, Axel Flessner, Klaus Luig, Michele Graziadei, Albrecht Cordes, William Ewald, David Johnston, Willem J. Zwalve, and Wolfgang Ernst in (1999) 7 *ZEuP* 494 ff.

[225] Emil Seckel, 'Die Neuordnung des juristischen Ausbildungsganges in Preußen', 1902 *DJZ* 58. Cf. also Kipp, (1924) 44 *ZSS* (*RA*) p. x: 'Seckel never failed to appreciate that historical insights, for the lawyer, serve the better perception of contemporary law.'

with impunity be snapped asunder.' Otto Lenel was prepared to disencumber the teaching of Roman law of those subject-matters which were no longer relevant for modern law. But as far as the greatest part, by far, of the general doctrines and of the law of obligations and of property law was concerned, he advocated the retention of a comprehensive course in the pandectist, or doctrinal, mould. The study of Roman law, he emphasized, does not serve a merely pedagogic purpose but it is pursued 'because our present and our future law has emerged essentially from Roman law and Romanistic legal scholarship and can only on that basis be interpreted in a scholarly manner'.[226] The same view was expressed by Theodor Mommsen.[227]

Ludwig Mitteis was, in certain respects, a tragic figure. Much of what he had unleashed filled him with a feeling of uneasiness.[228] This is true, in particular, of the concept of a universal history of classical antiquity which, to Mitteis's mind, dethroned Roman law and failed to recognize its outstanding and universal significance.[229] Studies in the cuneiform laws did not interest him.[230] Instead, he was apparently the only German Romanist[231] who continued, in

[226] Otto Lenel, 'Zur Reform des Rechtsunterrichts', 1896 *DJZ* 389. See also idem, in Hans Planitz (ed.), *Die Rechtswissenschaft der Gegenwart in Selbstdarstellungen*, vol. i (1924), 150: 'I know from experience how much is to be gained for the development of our private law from the knowledge of Roman law, that has been deepened so much today'; and see Fritz Pringsheim, 'Römisches Recht in Freiburg nach 1900', in *Aus der Geschichte der Rechts- und Staatswissenschaften zu Freiburg i. Br.*, ed. H. J. Wolff (1957), 127, who stresses that both Lenel and Partsch have always 'felt themselves to be nothing but lawyers'. For an emphatic plea for the reintroduction of a course in a contemporary pandectist mould, see Julius G. Lautner, *Zur Bedeutung des römischen Rechts für die europäische Rechtskultur und zu seiner Stellung im Rechtsunterricht* (1976), pp. 156 ff.

[227] See Otto Lenel's obituary to Theodor Mommsen, 1903 *DJZ* 515.

[228] '. . .not enchanted with the spirits he had summoned': Paul Koschaker, *Europa und das römische Recht* (4th edn., 1966), 301.

[229] For a detailed assessment, see Evelyn Höbenreich, 'A propos "Antike Rechtsgeschichte": Einige Bemerkungen zur Polemik zwischen Ludwig Mitteis und Leopold Wenger', (1992) 109 *ZSS* (*RA*) 547 ff.

[230] Koschaker (n. 228) 301 n. 2: 'From my own memory I can report that, at best, Mitteis tolerated my research into the cuneiform laws, he never approved of them.'

[231] See Koschaker (n. 228) 294; Lautner (n. 226) 138.

Leipzig, to give a course in the pandectist tradition ('Pandekten als Einführung in das bürgerliche Gesetzbuch') even after 1900; and he rejected a call to Berlin because the Prussian government did not have any sympathy for maintaining such a course.[232] In 1908 he published a textbook on *Römisches Privatrecht bis auf die Zeit Diokletians* (Roman Private Law up to the Time of Diocletian)[233] based on the pandectist system: first a general part and then the division into family law and the law of persons, property law, the law of succession, and the law of obligations.[234] 'Even though its content was entirely historical, there is a strongly dogmatic element pervading the book', Paul Koschaker writes,[235] 'since the point of departure is not a specifically historical one. For the author is not interested in Roman private law up to Diocletian's time as such but in the question whether, and how far, the concepts used in the general part of the BGB were present or prefigured in classical Roman law. The problem is stated from the point of view of modern law but the answer is given by employing the modern historical methods.' Roman law and the modern Civil Code, for Mitteis, were not two different worlds and he was not prepared to accept, for himself, the distinction between legal historian and legal dogmaticist.[236] Mitteis's pupil Ernst Rabel attempted to achieve a synthesis between history and legal doctrine in his two great works on the law

232 Josef Partsch, (1922) 43 *ZSS (RA)* p. xviii.

233 Only one volume appeared, dealing with basic concepts and the doctrine of juristic persons.

234 Partsch (n. 232) p. xxiv. Characteristically, also, the third chapter of the first book is entitled 'Das Rechtsgeschäft' (Legal Acts). This abstract notion had been developed by the pandectists; it had been alien to Roman law itself.

235 Koschaker (n. 228) 344.

236 Partsch (n. 232) p. xi. Cf. also Walter Selb, (1994) 17 *NDB* 577: 'Mitteis' continued study of contemporary law, in Leipzig, led in later years to his historical works carrying the stamp of a strictly doctrinal approach'; Okko Behrends, 'Der Romanist Henryk Kupiszewski', in *Le Droit romain et le monde contemporain: Mélanges à la mémoire de Henryk Kupiszewski* (1996), 35 ff., who draws attention to the 'specifically juristic character' of Mitteis and his school. Mitteis himself writes about his academic teacher Adolf Exner (on whom see p. 31, n. 138) that he was 'a born jurist' and 'what one calls a doctrinalist (*Rechtsdogmatiker*)' (Ludwig Mitteis, *Erinnerung an Adolf Exner* (1894), 7).

of sale,[237] and another of his pupils, Paul Koschaker, in his inspiring book on *Europe and Roman Law* provided the programmatic underpinnings.[238] This programme is still as timely and as apposite today as ever.

This is true even for the national legal systems prevailing today. Already in the middle of the 1950s Max Kaser, when looking at contemporary private law doctrine, had diagnosed the first signs of exhaustion.[239] The rich intellectual harvest, he said, which scholars had produced over the first half of this century was easily available in the big commentaries and textbooks.[240] But it had been a scholarship which had accepted the *lex positiva* as an immovable boundary of its endeavours and which had attempted to solve all problems arising on the basis, and within the confines, of the Code.[241] Kaser therefore hoped that 'our ossified private law scholarship may consider taking up a new task'.[242] It would have to aim to move beyond the Code so as to advance (just as the classical Roman jurists had done) 'for each problem, independent of the letter of a specific law, to the idea of justice as such'.[243] In the process, he thought, legal history and comparative law could be 'exploited to a much greater extent than is hitherto accepted'.[244] Legal historians were therefore called

[237] *Die Haftung des Verkäufers wegen Mangels im Rechte* (1902); *Das Recht des Warenkaufs*, 2 vols. (1936 and 1958). For a more detailed assessment see Reinhard Zimmermann, ' "In der Schule von Ludwig Mitteis": Ernst Rabels rechtshistorische Ursprünge', (2001) 65 *RabelsZ* in preparation (7th Ernst Rabel memorial lecture).

[238] 4th edn., 1966. The importance of Koschaker's book (which has recently been translated into Dutch) is emphasized also by Zwalve, (1997) 5 *ZEuP* 399. Views similar to those by Koschaker have been expressed by Heinrich Mitteis, 'Die Geschichte der Rechtswissenschaft im Rahmen der allgemeinen Kulturgeschichte', 1951 *JZ* 677 f.; Lautner (n. 226) *passim*.

[239] Max Kaser, 'Wege und Ziele der deutschen Zivilrechtswissenschaft', in *Europa e il diritto romano: Studi in memoria di Paolo Koschaker*, vol. i (1954), 567, 574.

[240] Ibid. 568.

[241] Ibid. 573.

[242] Ibid. 576. Cf. also Max Kaser, 'Gegenwartsbedeutung des römischen Rechts', (1972) 18 *Labeo* 154 ('. . .does it become necessary to look for new paths outside of the system of the codifications'); 'Nachwort', in Lautner (n. 226) 209.

[243] *Studi Koschaker* (n. 239) 576.

[244] Ibid. 577.

upon to turn their attention to the history of legal doctrines and institutions so as to prepare the foundations for a contemporary comparative scholarship in private law.[245]

[245] See Max Kaser, 'Der römische Anteil am deutschen bürgerlichen Recht', 1967 *JuS* 344; idem, *Studi Koschaker* (n. 239) 578; 'Nachwort' (n. 242) 206 ff.

Lecture Three—
A Change in Perspective: European Private Law and its Historical Foundations

I. HISTORICAL SCHOLARSHIP AND THE NEW *IUS COMMUNE*

It is remarkable that Max Kaser, who himself devoted all his energies to the reconstruction of Roman private law as it had prevailed in antiquity, emphasized the necessity of a new synthesis between legal history and legal system, and that he also saw the need for establishing an intellectual link between legal history and comparative law.[1] What Kaser postulated half a century ago is even more important today. The age of more or less autonomous systems of national law is slowly drawing to its close. The directives enacted by the Council of the European Union,[2] the case law emanating from the European Court of Justice,[3] the

[1] For a more detailed examination of Kaser's views, see Reinhard Zimmermann, 'Max Kaser und das moderne Privatrecht', (1998) 115 *ZSS (RA)* 99 ff.

[2] For a collection of all directives (and other relevant legal texts) affecting the law of obligations, see Reiner Schulze and Reinhard Zimmermann (eds.), *Basistexte zum europäischen Privatrecht* (2000). Cf. also Stefan Grundmann, *Europäisches Schuldvertragsrecht* (1999).

[3] On the importance and character of which see, for instance, the contributions by David A. O. Edward and Lord Mackenzie Stuart, both in David L. Carey Miller and Reinhard Zimmermann (eds.), *The Civilian Tradition and Scots Law: Aberdeen Quincentenary Essays* (1997), 307 ff., 351 ff.; most recently see the comprehensive analysis by Martin Franzen, *Privatrechtsangleichung durch die Europäische Gemeinschaft* (1999), 291 ff. For general background on legal unification by means of appeal court decisions in states with several legal systems, see the symposium edited by Klaus Luig, (1997) 5 *ZEuP* 762 ff. For a regular review of decisions by the European Court of Justice affecting private law, see Christian Kohler and Waltraud Hakenberg, (1995) 3 *ZEuP* 482 ff.; (1996) 4 *ZEuP* 452 ff.; (1997) 5 *ZEuP* 1030 ff.; (1998) 6 *ZEuP* 909 ff.; (1999) 7 *ZEuP* 849 ff.

legal problems arising from the application of the United Nations Convention on Contracts for the International Sale of Goods:[4] these all increasingly affect the legal situation in most Western European countries. Private law in Europe is in the process of reacquiring a transnational character.[5] The first textbooks have appeared which analyse particular areas of law under a European perspective and deal with the rules of English, French, or German law as local variations of a common theme.[6] Several legal periodicals are competing for the attention of lawyers interested in the development of European private law; and a number of international groups of academics are busy drafting 'Restatements' or 'Principles' of European contract,[7] tort,[8]

[4] On the application in Germany, see the regular contributions by Ulrich Magnus, (1993) 1 *ZEuP* 79 ff.; (1995) 3 *ZEuP* 202 ff.; (1997) 5 *ZEuP* 823 ff.; (1999) 7 *ZEuP* 642 ff. The Convention has been adopted by close to 50 states, among them ten member states of the European Union. Concerning Great Britain, see the comments by Barry Nicholas, *The United Kingdom and the Vienna Sales Convention: Another Case of Splendid Isolation?* (1993).

[5] See, e.g., Martin Gebauer, *Grundfragen der Europäisierung des Privatrechts* (1998); Jan Smits, *Europees Privaatrecht in wording* (1999); and the contributions in Nicolò Lipari (ed.), *Diritto privato europeo* (1997); Thomas G. Watkin (ed.), *The Europeanisation of Law* (1998) (also covering other areas of the law); Arthur Hartkamp and Martijn Hesselink et al. (eds.), *Towards a European Civil Code* (2nd edn., 1998); Peter-Christian Müller-Graff (ed.), *Gemeinsames Privatrecht in der Europäischen Gemeinschaft* (2nd edn., 1999); on contract law, see Jürgen Basedow, 'The Renascence of Uniform Law: European Contract Law and its Components', (1998) 18 *Legal Studies* 121 ff.

[6] Cf. the programme sketched by Hein Kötz, 'Gemeineuropäisches Zivilrecht', in *Festschrift für Konrad Zweigert* (1981), 498, and now implemented in Hein Kötz, *Europäisches Vertragsrecht*, vol. i (1996) (English translation by Tony Weir [1997]; Christian von Bar, *Gemeineuropäisches Deliktsrecht*, vol. i (1996) (an English translation appeared in 1998), vol. ii (1999) (an English translation is in preparation); Filippo Ranieri, *Europäisches Obligationenrecht* (1999).

[7] Ole Lando and Hugh Beale (eds.), *Principles of European Contract Law* (2000) (incorporating a previously published part I [1995]; for comment, see Reinhard Zimmermann, 'Konturen eines Europäischen Privatrechts', 1995 *JZ* 477 ff.; Hugh Beale, 'The Principles of European Contract Law and Harmonisation of the Law of Contract', in *Festskift til Ole Lando* (1997), 21 ff.; Ralf Michaels, 'Privatautonomie und Privatkodifikation', (1998) 62 *RabelsZ* 580 ff. Cf. also the contributions in Hans-Leo Weyers (ed.), *Europäisches Vertragsrecht* (1997), and Jürgen Basedow (ed.) *Europäische Vertragsrechtsvereinheitlichung und deutsches Recht* (2000).

[8] See now Jaap Spier and Olav A. Haazen, 'The European Group on Tort Law ("Tilburg Group") and the European Principles of Tort Law', (1999) 7 *ZEuP* 469 ff.

or trust law.[9] We are living in an age of post-positivism.[10] The narrowness, but also the security, of a national codification (or common law) is increasingly left behind and we are moving towards a new *ius commune*.

This new *ius commune* will have to be built around shared values and generally recognized legal methods[11] as well as common principles[12] and guiding maxims, and it will have to be shaped by judges, legislators, and professors,[13] acting in cooperation with each other. But since, in the words of Savigny, there is no autonomous human existence entirely isolated from the past, we cannot freely fashion our own existence, including our laws: we always, and necessarily, do it 'in indissoluble community with the entire past';[14] and unless we want unconsciously to be governed by the past[15] we should explore it in order to understand how we got to where we are. Historical scholarship (which will itself have to abandon its focus on national legal history[16]) may thus

Hitherto, the following volumes have appeared: Jaap Spier (ed.), *The Limits of Liability* (1996); idem (ed.), *The Limits of Expanding Liability* (1998); Helmut Koziol (ed.), *Unification of Tort Law: Wrongfulness* (1998); for general background, see Ulrich Magnus, 'Elemente eines europäischen Deliktsrechts', (1998) 6 *ZEuP* 602 ff. with further references.

[9] See D. J. Hayton, S. C. J .J. Kortmann and H. L. E. Verhagen (eds.), *Principles of European Trust Law* (1999); cf. also (1999) 7 *ZEuP* 745 ff.

[10] See Jürgen Basedow, 'Rechtssicherheit im europäischen Wirtschaftsrecht: Ein allgemeiner Rechtsgrundsatz im Lichte der wettbewerbsrechtlichen Rechtsprechung', (1996) 4 *ZEuP* 570 ff.; Eugen Bucher, 'Recht—Geschichtlich keit—Europa', in Bruno Schmidlin (ed.), *Vers un droit privé européen commun? Skizzen zum gemeineuropäischen Privatrecht* (1994), 23.

[11] See, most recently, Jürgen Basedow, 'Anforderungen an eine europäische Zivilrechtsdogmatik', in Reinhard Zimmermann, Rolf Knütel and Jens Peter Meincke (eds.), *Rechtsgeschichte und Privatrechtsdogmatik* (2000), 79 ff.

[12] See Reiner Schulze, 'Allgemeine Rechtsgrundsätze und europäisches Privatrecht', (1993) 1 *ZEuP* 442 ff.

[13] They have traditionally been responsible for the development of European private law; see the classic study by R. C. van Caenegem, *Judges, Legislators and Professors* (1987); idem, *A Historical Introduction to Private Law* (1988), 170 ff.

[14] 'Ueber den Zweck dieser Zeitschrift', (1815) 1 *Zeitschrift für geschichtliche Rechtswissenschaft* 1 ff. For a critical exploration of Savigny's views, see the literature quoted supra p. 12 (n. 42).

[15] Friedrich Carl von Savigny, *System des heutigen römischen Rechts* (1840), vol. i, preface, pp. xv f.

[16] Cf. also Harold J. Berman, *Law and Revolution: The Formation of the Western*

enable us to take stock of our present legal condition. It may help us to map out, and to become aware of, the common ground still existing between our national legal systems as a result of a common tradition, of independent but parallel developments, and of instances of intellectual stimulation or the reception of legal rules or concepts. At the same time, it will be able to explain discrepancies on the level of specific result, general approach, and doctrinal nuance.[17] It is this kind of comprehension that paves the way for rational criticism and organic development of the law.[18] The past, of course, does not justify itself; nor does it necessarily contain the solutions for present-day problems.[19] But an understanding of the past is a first and essential prerequisite for devising the most appropriate solutions.[20] This is as true within a given national legal system as it is for the formation of a European law. And just as legal history informs the development of private law doctrine in the one case, so it constitutes the basis for comparative scholarship in the other.[21] European private law requires a combination of comparative and historical scholarship.

Legal Tradition (1983), 17: 'And in the late twentieth century we still suffer from the nationalist historiography that originated in the nineteenth century and that supported the disintegration of a common Western legal heritage. . . . It was simply assumed that history meant national history'; Reiner Schulze, 'Vom Ius commune bis zum Gemeinschaftsrecht: Das Forschungsfeld der europäischen Rechtsgeschichte', in idem (ed.), *Europäische Rechts- und Verfassungsgeschichte: Ergebnisse und Perspektiven der Forschung* (1991), 3 ff.

17 The point has been emphasized already in (1996) 112 *LQR* 596 ff.

18 On 'organic' development (or growth) as a characteristic of the European legal tradition see (apart, of course, from Savigny) Berman (n. 16) 1 ff.

19 Alfred Cockrell, 'Studying Legal History in South Africa: The Lesson of Lot's Wife', (1997) 5 *ZEuP* 438.

20 See, e.g., the moving statement (in the nature of a confession) by W. A. Wilson, 'The Importance of Analysis', in *Comparative and Historical Essays in Scots Law: A Tribute to Professor Sir Thomas Smith* Q.C. (1992), 171.

21 For clear statements to that effect, see Hein Kötz, 'Was erwartet die Rechtsvergleichung von der Rechtsgeschichte?', 1992 *JZ* 20 ff.; Axel Flessner, 'Die Rechtsvergleichung als Kundin der Rechtsgeschichte', (1999) 7 *ZEuP* 513 ff.

II. CIVIL LAW AND COMMON LAW: TWO WORLDS APART?

1. A Western Legal Tradition

It has, occasionally, been contended that this kind of programme, while it might suit the codified systems of continental Europe, would be unable to accommodate English law. In its most extreme form this view postulates, or presupposes, a *summa differentia* between the civil law and common law traditions, an 'epistemological chasm' which is irreducible and prevents any genuine understanding between lawyers schooled in either the one or the other of these traditions.[22] I do not share this view. Three important reasons may be very briefly stated as follows.

(i) There are a great number of lawyers who have in fact managed not only to understand both legal worlds but also to be at home in them. Their legal training in the one tradition has often sharpened their faculty of perception and contributed to new insights into the characteristics of the other tradition. I am not merely referring here to the great comparative lawyers of this generation and the last but, particularly, to those who were expelled from their home country, Germany, and had to re-establish themselves in England or in the United States: Fritz Kessler, Stefan Riesenfeld, Ernst Stiefel, Otto Kahn-Freund, Fritz A. Mann, Kurt Lipstein, and many others.[23] Also, all over Europe today international groups of lawyers, comprising both civil lawyers and common lawyers, are successfully collaborating on a whole range of projects: they are busy drafting 'restatements' of particular areas of European private law,[24]

[22] Pierre Legrand, 'Legal Traditions in Western Europe: The Limits of Commonality', in R. Jagtenberg, E. Örücü, and A. J. de Roo (eds.), *Transfrontier Mobility of Law* (1995), 63 ff.; idem, 'European Legal Systems are Not Converging', (1996) 45 *ICLQ* 52 ff.

[23] As to the influence of German émigré lawyers in the United States, see the contributions in Marcus Lutter, Ernst C. Stiefel, and Michael Hoeflich (eds.), *Der Einfluß deutscher Emigranten auf die Rechtsentwicklung in den USA und in Deutschland* (1993).

[24] The European Contract Law Commission has been inspired by the American 'restatement' idea. Cf. also Michael Joachim Bonell, *An International Restatement of*

searching for the 'common core' of European legal systems,[25] compiling casebooks,[26] etc.

(ii) The view mentioned above greatly exaggerates the insularity, or isolation, of the common law and its development. Roman law, Canon law, indigenous customary law, feudal law, the Law Merchant, Natural law theory: these were the most important ingredients in the development of continental law. All of them, in various ways, also shaped the English common law.[27] Protagonists of this development, on both sides of the Channel, have been Parliament, courts and academic writers.[28] English law, as Harold J. Berman says, was an integral part of 'the Western legal tradition'. This is becoming increasingly clear today. Wherever one chooses to look, one will find 'legal institutions, procedures, values, concepts and rules that English law shares with other Western legal systems'.[29] Hardly anything is sacred. Even Magna Carta, 'this most basic statement of English customary law and constitutional principle', was at least partly shaped by influences coming from the *ius commune*.[30]

2. Variations of a Theme

(iii) Any attempt to describe and analyse the Western legal world in terms of a civil law/common law dichotomy is in

Contract Law (1994) (referring to the Unidroit Principles of International Commercial Contracts). On the American restatements see, most recently, Thomas Schindler, 'Die Restatements und ihre Bedeutung für das amerikanische Privatrecht', (1998) 6 *ZEuP* 277 ff.

25 The Trento Common Core Project; it has been inspired by Rudolf Schlesinger et al., *Formation of Contracts: A Study of the Common Core of Legal Systems*, 2 vols. (1968).

26 See Walter van Gerven et al., *Tort Law: Scope of Protection* (1998).

27 For an attempt to summarize the intellectual connections between civil law and common law, see Reinhard Zimmermann, 'Der europäische Charakter des englischen Rechts: Historische Verbindungen zwischen civil law und common law', (1993) 1 *ZEuP* 4 ff.

28 See supra p. 109, n. 13.

29 Berman (n. 16) 18. For an evaluation of Harold J. Berman's views of a Western legal tradition, see R. H. Helmholz, 'Harold Berman's Accomplishment as a Legal Historian', (1993) 42 *Emory Law Journal* 475 ff.

30 R. H. Helmholz, 'Magna Carta and the Ius commune', (1999) 66 *University of Chicago Law Review* 297 ff. (quotation on p. 371).

great danger of considerably underrating the diversity existing within the civil law systems. The differences between French and German law may be as great, or even greater, than those between French and English, or German and English law: on the level both of substantive law[31] and legal style.[32] Even where both French and German law are based on Roman law, the solutions adopted by *code civil* and BGB may be quite different.[33] This is attributable to the specific nature of the Roman sources. Not infrequently do they contain two different sets of rules dealing with one and the same problem, one for the stipulation, another for the consensual contracts; and both have found their way into our modern codifications. In other cases, considerable variations presented in the modern codes are based on the fact that the relevant Roman texts, which have for centuries informed our discussion, are either unclear, or even contradictory. The *Digest* sometimes still retains different layers of legal tradition. Often we find ambiguities resulting from Justinian's attempts to streamline and interpolate what the classical jurists had written, or to devise a generalized doctrine that was no longer dictated by procedural niceties. Moreover, generalization of rules and institutions, concepts and criteria of Roman law is a characteristic feature of the civilian tradition. Often that process had already been started by the classical jurists, who built on the foundations of the ancient *ius civile*; it was carried on by Justinian; and it was further advanced by the jurists of the *ius commune* and the Natural lawyers. Sometimes a reaction occurred against generalizations which subsequently were regarded as too sweeping.

The codifications, of course, reflect the results of these developments; or, more precisely, the different stages that

[31] See, e.g., the examples provided in (1996) 112 *LQR* 593 ff.

[32] See, e.g., the remark by Lord Goff of Chieveley, à propos a meeting with German judges, that he found hardly any difference between English and German law, as far as application and development of the law by the judiciary are concerned (see (1994) 58 *RabelsZ* 443 and the report by Hans-Peter Kirchhof, (1994) 2 *ZEuP* 352).

[33] The argument is developed in Reinhard Zimmermann, 'The Civil Law in European Codes', in Carey Miller and Zimmermann (n. 3) 259 ff.

these developments had reached, when each codification was drafted. As a result of these specific features of the Roman sources, we have a general provision of delictual liability in France but not in Germany; an institution of *mora debitoris* in Germany but not in France; the abstract system of transfer of ownership in Germany, the consensual one in France; vicarious liability in France, fault-based delictual liability for others in Germany; set-off operating *ipso iure*, a uniform concept of 'inexécution' covering all forms of breach of contract, and *nemo potest precise cogi ad factum* in the one legal system, set-off by notice, a distinction between various types of breach of contract focusing on the concept of 'impossibility', and the general recognition of specific performance in the other.[34] Many more examples could be mentioned. In fact, it is not easy to think of a legal rule derived, directly or indirectly, from Roman law and expressed in exactly the same way in all European codes.[35] European private law, one might say pointedly, is characterized by its great variety of rules and solutions—but it is a variety within a fundamental intellectual unity. The same is true as far as a comparison between civil law and common law is concerned. The European legal landscape resembles a painting in many different shades and colours rather than a simple monochrome snapshot.

I would like to use the main part of my third lecture to illustrate the way in which I think we may gain a better understanding of private law in Europe and may be able to recreate an awareness of the historical foundations of a new *ius commune*. I am using the opportunity to present certain conclusions, or preliminary conclusions, of a number of research projects with which I have, in some or other way, been associated. The focus of the following observations is on (i) the vital connection that ties the present to the past; (ii) the intellectual link between legal history and comparative law; and (iii) connections existing between civil law and common law.

[34] For all references, see the article mentioned in the previous footnote.

[35] Zimmermann (n. 33) 267 f.

III. LEGAL HISTORY AS A MEANS OF UNDERSTANDING THE PRESENT STATE OF OUR LAW

1. Comparative Evidence and Historical Explanation

Anyone who considers a legal problem in comparative perspective will usually start by collecting the solutions to that problem in his own and other legal systems. If he should find, for instance, a majority of those systems adopting one solution, or one approach, and only one or a few of them endorsing another, his own view may be swayed by the greater number. In addition, he may try to develop an argument why the one solution is more reasonable, or more practicable, or rationally more convincing, or more in conformity with the needs of the business community than the other.[36] Such an argument will often be based on the comparative experiences of the various legal systems with the different solutions under consideration. Even this is, essentially, an enquiry of a historical nature. But it is not where the historical approach should end. Ultimately, the mere juxtaposition of the comparative evidence, and experience, remains unsatisfactory.[37] A better picture usually emerges on the basis of an investigation into the historical development of the modern rules. An example taken from German law will make this clear.

2. Restitution for Improvements Made on Another Person's Property

(a) A Jungle of Distinctions: Roman Law and German Law

The German Civil Code contains a number of rules (§§ 994 ff. BGB) dealing with the restitution for improvements made on another person's property within what is called an 'owner-possessor relationship' (*Eigentümer-Besitzer-Verhältnis*). This complex set of rules tends to baffle German law students as well as foreign lawyers. Nothing comparable can be found

[36] See Klaus Luig, 'Was kann die Rechtsgeschichte der Rechtsvergleichung bieten?', (1999) 7 *ZEuP* 521 ff.

[37] The point has been emphasized, most recently, by Luig, (1999) 7 *ZEuP* 525 ff.

in either French or English law. In Germany, these rules have become the subject of an extensive and elaborate scholarship devoted, partly, to ironing out conflicts of result and evaluation with the general restitution regime based on the law of unjustified enrichment (§§ 812 ff. BGB).[38] The German regulation contained in §§ 994 ff. BGB is squarely based on the Roman rules concerning restitution of *impensae* (expenses). These rules contain a 'jungle of distinctions'.[39] None the less, they used to fulfil a very necessary function, for if a person had made improvements on another's property he could not avail himself of the *condictio* as it was applied in classical Roman law.[40] Thus, the possessor was without protection at first. The rules concerning restitution for expenses, based on the *exceptio doli* (defence of fraud, or bad faith), served to provide such protection, if the owner demanded restoration of his property.[41]

With the generalization of liability for unjustified enrichment in the subsequent history of the *ius commune*, and from the point of view of Natural law,[42] the rules concerning restitution for expenses were bound to lose their original significance: if a claim based on unjustified enrichment was available to a possessor who had made improvements on another person's property, he no longer required any special protection. Still, however, the draftsmen of the BGB decided to maintain the Roman rules concerning restitution for expenses. But they turned their rationale upside down: a special set of rules was necessary, not in order to enable a possessor to claim restitution for improvements, but in

[38] See, for instance, the discussion and the literature quoted by Karl-Heinz Gursky, *Staudinger, Kommentar zum Bürgerlichen Gesetzbuch* (13th edn., 1993), preliminary notes to §§ 994–1003; or Hans-Josef Wieling, *Sachenrecht*, vol. i (1990), 574 ff.

[39] John P. Dawson, *Unjust Enrichment: A Comparative Analysis* (1951), 69.

[40] On the system of *condictiones*, see Reinhard Zimmermann, *The Law of Obligations: Roman Foundations of the Civilian Tradition* (paperback edn. 1996), 834 ff.

[41] For details see, most recently, Dirk A. Verse, *Verwendungen im Eigentümer-Besitzer-Verhältnis* (1999), 13 ff.

[42] See Zimmermann (n. 33) 282 f.

order to define and specify the situations in which, exceptionally, no such claim was to be granted.[43] The policy focus, in other words, had shifted from the position of the possessor to that of the owner who was to be protected, wherever reasonable, from having to accept—and pay for—an imposed benefit. But the decision to retain the Roman rules within a changed doctrinal environment, and in terms of a reversed policy perspective, was a recipe for disaster. It has made the §§ 994 ff. BGB a minefield of legal problems.[44]

(b) Liability for Unjustified Enrichment: French Law and English Law

Other legal systems have jettisoned the Roman rules concerning restitution for improvements on another person's property, among them, most prominently, French law. Here we find a much simpler and more straightforward legal regime devised under the auspices and within the framework of the generalized liability for unjustified enrichment.[45] English law too since *Greenwood* v. *Bennett*[46] approaches the problem of restitution for improvements from the point of view of the 'principle of unjust enrichment'. Even German law reaches entirely satisfactory solutions in cases where §§ 994 ff. BGB are not applicable and where, therefore, resort must be had to the general enrichment regime. Thus, for instance, it is widely accepted that in cases of imposed benefits the enrichment has to be defined not just as a rise in market value but with regard to the particular recipient.[47] Once again, this is a solution with a long pedigree: it was applied in the German *ius commune* and has resurfaced in the interpretation of the Code even

[43] See Verse (n. 41) 36 ff. with full references.

[44] This is demonstrated, in detail, by Verse (n. 41) *passim*.

[45] Analysed by Verse (n. 41) 65 ff.

[46] [1973] 1 QB 195. The position in England is analysed by Verse (n. 41) 89 ff. For a comparative analysis, cf. also idem, 'Improvements and Enrichment: A Comparative Analysis', (1998) 6 *Restitution Law Review* 85 ff.; Werner Lorenz, 'Der Schutz vor aufgedrängter Bereicherung: Eine vergleichende Betrachtung des deutschen und englischen Rechts', in *Festschrift für Dieter Medicus* (1999), 367 ff.

[47] See, e.g. Dieter Medicus, *Bürgerliches Recht* (18th edn., 1999), n. 899; Werner Lorenz, in *Staudinger, Kommentar zum Bürgerlichen Gesetzbuch*, revised version of the 13th edn. (1999), preliminary remarks to §§ 812 ff. n. 46.

though it was not specifically adopted by it.[48] It has convincingly been demonstrated that §§ 812 ff. BGB would also provide more flexible and more appropriate solutions in cases where we have an 'owner-possessor relationship'.[49] By discarding §§ 994 ff. BGB, German legal doctrine could not only be considerably simplified; German law could, in this respect, also be brought in line, again, with mainstream European legal thinking.

3. The Retroactive Effect of Set-Off

The law of set-off provides another example of how our modern legal thinking is, arguably, still unconsciously dominated by Roman law. In continental Europe we essentially have two different regimes concerning the effect of set-off.[50] The more traditional one prevails in French law. As soon (and as far) as two obligations capable of being set off against each other confront each other, both of them are extinguished.[51] Set-off, in other words, takes effect *ipso iure* and it operates retrospectively. This approach is based on a tradition reaching back to Roman law. '. . .ut actiones ipso iure minuant' is how Justinian described the effect of set-off in Inst. IV, 6, 30. The other solution is the one implemented in the German Code: set-off has to be asserted by an extrajudicial, informal, and unilateral declaration to the other party.[52] This approach today is widely regarded as preferable since it considerably enhances legal certainty without being unduly formalistic.[53] Somewhat strangely, however, it is generally accepted that the declaration has retroactive effect: the obligations, as far as they are coextensive, are deemed to have been discharged at the moment at which, being suitable for set-off, they first

48 See Verse, (1998) 6 *Restitution Law Review* 89.

49 Verse (n. 41) 119 ff., 158 ff.

50 See *Law of Obligations* (n. 40) 760 f.

51 Art. 1290 *code civil*.

52 § 388 BGB.

53 See, e.g., the position in Austrian (Helmut Koziol and Rudolf Welser, *Grundriß des bürgerlichen Rechts*, vol. i [10th edn., 1995], 279, 280 f.), Greek (art. 441 Astikos Kodikas), Dutch (arts. 6: 127 I, 129 BW) and Italian law (Giorgio Cian, 'Hundert Jahre BGB aus italienischer Sicht', (1998) 6 *ZEuP* 220 f.).

confronted each other.[54] Even though the artificial notion of a retroactive declaration of set-off is not practicable without recognizing a number of exceptions, and is detrimental to legal certainty,[55] it has hardly ever been questioned.[56] Nor have any good policy reasons been advanced in favour of it. Instead, retroactivity seems to be regarded as being somehow intrinsically related to the 'essence' of set-off.[57] In reality, we seem to be dealing here with (indirect) consequences of the *ipso iure* doctrine still overshadowing our perception of set-off. This suspicion is confirmed if we turn our attention to those European legal systems that have, in this respect, remained unencumbered by the Justinianic heritage: English and Nordic law. They merely attribute ex nunc effect to set-off.[58]

4. *Periculum Emptoris*

(*a*) *Consensual Contracts of Sale in Roman Law*

New and interesting insights can even be gained in areas which have traditionally attracted much more scholarly attention than set-off or restitution for improvements. *Periculum est emptoris* is a rule of Roman law that can still be found in modern legal systems.[59] Once again, however,

[54] See, for Germany, § 389 BGB. The same applies in the other legal systems mentioned in the previous note.

[55] For details, see Reinhard Zimmermann, 'Die Aufrechnung: Eine rechtsvergleichende Skizze zum Europäischen Vertragsrecht', in *Festschrift für Dieter Medicus* (1999), 721 ff.

[56] But see Peter Bydlinski, 'Die Aufrechnung mit verjährten Forderungen: Wirklich kein Änderungsbedarf?', (1996) 196 *AcP* 281 ff.; and see now the historical analysis by Pascal Pichonnaz, 'The Retroactive Effect of Set-Off', (2000) 48 *TR* (in preparation).

[57] See the references in Joachim Gernhuber, *Die Erfüllung und ihre Surrogate* (2nd edn., 1994), 229.

[58] This follows from the procedural nature of set-off in English law. For a comparative discussion, see Zimmermann (n. 55) 710 ff.

[59] For Roman law, see *Law of Obligations* (n. 40) 281 ff.; Martin Bauer, *Periculum Emptoris: Eine dogmengeschichtliche Untersuchung zur Gefahrtragung beim Kauf* (1998), 26 ff. The rule was applied in Germany down to the days of the pandectists; a modern codified version of it can be found in art. 185 I OR. See, in this context, the observations by Eugen Bucher, 'Die Eigentums-Translativwirkung von Schuldverträgen: Das "Woher" und "Wohin" dieses Modells des Code Civil',

what worked well in Roman law does not provide a reasonable solution in modern law. The Roman rule was intimately linked up with the concept of *custodia*: since the seller was under a particularly strict type of liability—including accidents which were regarded as being typically avoidable by him—the buyer effectively only had to carry the risk of *vis maior*.[60] Moreover, the risk rule followed logically from the structure of *emptio-venditio* as a transaction involving a reallocation of value: as between the parties, the object of the sale was allocated to the buyer, once the contract had been concluded.[61] Thus, whilst he could reap the fruits of the object and other benefits, he also had to carry the risk.[62] Another consequence of this specific structure of the consensual sale of classical Roman law was that it could only relate to one or the other specific object; generic sales were inadmissible.[63]

Justinian's compilers took over the risk rule of classical law. At the same time, however, they demolished one of its cornerstones. For, on the one hand, they converted the classical concept of *custodia* into a fault-based liability: liability for accidents which can typically been avoided (i.e. for all accidents except for *vis maior*) was turned into the duty to display the strictest diligence.[64] On the other hand, the compilers generalized the idea that the degree of diligence one party to a contract may reasonably expect from the other is to be determined by considerations of 'utility' (*Utilitätsprinzip*).[65] In view of the fact that a contract of sale benefits both the seller and the buyer, it was bound to appear unreasonable to subject the seller to a liability that was stricter than normal. His standard of liability was thus

(1998) 6 *ZEuP* 651 ff., 664 f. *Periculum est emptoris* also still applies in modern South African law; for all details, see Bauer, 185 ff.

60 See *Law of Obligations* (n. 40) 287 in connection with 192 ff.

61 See ibid. 290 f.

62 *Qui habet commoda ferre debet onera* (see Paul. D. 50, 17, 10 and *Law of Obligations* (n. 40) 290 f.).

63 For details, see *Law of Obligations* (n. 40) 236 ff., 239 f.

64 See, e.g., Gai. D. 13, 6, 18 pr.; Gai. D. 44, 7, 1, 4.

65 See *Law of Obligations* (n. 40) 198 ff.

reduced to *culpa*.[66] But this meant that the balance of risks inherent in the classical sale was upset considerably.

(b) The Development of the Generic Sale

The medieval jurists tied the Roman risk rule even more rigorously into a liability system dominated by the fault principle and considerations of utility. At the same time, they started to remove another of its cornerstones. As a result of a 'productive misunderstanding', they abandoned the idea that a consensual contract of sale could only relate to a specific object and read the (purely) generic sale into the sources of Roman law.[67] They thereby ensured that *emptio-venditio* became, and remained, the legal garment for the most important transaction of business life. But they also saddled the discussion of sales law for many centuries with the conceptual consequences of their misunderstanding.[68] One of these consequences was a new double meaning of the concept of risk: does the seller still have to deliver another object of the same class if the one that he intended to deliver is destroyed (*Leistungsgefahr*); and does the purchaser still have to pay even though he does not receive the object he has bargained for (*Gegenleistungsgefahr*)? The application to generic sales of a set of rules devised originally for the sale of specific goods led to considerable controversy and complex distinctions. All these distinctions and discussions, however, could only imperfectly hide the fundamental truth: *periculum est emptoris* was no longer justifiable on rational grounds.

5. Liability for Latent Defects

The rules relating to the seller's liability for latent defects as contained in the BGB (and other codifications) are characterized by a number of peculiarities: the buyer cannot ask for the defect to be remedied; he is confined, in principle, to

66 Bauer (n. 59) 86 ff.

67 See ibid. 98 ff. On the history of the generic sale, see Wolfgang Ernst, 'Kurze Rechtsgeschichte des Gattungskaufs', (1999) 7 *ZEuP* 583 ff.

68 For all details, see Bauer (n. 59) 113 ff. (on Roman-Dutch law).

claiming reduction of the purchase price (*Minderung*) or cancellation of the contract with the result that the parties have to return what they have given (*Wandelung*).[69] In two narrowly defined situations (a promised quality in the object of the sale is absent; the defect has been fraudulently concealed) a claim for damages is available.[70] And but for cases of fraudulent concealment, all claims based on a latent defect are subject to an exceptionally short prescription period.[71] Once again, it can easily be demonstrated that all these rules derive from Roman law.[72] There, indeed, they made good sense.[73] Liability under the aedilitian edict covered physical defects in slaves and livestock and certain defects of character in slaves. In nearly all these situations it would have been impossible to remedy the defect. In many of these situations it would have been, even after a few months, very difficult to determine whether the defect had existed at the time of sale. A type of liability which was based on the simple alternative of redhibition or reduction of the price and which, in particular, did not involve difficult enquiries as to fault or damages was well suited for everyday market transactions. And liability for *dolus* and *dicta vel promissa* had to be available in terms of what was required by the precepts of good faith. In their modern generalized form, these Roman rules have changed their function; they constitute peculiar deviations from the normal liability regime. They have led to unsatisfactory results and considerable doctrinal headache.[74] An integration of liability for latent defects into generalized liability rules for breach of contract is overdue.[75]

[69] §§ 459, 462 BGB.

[70] § 463 BGB.

[71] § 477 BGB.

[72] See *Law of Obligations* (n. 40) 305 ff.

[73] See, in particular, Dieter Medicus, 'Zur Geschichte der Sachmängelhaftung', in Zimmermann, Knütel, and Meincke (n. 11) 307 ff.

[74] See Medicus (n. 47) 307 ff.

[75] See Bundesminister der Justiz (ed.), *Abschlußbericht der Kommission zur Überarbeitung des Schuldrechts* (1992), 20 ff.

IV. THE DEVELOPMENT OF LEGAL IDEAS BY WAY OF GENERALIZATION

1. The Example of Delictual Liability for Others

Generalization of certain ideas contained in some or other Roman text is, as has been emphasized above, a characteristic feature of the civilian tradition.[76] A classical Roman lawyer would often have been very surprised by the end product of a process as a result of which the *ius commune* has managed to venture beyond Roman law by means of Roman law.[77] Vicarious liability provides an example of a vigorous modern institution created on extremely slender Roman foundations.

2. Johannes Voet

Of crucial importance, as far as continental Europe is concerned, was the recognition of the fact that the Roman system of noxal liability had become obsolete.[78] In the seventeenth and eighteenth centuries three approaches were competing as to how to fill that gap. 'Door de dienaers misdaed en werden de meesters ende vrouwen in't ghemeen niet verbonden dan zoo veel de onbetaelde huir maeg bedragen', we read in Grotius' *Inleiding*:[79] the master is 'vicariously' liable, but only up to the amount of unpaid wages. This kind of wage liability appears to have had its origin in Saxonian law[80] and was accepted also by a number of other authors. Others, however, regarded liability of the master as appropriate only if some fault could be attributed to him. Johannes van der Linden advocated this view[81] and he was clearly influenced by Natural law thinking in this

[76] See supra p. 113. [77] Supra p. 4 f.

[78] See *Law of Obligations* (n. 40) 1118 ff.

[79] (Masters and mistresses are not generally bound by their servants' wrongful acts, except to the amount of unpaid wages: translation by R. W. Lee, *The Jurisprudence of Holland*, vol. i (1926), 485). Hugo Grotius, *Inleiding tot de Hollandsche Rechtsgeleertheyd* (ed. R. W. Lee, 2nd edn., 1953), iii, xxxviii, 8.

[80] Cf. II, 32 *Sachsenspiegel*; Samuel Stryk, 'Specimen usus moderni pandectarum', in *Opera omnia* (1837 ff.), lib. IX, tit. IV, 4.

[81] *Supplementum ad Voet* (1793), ad lib. IX, tit. IV, 10.

respect. And finally there was the view that ultimately won the day: liability of the master for all the wrongs committed by the people in his service, as far as these wrongs were committed in the course of their employment. Johannes Voet was the most influential proponent of this view,[82] and he developed it on the basis of certain traces of this regime in the Roman sources:[83] the liability of a person from whose dwelling something was thrown down or poured onto the street so as to injure another (*actio de effusis vel deiectis*),[84] the liability of sea-carriers, innkeepers, and stable keepers for damage done by their employees to their customer's property (*receptum nautarum, cauponum, stabulariorum* and *actio furti vel damni in factum adversus nautos, caupones, stabularios*),[85] and the liability of tax collectors (*publicani*) for wrongs committed by a member of their *familia*.[86] The idea of the functional limitation of the master's liability was derived from the *actiones exercitoria* and *institoria* where the master of a ship and the owner of a shop had been held liable for debts incurred by others within the terms of their *praepositio*.[87]

3. Robert Joseph Pothier

'Ac primo quidem admonendi sumus, dominos ac patres in solidem teneri ex delictis famulorum ac filiorum . . . quoties illi delinquerunt in officio aut ministerio, cui a patre dominove fuerunt praepositi' (Firstly then we must take warning that masters and fathers are held liable *in solidum* on the wrongdoings of domestic servants and of sons . . . so often as those persons have done wrong in the duty or service in charge of which they were put by father or

[82] *Commentarius ad Pandectas* (1827/1829), lib. IX, tit. IV, 10.

[83] See Hartmut Wicke, *Respondeat Superior: Haftung für Verrichtungsgehilfen im römischen, römisch-holländischen, englischen und südafrikanischen Recht* (2000), § 2 III, § 3 II 1 and 3 (c).

[84] On which, see Reinhard Zimmermann, 'Effusum vel deiectum', in *Festschrift für Hermann Lange* (1992), 301 ff.

[85] *Law of Obligations* (n. 40) 16, 514 ff.

[86] Wicke (n. 83) § 2 III 3.

[87] See ibid., § 2 III 2 (d) and § 3 II 1 (a) (ee).

master.)[88] This was the general rule formulated by Voet around the turn of the seventeenth to the eighteenth century. A few decades later Robert-Joseph Pothier was also inspired by some of the Roman texts to state the same principle in his *Traité des obligations* ('Quiconque a commis quelqu'un à quelque fonction est responsable des délits et quasi-délits que son préposé a commis dans l'exercice des fonctions auxelles il était préposé')[89] and thus to lay the foundations of art. 1384 *code civil*.[90] The idea of a generalized but functionally limited vicarious liability was clearly 'in the air'.

4. Lord Holt

This was not only true of continental legal systems but also of the common law. For at about the same time when Voet wrote his *Commentarius ad Pandectas* Chief Justice Holt handed down the two decisions of *Boson* v. *Sandford* (1691)[91] and *Turberville* v. *Stampe* (1698)[92] which established the modern English concept of vicarious liability. He, too, obviously drew his inspiration from some of the Roman precedents (the *actio de effusis vel deiectis* and the liability of the sea-carrier)[93] and thus it is hardly surprising that the headnote in *Turberville* v. *Stampe* reads like an English rendition of the words used by Johannes Voet: 'A master is responsible for all acts done by his servant in the course of his employment'; and in order to demarcate the new rule from the old common law principle the phrase 'though without particular direction' was added. This, essentially, has

[88] Translation by Percival Gane, *The Selective Voet*, vol. ii (1955), 606.

[89] ('Whoever has entrusted some function to someone's care is responsible for the wrongs and quasi-wrongs which that person commits in the exercise of the functions in charge of which he was placed'.) 'Traité des obligations', in *Œuvres* (1835), n. 453.

[90] On the application of which, see Konrad Zweigert and Hein Kötz, *An Introduction to Comparative Law*, tr. Tony Weir (3rd edn., 1998), 635 ff.

[91] (1691) 2 Salkeld 440.

[92] (1698) 1 Ld Raym 264.

[93] See Zimmermann, *Festschrift Lange* (n. 84) 319 ff. and Wicke (n. 83) § 4 V. Wicke also draws attention, i.a., to Christopher St. Germain, *Doctor and Student*, ed. Theodore F. Plucknett and J. L. Barton, Selden Society 91 (1974), 265 f.

remained the common law rule.[94] But, more than that, it has become one of the basic structural features of European private law.[95]

Characteristically, South African courts and legal writers[96] did not find it too difficult to amalgamate the Roman-Dutch and English strands of the European tradition.[97] In the process, South African law was saved from the artificial restriction of the 'common employment' doctrine which the courts in England introduced in the course of the nineteenth century:[98] a step taken for essentially the same reason for which contemporary German lawyers opted for the introduction of the requirement of fault into § 831 BGB.[99] English law has, in the meantime, re-established its general of vicarious liability regime; German law has, so far, failed to do so.

V. LESSONS FROM MIXED LEGAL SYSTEMS

1. 'The Third Legal Family'

The establishment of an intellectual connection between civil law and common law is widely regarded as the most

[94] P. S. Atiyah, *Vicarious Liability in the Law of Torts* (1967), 12, refers to 'one of the most firmly established legal principles throughout the common law world'.

[95] The point is emphasized by Wicke (n. 83) *passim*.

[96] On the significance of South African private law at the intersection between civil law and common law, cf. infra pp. 128 ff.

[97] For all details, see Wicke (n. 83) § 6.

[98] *Priestley* v. *Fowler* (1837) 3 M & W 1; see Wicke (n. 83) § 4 V 9. That South African law did not receive the common employment doctrine is due, essentially, to a decision by J. G. Kotzé, the most influential judge, by far, in the 19th-century South African Republic (Transvaal): *Lewis* v. *The Salisbury Gold Mining Company* (1894) 1 OR 1; on which, see Reinhard Zimmermann and Philip Sutherland, ' "a true science and not a feigned one": J. G. Kotzé (1849–1940), Chief Justice der Südafrikanischen Republik (Transvaal)', (1999) 116 *ZSS (RA)* 147 ff. (180 ff.). Scots law took a different course (*Bartonshill Coal Company* v. *Reid* (1858) 3 Macq 266 (285)), not to its advantage: see the analysis by Philip Simpson, 'Vicarious Liability', in Reinhard Zimmermann and Kenneth Reid (eds.), *A History of Private Law in Scotland*, vol. ii, in preparation.

[99] See Hans Hermann Seiler, 'Die deliktische Gehilfenhaftung in historischer Sicht', 1967 *JZ* 527 ff.; cf. also supra pp. 72 f.

important prerequisite for the emergence of a genuinely European legal scholarship.[100] Thus, it should be of the greatest interest for legal scholars in Europe to see that such connection has already been established, on an intellectual as well as practical level, in a number of 'mixed' legal systems. They provide a wealth of experience of how these two branches of the European legal tradition may be accommodated within one legal system. Comparative lawyers have indeed started to pay attention to mixed legal systems as potential models for 'procur[ing] a gradual approximation of Civil Law and Common Law'.[101] First attempts are even made to compare mixed legal systems with each other,[102] to explore their similarities and differences, and to present them as 'a third legal family'.[103] Some members of that family have codified their private law.[104] Others are still largely based today on common (in the sense of uncodified) law. They present the particularly fascinating picture of courts and legal writers still having to

[100] This has repeatedly been emphasized by Ernst Rabel; cf. the essays 'On Comparative Research in Legal History and Modern Law', 'Private Laws of Western Civilization', and 'Deutsches und amerikanisches Recht', all in Ernst Rabel, *Gesammelte Aufsätze*, ed. Hans G. Leser, vol. iii (1967), 258, 276, 342; cf. also, for instance, Helmut Coing, 'Die Bedeutung der europäischen Rechtsgeschichte für die Rechtsvergleichung' (1967), in idem, *Gesammelte Aufsätze zu Rechtsgeschichte, Rechtsphilosophie und Zivilrecht*, vol. ii (1982), 176; Mathias Reimann, 'Towards a European Civil Code: Why Continental Jurists Should Consult their Transatlantic Colleagues', (1999) 73 *Tulane Law Review* 1341; Flessner, (1999) 7 *ZEuP* 518 f.

[101] Zweigert and Kötz (n. 90) 204. This approach is now forcefully advocated by Smits (n. 5) 117 ff.

[102] See, e.g., Esin Örücü, Elspeth Attwooll, and Sean Coyle (eds.), *Studies in Legal Systems: Mixed and Mixing* (1996); on Scots and South African law, see the literature quoted infra n. 310, in particular the essays by Visser and Du Plessis.

[103] Vernon V. Palmer (ed.), *Mixed Jurisdictions of the World: The Third Legal Family*, forthcoming.

[104] On the history of codification in Louisiana, and on Louisiana's mixed legal system in general, see Joachim Zekoll, 'Zwischen den Welten: Das Privatrecht von Louisiana als europäisch-amerikanische Mischrechtsordnung', in Reinhard Zimmermann (ed.), *Amerikanische Rechtskultur und europäisches Privatrecht: Impressionen aus der Neuen Welt* (1995), 11 ff.; Vernon V. Palmer, *Louisiana: Microcosm of a Mixed Jurisdiction* (1999); for Quebec see, e.g., H. Patrick Glenn, 'Quebec: Mixité and Monism', in Örücü, Attwooll, and Coyle (n. 102) 1 ff.; cf. also Reimann, (1999) 73 *Tulane Law Review* 1341 ff.

grapple with the historical sources of the *ius commune* and of the English common law and thus being faced with the specific problems and challenges arising from a living interaction between civil law and common law.

2. Southern Cross

(a) *Civil Law and Common Law in South Africa*

A few years ago, the first large-scale attempt was made to trace the history of legal doctrine in South African law: one of the two major uncodified mixed legal systems in the world. *Southern Cross,*[105] I think, provides stimulating insights into how a modern legal system with its own peculiar flavour emerged from civilian as well as common law roots.[106] It shows how the Dutch variant of the European *ius commune* that was transplanted to the Cape of Good Hope in the seventeenth century came under the influence of English law in the course of the nineteenth and early twentieth centuries and has, in the process, acquired an identity which is neither purely Roman-Dutch nor purely English.[107] Of course, there are entire areas of the law where the balance has been tilted very much in one direction. The law of evidence, procedural law, and large parts of commercial law (especially those governed by statute) are mainly English. The law of things (property law) and succession, on the other hand, remain mainly Roman-Dutch.

But even here we do not usually find the one strand of legal tradition continuing to exist in clinical purity. The law of procedure provides a good example. For, on the one hand, a particularly characteristic aspect of the English procedural model, the distinction between courts of law and courts of equity and the concomitant distinction

[105] Reinhard Zimmermann and Daniel Visser (eds.), *Southern Cross: Civil Law and Common Law in South Africa* (1996).

[106] See now also Smits (n. 5) 157 ff.

[107] For a general account, see Reinhard Zimmermann, *Das römisch-holländische Recht in Südafrika* (1983), 1 ff.; Eduard Fagan, 'Roman-Dutch Law in its South African Historical Context', in Zimmermann and Visser (n. 105) 33 ff.

between two distinct bodies, or levels, of law, was never received in South Africa.[108] On the other hand, the superimposition of a judicial and procedural framework of common law origin upon the Roman-Dutch law had a decisive influence on South African judicial style which, in turn, could not fail to colour the way in which substantive rules of law were perceived and applied, even where they were of Roman-Dutch origin.[109] None the less, the law of obligations is probably that part of the law where the most complex process of blending of the two traditions has occurred. Here too, of course, there has sometimes been a competition of approaches resulting, ultimately, in the rejection of one of them. Thus, South African law recognizes contracts in favour of third parties[110] and penalty clauses,[111] and it has rejected the doctrine of consideration.[112] In all three respects, the development of South African law has foreshadowed that of modern European private law.[113] More often, however, we find a complex process of interaction: an interaction prefigured, not rarely, in the development of the respective English legal doctrine. A few examples will have to suffice.

(*b*) *Offer and Acceptance*

The modern South African law on offer and acceptance may fairly be regarded as 'an anglicized version of an

[108] See Reinhard Zimmermann, 'Good Faith and Equity', in Zimmermann and Visser (n. 105) 217 f.

[109] For details, see the analysis by H. J. Erasmus, 'The Interaction of Substantive Law and Procedure', in Zimmermann and Visser (n. 105) 141 ff.

[110] See David J. Joubert, 'Agency and Stipulatio Alteri', in Zimmermann and Visser (n. 105) 335 ff.

[111] See Schalk van der Merwe, L. F. van Huyssteen, M. F. B. Reinecke, G. F. Lubbe, and J. G. Lotz, *Contract: General Principles* (1993), 315 ff.

[112] The story of the rejection of the doctrine of consideration is told by Dale Hutchison, 'Contract Formation', in Zimmermann and Visser (n. 105) 166 ff.; cf. also Zimmermann and Sutherland, (1999) 116 *ZSS (RA)* 175 ff.

[113] See, as far as the Principles of European Contract Law are concerned, arts. 6:110 (Stipulation in Favour of a Third Party), 9:509 (Agreed Payment for Non-Performance), and 2:101 (Conditions for the Conclusion of a Contract); cf. also the comparative analysis (on the first two issues) presented in 1995 *JZ* 483 and 487 f. Generally on South African law as a potential model for legal harmonization of European contract law, see Smits (n. 5) 189 ff.

essentially civilian doctrine'.[114] For as it is recognized that (*a*) contracts are based on an agreement (*consensus*) between the parties, (*b*) such agreement must be manifested by two coinciding declarations of intention, namely offer and acceptance, and (*c*) an offer is freely revocable until it has been accepted, South African law moves as much within the thinking patterns established by the Natural lawyers as does English law.[115] Commercial convenience prompted South African courts to accept the English 'mailbox-rule' established in *Adams* v. *Lindsell*:[116] contrary to general principle, a contract to be concluded by post is formed already at the moment when the letter accepting the offer is dispatched. Kotzé, JP, attempted to explain that rule in terms of the nature of contractual *consensus*: a contract comes into existence when the will to accept an offer has been manifested and the act dispatching the letter accepting the offer is nothing more than the typical manifestation of such will to be bound by the contract.[117] In the process, Savigny, Mühlenbruch, Friedrich Ludwig Keller, and others became early protagonists of a continental mailbox theory;[118] but it is noticeable that the Court in *Adams* v. *Lindsell* advanced a very similar argument.[119]

(*c*) *Mistake*

Contractual theory may emphasize the correspondence either of the will of the two parties to the contract (there has to be *consensus ad idem*) or of the declarations expressing

[114] Hutchison (n. 112) 173.

[115] See A. W. B. Simpson, 'Innovation in Nineteenth Century Contract Law', (1975) 91 *LQR* 257 ff.; *Law of Obligations* (n. 40) 565 ff.; James Gordley, *The Philosophical Origins of Modern Contract Doctrine* (1991), 112 ff., 139 f., 175 ff.

[116] (1818) 1 B & Ald 681, 106 ER 250; confirmed by the House of Lords in *Dunlop* v. *Higgins* (1848) 1 HLC 381, 9 ER 805. See, e.g., G. H. Treitel, *The Law of Contract* (10th edn., 1999), 23 ff.; Zweigert and Kötz (n. 90) 358 f.

[117] *Cape Explosives Works, Ltd.* v. *South African Oil and Fat Industries, Ltd.* 1921 CPD 244; on this decision, and its background, see Zimmermann and Sutherland, (1999) 166 *ZSS (RA)* 169 ff.

[118] *Cape Explosives Works, Ltd.* v. *South African Oil and Fat Industries, Ltd.* 1921 CPD 244 (260, 261).

[119] (1818) 1 B & Ald 681, 106 ER 250; and see Treitel (n. 116) 24 n. 73.

such will.[120] Continental legal systems have usually accepted the will theory as their basic premise.[121] It was supported, influentially, by Savigny and Grotius but its intellectual ancestry has been traced back to Thomas Aquinas.[122] English courts, however, in spite of their frequent use of will-related terminology,[123] traditionally look at the expression of the will in order to determine whether (and with what content) a contract has been concluded.[124] But the objective approach has also found support in continental Natural law theory[125] and has characteristically influenced the Austrian General Civil Code.[126]

Obviously, both approaches differ in their analysis of the problem of mistake. Taken to their logical extremes, the will theory would have to regard every error as operative as far as it has affected the contractual intention of one of the parties whereas, according to the declaration theory, a unilateral mistake cannot, in principle, have any effect at all as long as both parties have declared the same thing. However, while it may be equitable to stress the individual will, certainty of the law will be detrimentally affected. Sole emphasis on the external manifestation of the intention, in turn, is bound to lead to harsh and inequitable results. This is why every developed legal system attempts to find some balance between these two positions. If it proceeds from the will theory it will usually *limit* the range of mistakes that will afford an escape from the contract. If it subscribes to the declaration theory, it has to accommodate the interests

[120] On the shift from *verba* to *voluntas* in Roman law, see *Law of Obligations* (n. 40) 583 ff., 621 ff.

[121] On the rise of the will theory, see Gordley (n. 115) 161 ff.

[122] For details, and references, see Martin Josef Schermaier, 'Europäische Geistesgeschichte am Beispiel des Irrtumsrechts', (1998) 6 *ZEuP* 60 ff., 67 ff.

[123] See P. S. Atiyah, *The Rise and Fall of Freedom of Contract* (1979), 407 ff.; *Law of Obligations* (n. 40) 601.

[124] See, e.g., the references in *Law of Obligations* (n. 40) 601 n. 72.

[125] Schermaier, (1998) 6 *ZEuP* 73 ff.

[126] See Helmut Coing, *Europäisches Privatrecht*, vol. ii (1989), 448; *Law of Obligations* (n. 40) 613; and see, most recently, Franz Bydlinski, 'Mistake in Austrian Private Law Viewed in Terms of a "Flexible System" Approach', in Herbert Hausmaninger, Helmut Koziol, Alfredo M. Rabello, and Israel Gilead (eds.), *Developments in Austrian and Israeli Private Law* (1999), 21 ff.

of the mistaken party by *allowing* a defence of mistake in a limited number of situations.[127] In particular, a mistake may be operative in cases where it has been caused by the other party and where that other party cannot therefore reasonably rely on the validity of the contract.[128]

In South African law, will theory and declaration theory have, for a long time, been vying for recognition. Today the will theory is widely regarded as the proper point of departure[129] but it has been considerably modified by reliance-based considerations. A unilateral mistake renders a contract void if it is 'material'. In this regard the Roman classification of relevant errors has been of some assistance to the courts, though some of the Roman categories have been considerably modified.[130] Generally speaking an error is material if it relates to one of the essential elements of the contract and thus excludes *consensus*; and it is not material if it relates only to a person's reasons for contracting. This distinction is obviously based on Savigny's analysis of error.[131]

In addition to being material, however, the mistake also has to be reasonable (*iustus error*). But when is a mistake reasonable? This remained unclear for a long time.[132] From the late 1920s, however, a new approach gained ground. Rather than asking whether the error was *iustus*, it required the courts to establish whether the other party's belief in the existence of *consensus* was reasonable, for in the absence of mutual assent a contract might none the less be established on the basis of 'quasi-mutual assent'.[133] This was, essentially, the principle established by Blackburn, J, in the famous

[127] See *Law of Obligations* (n. 40) 584 ff. For a comparative overview, see Kötz (n. 6) 171 ff.; Bruno Schmidlin, in *Berner Kommentar zum schweizerischen Privatrecht*, vol. vi, first part (1993), nn. 60 ff.; Ernst A. Kramer, *Der Irrtum beim Vertragsschluß: Eine weltweit rechtsvergleichende Bestandsaufnahme* (1998).

[128] Kötz (n. 6) 191 ff.

[129] See, in particular, *Saambou-Nasionale Bouvereniging* v. *Friedman* 1979 (3) SA 978 (A) 993 (995 f.).

[130] Hutchison (n. 112) 183 f.

[131] For details, see Klaus Luig, 'Savignys Irrtumslehre', (1979) 8 *Ius Commune* 36 ff.; Horst Hammen, *Die Bedeutung Friedrich Carl von Savignys für die allgemeinen dogmatischen Grundlagen des deutschen Bürgerlichen Gesetzbuches* (1983), 111 ff.; *Law of Obligations* (n. 40) 614 ff.

[132] For a historical analysis, see Hutchison (n. 112) 184 ff.

[133] Ibid. 187.

English case of *Smith* v. *Hughes*[134] 'and it was now embraced with enthusiasm by the South African courts'.[135] The path towards a reconciliation between the *iustus error* requirement and the doctrine of quasi-mutual assent was eventually paved by Fagan, CJ, in the case of *George* v. *Fairmead (Pty.) Ltd.*, where he said:[136] 'As I read the decisions, our Courts, in applying the test [of *iustus error*], have taken into account the fact that there is another party involved and have considered his position. They have, in effect, said: Has the first party—the one who is trying to resile—been to blame in the sense that by his conduct he has led the other party, as a reasonable man, to believe that he was binding himself? . . . If his mistake is due to a misrepresentation, whether innocent or fraudulent, by the other party, then, of course, it is the second party who is to blame and the first party is not bound.' Or, to put the matter slightly differently: an error is *iustus* when the other party, due to his unreasonable reliance, cannot uphold the contract on the basis of quasi-mutual assent.[137]

(d) Misrepresentation

A misrepresentation is a false statement of fact made by one party to the other before or at the time of the contract.[138] It is obvious that a claim for damages lies whenever such misrepresentation was fraudulent; and the scope of the Aquilian action, as extended by the Appellate Division in *Administrateur, Natal* v. *Trust Bank van Afrika Bpk.*,[139] appears to be broad enough to allow also the recovery of damages in cases of negligent misrepresentations.[140] But what about

134 (1871) LR 6 QB 597, at 607.

135 Hutchison (n. 112) 187.

136 1958 (2) SA 465 (A) 471.

137 See Hutchison (n. 112) 192 f. with references.

138 Dale Hutchison (ed.), *Wille's Principles of South African Law* (8th edn., 1991), 440.

139 1979 (3) SA 824 (A), the 'Hedley Byrne' of South African law in which recoverability in delict for pure economic loss was authoritatively (re-)established. See Dale Hutchison, 'Aquilian Liability II (Twentieth Century)', in Zimmermann and Visser (n. 105) 629 ff.

140 See *Bayer South Africa (Pty.) Ltd.* v. *Frost* 1991 (3) SA 559 (A); on which, see Dale Hutchison and Reinhard Zimmermann, 'Fahrlässige Angaben im vorvertraglichen Bereich nach modernem römisch-holländischem Recht', (1995) 3 *ZEuP* 271 ff.

the *contract* that was induced by the misrepresentation? Is it still enforceable, is it void, or can it be rescinded? In classical Roman law no action could be granted on the basis of *negotia bonae fidei* affected by fraud; in all other cases relief had to be sought by raising the *exceptio doli* or by instituting the *actio de dolo*.[141] With the advent of the modern general law of contract the regime applicable to *iudicia bonae fidei* should ultimately have prevailed. However, for a variety of reasons *ipso iure* invalidity of the contract induced by fraud did not appear to be a suitable solution, and thus it came to be recognized that the effect of fraud was at most to render the contract voidable at the instance of the innocent party.[142] But does this kind of rescission really depend on fraudulent behaviour, *stricto sensu*, on the part of the other party to the contract? In other words, does it require an intentional misstatement of an existing material fact?

This was the problem addressed by Solomon, J, in *Viljoen* v. *Hillier*, decided in 1904.[143] The judge not only rejected the proposition that, in order successfully to defend himself against the contractual claim, the defendant had to prove a fraudulent misrepresentation on the part of the plaintiff; he did not even regard proof of negligence as necessary. Fault was thus considered to be entirely irrelevant. Under Roman law, Solomon, J, argued, the defendant could have raised the *exceptio doli* under such circumstances, 'the dolus consisting not in fraud at the initiation of the contract, but in the fact that it is against good faith for a man to insist upon enforcing a contract which he has secured by his own misrepresentation'.[144] The *exceptio doli*, here as in many other cases,[145] provided a convenient screen behind which

[141] *Law of Obligations* (n. 40) 663 f.

[142] Ibid. 671 f. As far as the requirements for rescission in modern South African law are concerned, see David J. Joubert, *General Principles of the Law of Contract* (1987), 93 ff.; Gerhard Lubbe and Christina Murray, *Farlam and Hathaway, Contract: Cases, Materials and Commentary* (1988), 335 ff.

[143] 1904 TS 312.

[144] *Viljoen* v. *Hillier* 1904 TS 312 (315 f.). On the development leading up to, and following, *Viljoen* v. *Hillier*, see Gerhard Lubbe, 'Voidable Contracts', in Zimmermann and Visser (n. 105) 276 ff.

[145] For details, see Zimmermann (n. 108) 217 ff.

an entirely new doctrine could be introduced into the emerging South African version of Roman-Dutch law. For Solomon, J, quite clearly took his lead from English law and simply adopted the doctrine of innocent misrepresentation, as he perceived it to have been developed in equity. This is evident from his conspicuous remark that in his opinion 'by our law as well as by the English law the facts above enumerated would constitute a good defence';[146] and also, particularly, from his reference to the decision of the Chancery Division in *Redgrave* v. *Hurd*, where Jessel, MR, had stated that it would be a 'moral delinquency' if the law were to allow a man to enforce a contract obtained by a statement which he *now* knew to be false (*ex post facto fraud*).[147] The impact on South African law of importing the doctrine of innocent misrepresentation has been profound.[148] It has, effectively, meant that unilateral mistakes of motive, induced by the other party, are to be accorded legal effect; for if the mistake induced by the misrepresentation relates to one of the material elements of the contract, lack of *consensus* prevents the formation of a contract in the first place.

Obviously, rescission of a contract in cases of a material misrepresentation fits in well with the fundamental premisses of contemporary Roman-Dutch law for there can be no doubt that the Labeonic conception of fraud,[149] as it defined the range of application of the *exceptio doli* in Roman law and under the *ius commune*, had been consistently applied by South African courts.[150] Nor is this correspondence surprising in view of the fact that 'the doctrine of equitable fraud [as developed by nineteenth-century English courts] seems not only to have proceeded originally

146 *Viljoen* v. *Hillier*, 1904 TS 312 (315 f.).

147 (1881) 20 Ch D 1 (12 f.).

148 Lubbe (n. 144) 284.

149 See Ulp. D. 4, 3, 1, 2 ('dolum malum esse omnem calliditatem fallaciam machinationem ad circumveniendum fallendum decipiendum alterum adhibitam'; [and so he himself defines] malice or fraud as being every kind of cunning, trickery, or contrivance practiced in order to cheat, trick or deceive another); *Law of Obligations* (n. 40) 664 ff.

150 Lubbe (n. 144) 264 ff., 286.

from a premise similar to that of the civil law but actually to have been inspired by it'.[151]

(e) Undue Influence

The notion of *dolus* also played a key role in the decision of the Appellate Division of the South African Supreme Court in *Preller* v. *Jordaan*.[152] Referring to Labeo's famous definition,[153] Fagan, JA, expressed the opinion that it was broader than the concept of fraud since it did not carry such a strong connotation of moral censure.[154] He pointed out that *dolus* in terms of the *exceptio doli* was taken to comprise conduct that could merely be described as inequitable and quoted a judgment by Kotzé, JA,[155] who had in turn relied on Savigny and Heumann for the proposition that *dolus* indicated 'anything which the law does not allow, anything inequitable, done with the consciousness that one is acting contrary to the law and good faith'. Fagan, JA, then explored the range of application of the term *dolus* among the 'classical' Roman-Dutch authors and finally came to the conclusion that it was broad enough to cover the case 'where one person obtaining an influence over another which weakens the latter's resistance and makes his will pliable, and where such a person then brings his influence to bear in an unscrupulous manner in order to prevail upon the other to agree to a prejudicial transaction which he would not normally have entered into of his own free will'.[156] The innocent party, under these circumstances, may rescind the contract and claim *restitutio in integrum*.

[151] Ibid. 302; for an analysis of the development of the doctrine of innocent misrepresentation, and its sources, see ibid. 270 ff., 298 ff. Of particular interest, in this context, are *Redgrave* v. *Hurd* (1881) 20 Ch D 1 and *Derry* v. *Peek* (1889) 14 App Cas 337.

[152] 1956 (1) SA 483 (A).

[153] Supra n. 149.

[154] *Preller* v. *Jordaan* 1956 (1) SA 483 (A) 491.

[155] *MacDuff & Co. Ltd. (in liquidation)* v. *Johannesburg Consolidated Investment Co. Ltd*. 1924 AD 573 (610).

[156] *Preller* v. *Jordaan* 1956 (1) SA 483 (A) 492 (tr. from the Afrikaans original). Cf. also already Sir John Wessels, *The Law of Contract in South Africa*, vol. ii (2nd edn., 1951), § 1209 ('This our courts call undue influence, though the Roman-Dutch lawyers merely regarded it as one of the Protean forms of dolus').

Preller v. *Jordaan* constitutes the most serious, and ultimately successful, attempt to domesticate a doctrine which had already been repeatedly acknowledged and in some cases even applied:[157] the doctrine of undue influence, as developed by the English courts of equity.[158] Again, therefore, *dolus* has proved to be the most suitable port of entry for an equitable doctrine which has become an established part of South African private law.[159] Undue influence, like innocent misrepresentation, is an emanation of a general norm requiring proper behaviour, particularly *in contrahendo*.[160] It has supplemented the comparatively narrow concept of *metus* as a ground of vitiating a contract[161] and has played a vital, corrective role in a number of distinctive areas.[162] In the English common law, at least since the nineteenth century, duress used to be about as narrowly defined as *metus* in the earlier *ius commune*.[163] This is what induced the courts of equity to step in and grant relief in cases of undue influence.[164] Again, there is an unmistakable intellectual link with civilian legal literature, especially Pothier's *Traité des obligations*.[165] Thus it may be said that

157 Cf. *Executors of Cerfontein* v. *O'Haire* (1873) 3 SC 476; *Armstrong* v. *Magid* 1937 AD 260 (273, 276); *Katzenellenbogen* v. *Katzenellenbogen and Joseph* 1947 (2) SA 528 (W) 540; *Mauerberger* v. *Mauerberger* 1948 (4) SA 902 (C) 910. But cf. Van den Heever, JA, in *Preller* v. *Jordaan* 1956 (1) SA 483 (A) 504 ff.; L. F. van Huyssteen, *Onbehoorlike Beinvloeding en Misbruik van Omstandighede in die Suid-Afrikaanse Verbintenisreg* (1980), 108 ff. See now, in particular, the analysis by Lubbe (n. 144) 286 ff.

158 Cf. Treitel (n. 116) 378 ff.; Wessels (n. 156) §§ 1208 ff.

159 *Patel* v. *Grobbelaar* 1974 (1) SA 532 (A); Wessels (n. 156) §§ 1208 ff.; Joubert (n. 142) 116 ff.; Lubbe and Murray (n. 142) 374 ff.; Hutchison, in Wille (n. 138) 448 ff.; Van der Merwe, Van Huyssteen et al. (n. 111) 91 ff.

160 Lubbe (n. 144) 293.

161 See Lubbe and Murray (n. 142) 355 ff.; Hutchison, in Wille (n. 138) 446 ff.; Van der Merwe, Van Huyssteen, et al. (n. 111) 85 ff.

162 Lubbe (n. 144) 288 ff.

163 A contract may be avoided, if there has been a threat of physical violence to, or unlawful constraint of, the person of one of the contracting parties: see Treitel (n. 116) 375. According to Atiyah (n. 123) 434 ff., duress (and mistake) 'were whittled away in the nineteenth century as defences to actions on executory contracts till virtually nothing was left of them'. He sees the 'severe limitations now imposed on the concept of duress [as] a natural corollary of the will theory'.

164 Treitel (n. 116) 378 ff.

165 See the analysis by Lubbe (n. 144) 296 ff.

'[a]s in the case of misrepresentation, the English law of undue influence constituted the impulse for a South African development which, rather than leading to the reception of a foreign doctrine, entailed the rediscovery' and adaptation of a general principle inherent in the broad civilian definition of *dolus*.[166]

(f) Anticipatory Repudiation

Where a party to a contract manifests an unequivocal intention not to perform his obligation, the other party should not be expected to wait until the due date before taking legal action.[167] Modern legal systems, therefore, tend to grant to that other party a remedy for breach of contract *in anticipando*.[168] South African courts took over and applied the English doctrine of repudiation as it had been established in the mid-nineteenth century.[169] They did not, at first, realize that 'an entirely new doctrine, unknown to Roman-Dutch law, thereby came to form part and parcel of South African law'. English authorities were regularly quoted 'and so it hardly occasions surprise that not only the principle, but the underlying reasons for the principle as expressed in the leading English cases, were adopted'.[170] The introduction of this specific type of breach of contract was generally welcomed as both 'useful and

[166] Ibid. 293, 302. As far as modern European law is concerned, see art. 4:109 PECL.

[167] Cf. the policy considerations advanced by Lord Campbell in *Hochster* v. *De la Tour* (1853) 2 El & Bl 678.

[168] In German law the rules relating to 'positive malperformance' are usually applied: cf. Volker Emmerich, in *Münchener Kommentar zum Bürgerlichen Gesetzbuch*, vol. ii (3rd edn., 1994), Vor § 275 nn. 274 ff. On historical and comparative aspects of the doctrine of anticipatory breach, see Francis Dawson, 'Metaphors and Anticipatory Breach', (1981) 40 *Cambridge Law Journal* 83 ff.; James C. Gulotta Jr., 'Anticipatory Breach: A Comparative Analysis', (1975/6) 50 *Tulane Law Review* 927 ff.

[169] See P. M. Nienaber, 'The Effect of Anticipatory Repudiation: Principle and Policy', (1962) 20 *Cambridge Law Journal* 213 ff.; idem, 'Enkele Beskouinge oor Kontrakbreuk in anticipando', (1963) 26 *THRHR* 22 ff. The leading case is *Hochster* v. *De la Tour* (1853) 2 El & Bl 678.

[170] The quotation is from Holmes, JA, in *Crest Enterprises (Pty.) Ltd.* v. *Rycklof Beleggings (Edms.) Bpk.*, 1972 (2) SA 863 (A) 869. On the position in Roman-Dutch law see Nienaber, (1963) 26 *THRHR* 29 f.

convenient'[171] while being at the same time consonant with the basic principles of Roman-Dutch law.[172] Final confirmation came with the decision of the Appellate Division in *Novick* v. *Benjamin*.[173]

However, there were always pecularities arising, by and large,[174] from the specific way in which the English courts had attempted to explain the fact that the creditor, confronted with the debtor's declared intention not to perform by the due date, was entitled to terminate the contract. Termination, it was argued, required an agreement between the parties to that effect; and so repudiation came to be interpreted as an offer which still had to be accepted by the other party. Thus, the perception gained ground that repudiation, unlike all other forms of breach of contract, required 'acceptance'.[175] Only slowly did the South African courts manage to disentangle themselves from this kind of theoretical framework and to recognize that repudiation is in itself a breach of contract.[176] The innocent party may now decide either to stand by the contract or to terminate it. By ignoring the repudiation he chooses the first alternative. By 'accepting' it, he exercises his election to terminate the contract. Thus, it is not the repudiation that terminates the contract;[177] nor does the contract come to an end as a result of an agreement

[171] Joubert (n. 142) 211.

[172] J. C. de Wet and A. H. van Wyk, *Kontraktereg in die Suid-Afrikaanse Reg*, vol. i (5th edn., 1992), 169: 'This . . . does not conflict with the basic principles of our law'.

[173] 1972 (2) SA 842 (A) (per Jansen, JA, and Trollip, JA). Cf. *Crest Enterprises (Pty.) Ltd.* v. *Rycklof Beleggings (Edms.) Bpk.* 1972 (2) SA 863 (A) (per Holmes, JA).

[174] Cf. the analysis by Nienaber, (1963) 26 *THRHR* 27 ff.; also Hutchison, in Wille (n. 138) 512 f.

[175] Cf., e.g., apart from *Hochster* v. *De la Tour* (supra nn. 167, 169), *White & Carter (Councils) Ltd.* v. *McGregor*, [1961] 3 All ER 1178 (1181) (per Lord Reid); *Denmark Productions Ltd.* v. *Boscobel Productions Ltd.*, [1968] 3 All ER 513 (CA).

[176] Cf. generally *Nash* v. *Golden Dumps (Pty.) Ltd.*, 1985 (3) SA 1 (A) 22 (per Corbett, JA); Joubert (n. 142) 210 ff.; Lubbe and Murray (n. 142) 476 ff.; Hutchison, in Wille (n. 138) 510 ff.; and, specifically, P. M. Nienaber, 'Kontrakbreuk in anticipando in retrospek', 1989 *TSAR* 1 ff.; Alfred Cockrell, 'Breach of Contract', in Zimmermann and Visser (n. 105) 303 ff.

[177] As had been thought by the Court in *Kameel Tin Co. (Pty.) Ltd.* v. *Brollomar Tin Exploration Ltd.* 1928 TPD 726.

between the parties.[178] Termination of the breach does not prevent the innocent party from claiming damages (for breach of contract); the ordinary principles governing assessment of his loss apply.[179] In *Tuckers Land and Development Corporation (Pty.) Ltd.* v. *Hovis*,[180] Jansen, JA, essentially accepted these principles and proposed, 'in order to obtain clarity of thought', finally 'to jettison the terminology of offer and acceptance'.

But he went much further. For he took the opportunity to redefine the doctrinal foundations of repudiation:

> It could be said that it is now, and has been for some time, felt in our domain, no doubt under the influence of English law, that in all fairness there should be a duty upon a promisor not to commit an anticipatory breach of contract, and such a duty has in fact often been enforced by our courts. It would be consonant with the history of our law, and also legal principle, to construe this as an application of the wide jurisdiction to imply terms conferred upon a court by Roman law in respect of the *judicia bonae fidei*. It would not then be inapt to say, elliptically, that the duty flows from the requirement of *bona fides* to which our contracts are subject, and that such duty is implied in law and not in fact.[181]

The decisive step[182] in Jansen's process of reasoning is the return to classical Roman law and the resuscitation of the power of the Roman *iudex*, within the framework of *iudicia bonae fidei*, to decide in accordance with what appears to be equitable under the circumstances. In principle, according to Jansen, JA,[183] this meant that the Dutch courts should

[178] As suggested in *Myers* v. *Abramson* 1952 (3) SA 121 (C); cf. now *Stewart Wrightson (Pty.) Ltd.* v. *Thorpe* 1977 (2) SA 943 (A).

[179] In principle, damages must therefore be calculated from the date of performance rather than from the breach: *Novick* v. *Benjamin* 1972 (2) SA 842 (A).

[180] 1980 (1) SA 645 (A).

[181] *Tuckers Land & Development Corporation (Pty.) Ltd.* v. *Hovis* 1980 (1) SA 645 (A) 652.

[182] See D. L. Carey Miller, 'Judicia Bonae Fidei: A New Development in Contract?', (1980) 97 *SALJ* 532. For further comment on Jansen's views of repudiation, see Nienaber, 1989 *TSAR* 8 f.; Carole Lewis, 'Towards an Equitable Theory of Contract: The Contribution of Mr Justice E L Jansen to the South African Law of Contract', (1991) 108 *SALJ* 249 ff.; Cockrell (n. 176) 314 ff.

[183] *Tuckers Land & Development Corporation (Pty.) Ltd.* v. *Hovis* 1980 (1) SA 645 (A) 652.

have had the same wide powers to read into a contract any term that justice required; and in spite of the fact that the Dutch courts do not seem to have made any creative use of these powers,[184] they still vest in the modern South African courts.[185]

(g) Cancellation as a Remedy for Breach of Contract

A general right of cancellation for breach of contract[186] was never recognized in Roman law. This 'iron rule'[187] had been retained in Roman-Dutch law and it still dominated, as we have seen,[188] the nineteenth-century German *ius commune*. A remedy of cancellation was only available if it had expressly been conferred by way of a *lex commissoria*. From the last two or three decades of the nineteenth century, however, we find judicial statements in South Africa allowing for cancellation 'where time is of the essence of the contract'.[189] At about the same time, South African courts also started to grant a right of cancellation in cases of 'positive malperformance' (i.e. performance in a manner that fails to correspond with the content of the contractual duty), provided the defective performance concerned 'a vital part of the contract', or amounted 'to a failure to substantially perform', or constituted a 'breach of condition' or, as it is usually put today, goes 'to the root of the contract'.[190]

This generalized right of cancellation for material breach of contract was clearly taken over from English law; it has

[184] See Jansen, JA, in *Tuckers Land & Development Corporation (Pty.) Ltd.* v. *Hovis* 1980 (1) SA 645 (A) 652.

[185] According to Cockrell (n. 176) 315, Jansen's judgment 'stands out as a remarkably innovative instance of doctrinal fusion in that it resurrected a Roman-Dutch doctrine often marginalized within mainstream contract law in order to effect the graft'.

[186] As opposed to specific instances of such right, such as the *actio redhibitoria* for latent defects in contracts of sale. For details, see *Law of Obligations* (n. 40) 578.

[187] Fritz Schulz, *Classical Roman Law* (1951), 532.

[188] Supra p. 94.

[189] See Cockrell (n. 176) 307 f. with references.

[190] Ibid. 312 f. with references. For modern law see, e.g., *Oatarian Properties (Pty.) Ltd.* v. *Maroun* 1973 (3) SA 779 (A) 784; *Elgin Brown & Hamer (Pty.) Ltd.* v. *Industrial Machinery Suppliers (Pty.) Ltd.* 1993 (3) SA 424 (A) 430.

been described as the single most important development in the history of South African law relating to breach of contract.[191] The relevant rules in English law originated in two decisions of William Murray, Lord Mansfield—*Kingston* v. *Preston*[192] and *Boone* v. *Eyre*[193]— and they were based on the device of an implied condition.[194] Whether they were inspired by civilian models is uncertain, though distinctly possible. For the Canon lawyers had always been guided by the rule *frangenti fidem fides frangatur eidem:*[195] if a person had not been faithful to his promise it was not morally objectionable if the promisee did not keep his own promise towards him. This rule was read into the contract by means of an implied condition: *subintellegitur conditio 'si fides servetur'.*[196] The seventeenth- and eighteenth-century Natural lawyers argued along very similar lines:[197] it must be assumed that a party to a contract only wishes to honour his promise if the other party does what he has promised.[198]

This is, essentially, the idea of the 'concurrent conditions' that we find in English law. Like Lord Mansfield, the Natural lawyers invoked the hypothetical will of the parties and availed themselves of the device of a *condicio tacita*. Remarkably, therefore, in the course of the seventeenth and eighteenth centuries a right of cancellation for breach of

[191] Cockrell (n. 176) 321.

[192] See *Jones* v. *Barkley* (1781) 2 Doug 684 (690 f.), 99 ER 434.

[193] 1 H Bl 273 126 ER 148; cf. also 2 W Bl 1314, 96 ER 767.

[194] For details, see Zimmermann, (1993) 193 *AcP* 153 ff.

[195] See Georges Boyer, *Recherches historiques sur la résolution des contrats* (1924), 220 ff.; Hans Ankum, *De voorouders van een boze fee* (1964), 10 ff.; Friedrich Merzbacher, 'Die Regel "Fidem frangenti fides frangitur" und ihre Anwendung', (1982) 99 *ZSS (KA)* 339 ff.

[196] (The condition is implied 'provided the faith is kept'.) See, e.g., Decretales Gregorii IX, lib. II, tit. XXIV, cap. XXV (Innocent III).

[197] For details, see Karl Otto Scherner, *Rücktrittsrecht wegen Nichterfüllung: Untersuchungen zur deutschen Privatrechtslehre der Neuzeit* (1965), 92 ff.; cf. also Helmut Coing, *Europäisches Privatrecht*, vol. i (1985), 444.

[198] See, e.g., Hugo Grotius, *De jure belli ac pacis* (1642), lib. III, cap. XIX, XIV; Samuel Pufendorf, *De jure naturae et gentium libri octo* (1759), lib. V, cap. XI, § IX; Christian Wolff, *Jus naturae methodo scientifica pertractatum* (1743; reprint 1968), § 827.

contract was developed on both sides of the Channel that was quite comparable in its general structure and based on the same doctrinal (condition) and ideological (will theory) premisses.[199] On the Continent, this idea found its most mature expression in art. 1184 *code civil*: a resolutive condition is always implied in bilateral contracts to provide for the case where one of the parties does not fulfil his undertaking.[200] This provision, inspired by Domat[201] and Pothier,[202] tied in nicely with the practice which the French courts had been following anyway;[203] already since the days of Molinaeus, the courts had felt to be both entitled and compelled to move away from 'the rigour of these principles' (that is, the Roman rejection of a general right of cancellation).[204] Interestingly, while the recognition of such right in modern South African law is largely due to the influence of English law, Pothier's *Traité des obligations* has on a number of occasions been used as an alternative source.[205]

(*h*) *Specific Performance*

In continental legal systems a contractor is in principle entitled today to demand that his contract be performed *in specie*.[206] This was not always so; for many centuries the path towards recognition of this principle was obstructed by the Roman maxim *omnis condemnatio pecuniaria*.[207]

[199] For a more detailed discussion, see (1993) 193 *AcP* 160 ff.

[200] For historical context and background, see Boyer (n. 195) 381 ff., 11 ff.; Scherner (n. 197) 135 ff.; cf. also supra p. 95.

[201] Jean Domat, *Les loix civiles dans leur ordre naturel*, vol. i (1766), liv. I, tit. I, ss. IV, XI.

[202] Robert Joseph Pothier, *Traité des obligations*, in *Œuvres*, vol. i (1824), n. 672.

[203] Boyer (n. 195) 329 ff., 343 ff., 350 ff. Cf. also Coing (n. 197) 443 f.

[204] Pothier (n. 202) n. 476.

[205] See Cockrell (n. 176) 321 f. with references.

[206] Zweigert and Kötz (n. 90) 470 ff. As far as Italy is concerned see, most recently, Christian Resch, *Das italienische Privatrecht im Spannungsfeld von Code civil und BGB am Beispiel der Entwicklung des Leistungsstörungsrechts*, in preparation.

[207] For details, see *Law of Obligations* (n. 40) 770 ff.; Karin Nehlsen-von Stryk, 'Grenzen des Rechtszwangs: Zur Geschichte der Naturalvollstreckung', (1993) 193 *AcP* 529 ff.; Wolfgang Rütten, 'Zur Entstehung des Erfüllungszwangs im Schuldverhältnis', in *Festschrift für Joachim Gernhuber* (1993), 939 ff.; Tilman Repgen, *Vertragstreue und Erfüllungszwang in der mittelalterlichen Rechtswissenschaft* (1994).

Roman-Dutch law marks the decisive breakthrough towards the modern principle.[208] In England, on the other hand, the disappointed creditor has to make do with a claim for breach of contract. Only in exceptional situations may he demand specific performance. Although it is often emphasized that the grant of a decree of specific performance remains in the discretion of the judge, that discretion has, largely, come to be governed by fixed rules and principles.[209]

In nineteenth-century South Africa we find a number of judgments granting specific performance without, however, discussing the principles on which such ruling was based.[210] This only happened in a judgment by Kotzé, CJ, *Cohen* v. *Shires, McHattie and King*.[211] The judgment is based on a thorough enquiry of Roman-Dutch law which supported current South African practice: 'By the well established practice of South Africa, agreeing with the Roman-Dutch law, suits for specific performance are matters of daily occurrence.'[212] Thus, it appeared to be settled that the plaintiff had a right to specific performance and that South African courts could not, in their discretion, refer him to a claim for damages: 'where specific performance is claimable under our law, it is a legal right of which the person entitled to it may demand the enforcement.'[213]

Soon, however, another view inspired by English law started to gain ground. '[I]t is in the discretion of the court to grant . . . an order [for specific performance] or not', as

[208] See Reinhard Zimmermann, 'Roman-Dutch Jurisprudence and its Contribution to European Private Law', (1992) 66 *Tulane Law Review* 1698 ff.

[209] See *Law of Obligations* (n. 40) 776 ff. (historical); Zweigert and Kötz (n. 90) 479 ff. (comparative); Treitel (n. 116) 955 ff. (for details of the modern law).

[210] See, e.g., *Twentyman* v. *Hewitt* (1833) 1 Menz 156; *Wolhuter* v. *De Villiers* (1837) 2 Menz 37; *Knox* v. *Blackhurst* (1880) 1 NLR 73; *Trollip* v. *Tromp & Van Zweel* (1880) 1 NLR 166; *Kettles* v. *Bennett* (1893) 8 EDC 82. For what follows see, in particular, Cockrell (n. 176) 325 ff.; cf. also Barney Jordaan, 'Employment Relations', in Zimmermann and Visser (n. 105) 407 ff.; Zimmermann and Sutherland, (1999) 116 *ZSS (RA)* 166 ff.

[211] (1882) 1 SAR 41.

[212] *Cohen* v. *Shires, McHattie and King* (1882) 1 SAR 41 (45).

[213] *Amoils* v. *Amoils* 1924 WLD 88 (98), per Mason, JP; two other decisions along the same lines are quoted by Cockrell (n. 176) 327 n. 147.

was said by Innes, CJ, in 1904.[214] Also when it came to specifying the manner in which the discretion should be exercised, English law was referred to. Specific performance had to be refused, it was said, where it would be unjust,[215] where the Court would not be able to enforce such decree,[216] where damages would adequately compensate the plaintiff,[217] or where the contract was one of employment.[218]

The contradiction between these two approaches was, strangely, hardly recognized at first.[219] Kotzé, for instance, stated in a decision from 1914 that it was 'a well recognized rule of the Roman-Dutch law that in a case of purchase and sale the court would recognize a claim for specific performance'.[220] But he added that it was in the discretion of the court 'whether, under the circumstances before the court, it would be doing right to grant a claim for specific performance'.[221] The same tension is apparent in other decisions, most importantly in *Haynes* v. *Kingwilliamstown Municipality*,[222] for more than thirty years the leading case on the subject. On the one hand, again, the right to specific performance is recognized. On the other hand, however, the Court is given a discretion to refuse a decree of specific performance, the exercise of such discretion being determined by a list of typical situations, all of them borrowed from English law.

Only in the 1980s did the South African courts begin to reassess these principles. *Benson* v. *SA Mutual Life Assurance Society* re-established the right of every plaintiff to claim specific performance as 'the cornerstone of our law relating to specific performance'.[223] To this extent, therefore, the

214 *Shakinovsky* v. *Lawson and Smulowitz* 1904 TS 326 (330).

215 *Atkinson* v. *Vause's Executors* (1892) 13 NLR 85.

216 Cf., e.g., *Ingle Colonial Broom Co. Ltd.* v. *Hocking* 1914 CPD 495 (499).

217 See *Visser* v. *Neethling* 1921 CPD 176.

218 *Schierhout* v. *Minister of Justice* 1926 AD 99 (108), per Innes, C.J.

219 Cockrell (n. 176) 328.

220 *Manasewitz* v. *Oosthuizen* 1914 CPD 328 (331).

221 Ibid.

222 1951 (2) SA 371 (A) 378 f.; cf. also the extracts from this decision in Lubbe and Murray (n. 142) 531 ff.

223 1986 (1) SA 776 (A) 782; for comment, see Joubert (n. 142) 224 ff.; Lubbe and Murray (n. 142) 541 ff.; Cockrell (n. 176) 329 ff.

civilian principle has prevailed. Unlike their modern continental counterparts, however, the courts retain a discretion to refuse specific performance. This discretion obviously has its roots in English equity: but it is no longer subject to any rules save that it be judiciously exercised in order to prevent injustice. In particular, therefore, South African law has freed itself of the restrictive categories developed by the English courts.[224] While the right to specific performance has been given greater scope, there still remains a tension, at least on a theoretical level, between the recognition of such right and the endorsement of an overriding discretion of the court. This may be regarded as unsatisfactory.[225] At the same time, it is interesting to note that the comparative discussion in Europe also appears to be leading towards a pragmatic compromise.[226]

(j) Aquilian Liability

Delictual liability in modern continental legal systems can be regarded as a generalized version of Aquilian liability.[227] The same is true of South African law.[228] As elsewhere, however, it was very much disputed how far this process of generalization should be taken. Liability for negligent misstatements was one of the crucial issues. While South African courts were at first inclined to impose such liability,[229] they changed their view in the 1890s.[230] Undoubtedly this happened under the influence of the decision of the House of Lords in *Derry* v. *Peek*[231] which was (wrongly) taken to confine liability for damages to cases of fraudulent

224 *Benson* v. *SA Mutual Life Assurance Society* 1986 (1) SA 776 (A) 782 f. (785).

225 Cockrell (n. 176) 330.

226 See arts. 9:101 f. PECL; arts. 7.2.1 f. Unidroit PICC; and see the references in 1995 *JZ* 482.

227 For the historical development, see *Law of Obligations* (n. 40) 998 ff.

228 For the development in the 19th century, see Annél van Aswegen, 'Aquilian Liability I', in Zimmermann and Visser (n. 105) 559 ff.; Wolfgang Freiherr Raitz von Frentz, *Lex Aquilia und Negligence* (2000), 274 ff.

229 *Cape of Good Hope Bank* v. *Fischer* (1886) 4 SC 368.

230 *Dickson & Co.* v. *Levy* (1894) 11 SC 33 (36); *African Banking Corporation* v. *Goldbard* (1897) 4 OR 402; *De Kock* v. *Gafney* 1914 CPD 377.

231 (1889) 14 App Cas 337 (HL).

misrepresentation.[232] As in other jurisdictions, this cautious attitude was based on the fear of indeterminate liability; a fear which was increased by the fact that misstatements usually merely lead to purely patrimonial loss.[233] It was only after the famous decision in *Hedley Byrne* v. *Heller* had brought about a dramatic readjustment of English law,[234] that South African courts also started to reassess the situation. The decisive breakthrough occurred in 1979, in *Administrateur, Natal* v. *Trust Bank van Afrika Bpk.*[235] In this decision the Appellate Division of the Supreme Court at last recognized that, in principle, a negligent misstatement causing pure economic loss could give rise to a claim for delictual damages, provided that the normal elements of Aquilian liability were satisfied. The Court warned, however, that liability would have to be carefully controlled, in particular by a judicious manipulation of the elements of wrongfulness and causation.

Administrateur, Natal v. *Trust Bank van Afrika Bpk.* thus re-emphasized the key role of the old requirement of *iniuria*,[236] in its modern guise of wrongfulness, as distinct from and logically anterior to *culpa* (fault), in providing a niche for the open consideration of policy factors.[237] This development, in

[232] *Derry* v. *Peek* merely decided that in an action based on deceit, or fraudulent misrepresentation, actual fraud had to be proved. See *Hedley Byrne & Co. Ltd.* v. *Heller & Partners Ltd.*, [1964] AC 465 (HL).

[233] See D. B. Hutchison, 'Negligent Statements: Why the Reluctance to Impose Liability?', (1978) 95 *SALJ* 515 ff.

[234] [1964] AC 465 (HL). For comment, and for an analysis of the subsequent developments in English law, see Christian von Bar, 'Liability for Information and Opinions Causing Pure Economic Loss to Third Parties: A Comparison of English and German Case Law', in B. S. Markesinis (ed.), *The Gradual Convergence* (1994), 98 ff.; Dale Hutchison and Reinhard Zimmermann, 'Murphy's Law: Die Ersatzfähigkeit reiner Vermögensschäden innerhalb des "negligence"-Tatbestands nach englischem Recht', (1995) 94 *Zeitschrift für vergleichende Rechtswissenschaft* 42 ff.; Raitz von Frentz (n. 228) 108 ff.

[235] 1979 (3) SA 824 (A). For comment, see J. M. Burchell, 'The Birth of a Legal Principle: Negligent Misstatement Causing Pure Economic Loss', (1980) 97 *SALJ* 1 ff.; Hutchison (n. 139) 629 ff.; Raitz von Frentz (n. 228) 335 ff. The Court thus, essentially, re-established the position as it had prevailed under the older *ius commune*; see *Law of Obligations* (n. 40) 1022 ff., 1042 f.

[236] On which see *Law of Obligations* (n. 40) 998 ff., 1004 ff.; Hutchison (n. 139) 597 ff.

[237] Hutchison (n. 139) 634.

turn, was stimulated by the fact that South African courts had previously received the English notion of a 'duty to take care' into their formulations of Aquilian liability: a policy-based instrument that was seen to be 'basic to the development and growth of negligence and determin[ing] its scope, that is to say, the range of relationships and interests protected by it'.[238] A leading South African commentator has summarized the development in the following words:[239] 'If Aquilian liability is to be reduced to one general principle today, that principle would have to be that all patrimonial loss caused wrongfully and culpably is actionable . . . Expressing South African law in this sweeping way certainly emphasizes its inherently civilian nature and makes it look very different to that of England. . . . [Yet,] it is a notable fact that South African courts still refer far more frequently to English than to continental decisions in developing the law relating to liability for negligence.' This is a reflection, on the one hand, of the extent to which the English tort of negligence has been generalized this century;[240] on the other hand it demonstrates that South African courts, just as their English counterparts, ultimately favour an incremental approach in expanding the boundaries of delictual liability.[241]

(*k*) Actio Iniuriarum

The English tort of defamation is, in many respects, distinctly different from the civilian delict of *iniuria*. Yet, there is also at least one very obvious structural similarity. In both systems, a (prima facie) defamatory imputation (no matter whether *verbis* or *litteris*) may give rise to a cause of

[238] M. A. Milner, *Negligence in Modern Law* (1967), 230, quoted with approval by Rumpff, CJ, in *Administrateur, Natal* v. *Trust Bank van Afrika Bpk.* 1979 (3) SA 824 (A) 833. For the reception of the notion of the 'duty of care' into South African law, see Hutchison (n. 139) 620 ff.; Raitz von Frentz (n. 228) 282 ff.

[239] Hutchison (n. 139) 635.

[240] For details of the development, see David Ibbetson, *A Historical Introduction to the Law of Obligations* (1999), 188 ff.

[241] See Hutchison (n. 139) 637; Raitz von Frentz (n. 228) 346 ff. and *passim*; Smits (n. 5) 229 ff.; for English law, see Hutchison and Zimmermann, (1995) 94 *Zeitschrift für vergleichende Rechtswissenschaft* 75 ff.

action unless the person who has made the imputation is able to invoke one of a certain number of 'defences' or 'privileges'.[242] This basic similarity enabled South African courts and writers to graft many of the English rules of defamation onto the Roman-Dutch *actio iniuriarum* that had originally been transplanted to the Cape.[243] What has emerged, over the years, is a truly hybrid system that has emancipated itself from its Roman-Dutch and English roots and has, instead, acquired its own, South African, identity. Essentially, it is still the civilian *actio iniuriarum* that forms the basis of the law of defamation, and the gist of it is, as a rule, the presence of an *animus iniuriandi*.[244] Courts and legal writers have for some time toyed with the idea of a distinction, in principle, between libel and slander, but their view has failed to make an impact.[245] Truth alone is not a defence in South African law; as in Roman-Dutch law, the additional requirement of the public benefit must be satisfied.[246] On the other hand, however, English case law and writers continue to be cited by South African courts.[247] The test for determining what constitutes defamatory matter[248] and the defence of fair comment[249] are English in origin, and so is the element of 'publication' required for the modern South African version of *iniuria*.[250] Many details relating to the stereotyped or crystallized defences have

[242] See *Law of Obligations* (n. 40) 1078 ff. with references.

[243] See Bhadra Ranchod, 'Foundations of the South African Law of Defamation' (unpublished Dr. iur. thesis, Leiden, 1972), 135 ff.; Jonathan M. Burchell, 'The Protection of Personality Rights', in Zimmermann and Visser (n. 105) 640 ff.; Helge Walter, *Actio iniuriarum: Der Schutz der Persönlichkeit im südafrikanischen Privatrecht* (1996), 160 ff.

[244] The requirement of *animus iniuriandi* has been one of the major battlefields of the famous *bellum iuridicum* raging between 'pollutionists' on the one side and purists or antiquarians on the other. See *Law of Obligations* (n. 40) 1079 f.; Walter (n. 243) 174 ff.; Burchell (n. 243) 640 ff.

[245] See Walter (n. 243) 162.

[246] See Jonathan Burchell, *The Law of Defamation in South Africa* (1985), 206 ff.; Walter (n. 243) 169 f.

[247] See, for instance, Ben Beinart, 'The English Legal Contribution in South Africa: The Interaction of Civil Law and Common Law', 1981 *Acta Juridica* 58.

[248] Burchell (n. 246) 95 ff.; Walter (n. 243) 165 ff.

[249] Burchell (n. 246) 219 ff.; Walter (n. 243) 173 f.

[250] Burchell (n. 246) 67 ff.; Walter (n. 243) 163 f.

been taken over from English law, together with the term 'privilege' or 'privileged occasion'[251] and the distinction between an absolute and a qualified (or provisional) privilege.[252] The systematic division into defences rebutting the inference of unlawfulness (justification grounds) and those relating to the element of fault (that is: excluding the presence of *animus iniuriandi*)[253] is, however, of civilian (though not specifically Roman-Dutch) provenance.

Yet ultimately, and perhaps most importantly, it is still the civilian concept of *iniuria* that determines the scope and range of application of the *actio iniuriarum*. The starting point for an analysis of modern South African law is still Voet's (or, ultimately, Ulpian's[254]) triad of legal interests protected by the delict of *iniuria*: *corpus*, *dignitas*, and *fama*.[255] *Fama* leads us straight into the law of defamation. As far as the right to *corpus* is concerned, a distinction is usually drawn between the infringement of a person's physical (or bodily) integrity and an interference with his personal liberty.[256] Determination of the term *dignitas* has proved to be more difficult. Yet it is widely accepted today that it should not be strictly limited to dignity and honour, but should rather be seen as a 'general clause', or *nomen collectivum*, comprising all rights of personality not yet specifically identified in the sources of the Roman-Dutch common law: everything, that is, except the rights to *corpus* and *fama*.[257] It is within this broad framework that the protection of a person's right to his feelings of piety or chastity, of his right of identity, and, most importantly, his right to privacy find their place.[258] Infringement of the right

[251] See, for example, *Maisel* v. *Van Naeren* 1960 (4) SA 836 (C) 841.

[252] Burchell (n. 246) 237 ff.; Walter (n. 243) 170 ff.

[253] See Walter (n. 243) 167 ff. as opposed to 177 ff.

[254] Ulp. D. 47, 10, 1, 2.

[255] *Commentarius ad Pandectas* (n. 82) lib. XLVII, tit. X, I (tr. Melius de Villiers, *The Roman and Roman-Dutch Law of Injuries* (1899), 17). For a detailed analysis, see Walter (n. 243) 72 ff.

[256] Walter (n. 243) 151 ff.

[257] For details, see ibid. 186 ff.

[258] For all details, see J. Neethling, *Persoonlikheidsreg* (3rd edn., 1991), 193 ff.; Walter (n. 243) 186 ff.

to privacy, in particular, has been recognized by South African courts on various occasions as a 'dignitary wrong' in the broad sense of the word.[259] Unlike, particularly, German law with its restrictive list of rights and interests contained in § 823 I BGB,[260] South African law thus had at its disposal an instrument that could be adjusted suitably to cope with the problem of the ever increasing potential for intrusions upon a person's private sphere. The recognition of the modern action for invasion of privacy was inspired, at least to some extent, by American law; but it was also 'a logical development under the actio injuriarum'.[261]

3. Northern Cross

(a) *Civil Law and Common Law in Scotland*

A parallel project exploring the doctrinal history of the Scots law of obligations and property is on its way at the moment.[262] Like South African law Scots law has developed, since its inception, without codificatory intervention.[263] While the accession of King David I to the Scottish throne in 1124 initially thrust Anglo-Norman feudal law on the Scots,[264] the struggle over the succession to the Maid of Norway at the end of the thirteenth century, and the wars of independence which led to a Scottish victory at Bannockburn, created a strong and lasting feeling of antagonism towards the

[259] See the discussion, and the references, in David McQuoid Mason, *The Law of Privacy in South Africa* (1978); Walter (n. 243) 189 ff.; Burchell (n. 243) 650 ff.

[260] On the fate of the *actio iniuriarum* in German law, see *Law of Obligations* (n. 40) 1085 ff.; cf. also supra pp. 66 ff. English law, based essentially on a range of specific torts, is also often regarded as unsatisfactory in this respect; cf., e.g., Zweigert and Kötz (n. 90) 697 ff. Ibbetson (n. 240) 201, however, now refers to an 'embryonic tort of breach of privacy'. In addition, Peter Birks has drawn my attention to the law of enhanced damages which demonstrates that English law is very serious, albeit in a hidden way, about the protection of a human being's entitlement to respect.

[261] McQuoid Mason (n. 259) 86.

[262] Kenneth Reid and Reinhard Zimmermann (eds.), *A History of Private Law in Scotland*, vol. i: *Introduction and Property*; vol. ii: *Obligations*, in preparation.

[263] For an overview of Scottish legal history, see now John W. Cairns, 'Historical Introduction', in Reid and Zimmermann (n. 262) in preparation.

[264] See, in particular, Hector L. MacQueen, *Common Law and Feudal Society in Medieval Scotland* (1993).

English. This resulted in the Auld Alliance with France[265] and an orientation towards continental Europe. Connected with these was a gradual reception of the learned laws as they were taught at the European universities, which turned Scotland into a far-flung province of the *ius commune*.[266] In the same way that Grotius' *Inleidinge* laid down Roman-Dutch law in the mid-seventeenth century, Viscount Stair's *Institutions* some fifty years later in 1681 constituted Roman-Scotch law.[267] Stair was in turn followed by a series of institutional writers[268] and the eighteenth century was a flowering time for Scottish legal culture which lasted far into the first half of the nineteenth century. The law courses at the universities of Glasgow and Edinburgh flourished; Regius chairs for public law, natural law, and public international law (Edinburgh) and civil law (Glasgow) were created in both places. Lord Kames, David Hume, Adam Smith, and John Millar were among the most famous jurists and philosophers of the Scottish Enlightenment.

In the second half of the nineteenth century, however, Scotland became by comparison a somewhat backward province of the United Kingdom, and the level of the native legal culture, and legal education, descended to an equally low level. Stair's legal successors no longer went on the grand tour to France or Holland,[269] but to the Inns of Court in London. After the industrial revolution, England offered

[265] See William M. Gordon, 'Scotland and France: The Legal Connection', (1994) 22 *Index* 557 ff.

[266] See Peter Stein, 'Roman Law in Scotland', in *Ius Romanum Medii Aevi*, pars V, 13 b (1968); idem, 'The Influence of Roman Law on the Law of Scotland', 1963 *Juridical Review* 205 ff.; T. B. Smith, 'The Influence of the "Auld Alliance" with France on the Law of Scotland', in idem, *Studies Critical and Comparative* (1962), 28 ff.

[267] For the terminology, see John Cairns, 'The Civil Law Tradition in Scottish Legal Thought', in Carey Miller and Zimmermann (n. 3) 211.

[268] See, e.g., *The Laws of Scotland: Stair Memorial Encyclopedia*, vol. xii (1987), nn. 443 ff.; John W. Cairns, 'Institutional Writing Reconsidered', (1983) 4 *JLH* 76 ff. On the institutes of national law in contemporary Europe in general, see the references supra p. 2, n. 2.

[269] On the legal connection between Scotland and the Netherlands, see Robert Feenstra, 'Scottish-Dutch Legal Relations in the Seventeenth and Eighteenth Centuries', in T. C. Smout (ed.), *Scotland and Europe* (1986), 128 ff. (for a more

more attractive career possibilities due to its extended trade empire. As England's prestige grew, so did that of the common law. Its influence in Scotland became increasingly perceptible, as long as legal disputes ventured beyond the mosses and muirs of the Scottish highlands.

As in South Africa, a backlash occurred towards the middle of this century against what was perceived to be an English intrusion. Vigorous debates took place about the proper sources and the true nature of Scots private law and also about the way in which it had developed.[270] The relative importance of civil law and common law has been, and to some extent remains, a matter of keen controversy.[271] As a result of these debates, however, scholars became aware of the distinctiveness of the Scottish legal tradition, a tradition shaped by two equally fascinating and complex processes of reception, first of the civil law and later of the common law. Only about half a century ago, the institutional foundations were laid for a modern, genuinely Scottish legal culture, conforming to contemporary academic standards. The study of law was transformed into a full-time course, and the universities thus took over the reins of legal education from the professional bodies.[272] In the

recent version of the same article, see H. de Ridder-Symoens and J. M. Fletcher (eds.), *Academic Relations between the Low Countries and the British Isles 1450–1700* (1989) 25 ff.); John W. Cairns, 'Importing our Lawyers from Holland: Netherlands Influences on Scots Law and Lawyers in the Eighteenth Century', in Grant G. Simpson (ed.), *Scotland and the Low Countries 1124–1994* (1996), 136 ff.

[270] T. B. Smith, *A Short Commentary on the Law of Scotland* (1962); idem, *Studies Critical and Comparative* (1962); Lord Cooper of Culross, *The Scottish Legal Tradition*, reprinted in *The Scottish Legal Tradition* (1991), 65 ff.

[271] See, e.g., Robin Evans-Jones, 'Civil Law in the Scottish Legal Tradition', in idem (ed.), *The Civil Law Tradition in Scotland* (1995), 3 ff.; Niall R. Whitty, 'The Civilian Tradition and Debates on Scots Law', 1996 *Tydskrif vir die Suid-Afrikaanse Reg* 227 ff., 442 ff.; Alan Rodger, 'The Use of the Civil Law in Scottish Courts', in Carey Miller and Zimmermann (n. 3) 225 ff.; Hector L. MacQueen, 'Mixture or Muddle?: Teaching and Research in Scottish Legal History', (1997) 5 *ZEuP* 368 ff.; Robin Evans-Jones, 'Receptions of Law, Mixed Legal Systems and the Myth of the Genius of Scots Private Law', (1998) 114 *LQR* 228 ff.; idem, 'Roman Law in Scotland and England and the Development of one Law for Britain', (1999) 115 *LQR* 605 ff.

[272] See David M. Walker, 'Legal Education in Scotland 1889–1988', 1988 *Juridical Review* 184 ff.

process a body of legal literature has evolved[273] and become further important evidence of the new vitality of Scots law.[274]

Like its Roman-Dutch counterpart in South Africa, the modern Scots law of obligations shares a number of characteristic features with other civilian legal systems: it recognizes contracts in favour of third parties,[275] it accepts an order for specific performance ('specific implement') as the primary right of a creditor,[276] and it does not have a doctrine of consideration.[277] But we also find at least an equal number of rules and legal institutions that Scots law has in common with, i.e. usually borrowed from, English law: an essentially unified concept of breach of contract,[278] breach of contract by repudiation,[279] or the doctrine of the unidentified principal in the law of agency.[280] Hector MacQueen has drawn attention to the fact that in all these cases Scots law has anticipated the position eventually adopted by the European Contract Law Commission.[281] Again, I think, it will be most illuminating to see how Scots law has arrived, in the course of its historical development, at these solutions; how, in other words, it has arrived at its

[273] For an overview, see Reinhard Zimmermann and Johann Andreas Dieckmann, 'Das schottische Privatrecht im Spiegel seiner Literatur', (1995) 3 *ZEuP* 898 ff.

[274] See Kenneth G. C. Reid, 'The Third Branch of the Profession: The Rise of the Academic Lawyer in Scotland', in Hector L. MacQueen (ed.), *Scots Law into the 21st Century: Essays in Honour of W. A. Wilson* (1996), 39 ff.

[275] Hector L. MacQueen, 'Third Party Rights in Contract: Ius Quaesitum Tertio', in Reid and Zimmermann (n. 262) in preparation.

[276] Alastair Smith, 'Specific Implement', in Reid and Zimmermann (n. 262) in preparation.

[277] Gerhard Lubbe, 'Formation of Contract', in Reid and Zimmermann (n. 262) in preparation.

[278] See Hector L. MacQueen, 'Remedies for Breach of Contract: The Future Development of Scots Law in its European and International Context', (1997) 1 *Edinburgh Law Review* 200 ff.; David Johnston, 'Breach of Contract', in Reid and Zimmermann (n. 262) in preparation.

[279] William W. McBryde, *The Law of Contract in Scotland* (1987), 14-01 ff.

[280] See T. B. Smith, *Scotland: The Development of its Laws and Constitution* (1962), 774 ff.

[281] Hector L. MacQueen, *Scots Law and the Road to the New Ius Commune* (Ius Commune Lectures on European Private Law, vol. i, 2000).

present position at the crossroads between civil law and common law and whether it contains experiences which may be of interest for the new *ius commune*. Presently, I can merely give one example: the notion of a unilateral promise.

(b) *Unilateral Promise*[282]

Hugo Grotius, in his immensely influential work *De jure belli ac pacis*, had accepted the (unilateral) promise as the cornerstone of contractual doctrine.[283] This was a heritage of scholastic moral theology, where the binding nature of both the promissory oath and the simple promise had been emphasized:[284] breach of faith displeases God and is a sinful deviation from the precepts of honesty and truthfulness. Grotius blended this tradition with man's natural freedom to act or not to act in a specific manner. A binding promise thus has the effect of an 'alienatio particulae cuiusdam nostrae libertatis';[285] and such an alienation can ultimately find its legitimation only in the fact that it has been willed by the alienor. On the other hand, however, in order to be enforceable, the will to be bound has to find some external manifestation and there has to be an 'acceptatio' on

[282] There is a large body of literature; see T. B. Smith, 'Jus Quaesitum Tertio: Remedies of the "Tertius" in Scottish Law', in idem, *Studies Critical and Comparative* (1962), 183 ff.; idem, *Short Commentary* (n. 270) 746 f., 777 ff.; D. E. C. Ashton Cross, 'Bare Promise in Scots Law', 1957 *Juridical Review* 138 ff.; Alan Rodger, 'Molina, Stair and the Jus Quaesitum Tertio', 1969 *Juridical Review* 34 ff.; William W. McBryde, 'Promises in Scots Law', (1993) 42 *ICLQ* 48 ff.; Robert Black, in *The Laws of Scotland: Stair Memorial Encyclopedia*, vol. xv (1996), nn. 611 ff.; Reinhard Zimmermann and Phillip Hellwege, 'Belohnungsversprechen: "Pollicitatio", "Promise" oder "Offer"?', 1998 *Zeitschrift für Rechtsvergleichung, internationales Privatrecht und Europarecht* 133 ff.; W. D. H. Sellar, 'Promise in Scots Law', in Reid and Zimmermann (n. 262) in preparation.

[283] See, in particular, Malte Diesselhorst, *Die Lehre des Hugo Grotius vom Versprechen* (1958).

[284] See chs. 2 and 4 in James Gordley (n. 115).

[285] *De jure belli ac pacis* (n. 198) lib. II, cap. XI, 4; for comment, see Okko Behrends, 'Treu und Glauben: Zu den christlichen Grundlagen der Willenstheorie im heutigen Vertragsrecht', in L. L. Vallauri and G. Dilcher (eds.), *Christentum, Säkularisation und modernes Recht*, vol. ii (1981), 964 ff.; Bruno Schmidlin, 'Die beiden Vertragsmodelle des europäischen Zivilrechts: Das naturrechtliche Modell der Versprechensübertragung und das pandektistische Modell der vereinigten Willenserklärungen', in Zimmermann, Knütel, and Meincke (n. 11) 187 ff.

the part of the promisee.[286] Thus, according to Grotius, the unilateral promise as such does not create a right to sue in the person of the promisee: 'jus proprium alteri non dat.'[287] This view quickly gained ascendancy among the Natural lawyers;[288] via Pufendorf and Pothier it also found its way into English law.[289] Pothier, as usual, stated the conceptual distinctions most clearly. A contract includes the concurrence of intention in two parties, one of whom promises something to the other who, in turn, accepts such promise. A *pollicitatio*, on the other hand, is a promise not yet accepted by the person to whom it is made.[290] '[A]ux termes du pur droit naturel', it does not produce, without such acceptance, what can properly be called an obligation.[291]

This exposition (based as it was on Ulp. D. 50, 12, 3 pr.[292]) became the basis of the English doctrine of offer and acceptance.[293] A *pollicitatio* is 'a promise made but not accepted';[294] but only an accepted promise can give rise to a (contractual) obligation. As a result, promises of a reward,[295] or an advertisement promising to pay £100 to any user of a carbolic smoke ball who caught influenza,[296] presented special problems of analysis. The courts tried to squeeze their decisions into the new doctrinal straitjacket

[286] *De jure belli ac pacis* (n. 198) lib. II, cap. XI, 14. For commentary and background, see Gordley (n. 115) 71 ff., 81.

[287] *De jure belli ac pacis* (n. 198) lib. II, cap. XI, 3.

[288] See, most recently, Schmidlin (n. 285) 190 ff.

[289] A. W. B. Simpson, 'Innovation in Nineteenth Century Contract Law', (1975) 91 *LQR* 247 ff.; Gordley (n. 115) ch. 6; *Law of Obligations* (n. 40) 569 ff.

[290] Grotius had used the term 'pollicitatio' in a different sense; see *De jure belli ac pacis* (n. 198) lib. II, cap. XI, 3 and lib. II, cap. XI, 14. Cf. also Pufendorf, *De jure naturae et gentium* (n. 198) lib. III, cap. V, 6 ('imperfecta promissio').

[291] *Traité des obligations* (n. 202) 4.

[292] 'Pactum est duorum consensus atque conventio, pollicitatio vero offerentis solius promissum.' (A pact is an agreement and convention of two people, but an undertaking is the promise only of the person who makes it.)

[293] Simpson, (1975) 91 *LQR* 259.

[294] John Austin, *Lectures on Jurisprudence*, vol. ii (1885), 906.

[295] *Williams* v. *Carwardine* (1833) 4 B & Ad 621, ER 110, 590.

[296] *Carlill* v. *Carbolic Smoke Ball Company* [1892] 2 QB 484 and [1893] 1 QB 256. For all details, see A. W. B. Simpson, 'Quackery and Contract Law: The Case of the Carbolic Smoke Ball', (1985) 14 *Journal of Legal Studies* 345 ff.

and declared that the reward could be claimed only on the basis of a 'unilateral contract'. Like all contracts, it required the exchange of offer and acceptance. Consequently, the promise had to be taken to constitute an offer (*ad incertas personas*), which the person claiming the promised money accepts by performing the act specified. This, of course, he can only do if he has known about the offer. Thus, on the one hand, we have the somewhat strained construction of an acceptance which need not be communicated to the offeror.[297] On the other hand, 'it is hard to see what prejudice the offeror would suffer if he had to pay the reward to someone who had complied with the terms of the offer without being aware of it. The reasons for holding that there is no contract in such a case seem to be largely doctrinal.'[298]

Interestingly, the common law has been more rigid and blinkered by civil law doctrine than some of the modern civilian systems themselves. In the German Civil Code, for instance, special provision is made for the promise, by way of public notice, of 'a reward for the performance of an act, in particular for the production of a result'.[299] It is known as *Auslobung*, a unilateral act which need not be accepted. The Code endorsed a view propounded by a number of pandectist scholars:[300] a view for which there are but the faintest traces in the Roman sources.[301] Scotland alone did not have to rediscover the possibility of a unilaterally binding promise. Unencumbered by both the doctrine of consideration and a dogmatic adherence to contemporary Natural law contract theory, Viscount Stair distinguished between contract, which becomes binding as the result of an 'acceptance' following on an offer, and promise pure and simple which is 'now commonly held obligatory'.[302] This is clearly

297 See Simpson, (1985) 14 *Journal of Legal Studies* 378.

298 Treitel (n. 116) 34; cf. also Ewan McKendrick, *Contract Law* (3rd edn., 1997), 38.

299 § 657 BGB.

300 South African courts have not seen their way open to adopt a similar approach: *Bloom* v. *The American Swiss Watch Company* 1915 AD 100.

301 For details, see *Law of Obligations* (n. 40) 574 f.

302 Stair, *Institutions of the Law of Scotland*, ed. David M. Walker (1981), book I, title 10, 3 f.

based on Canon law[303] and it differs, as Stair himself acknowledges, from the view propounded by Grotius. Stair's views on *stipulatio alteri* (*ius quaesitum tertio*), incidentally, are a direct consequence of his treatment of promise: the third party acquires a right to sue even if he is 'neither present nor accepting'.[304] Again, this was contrary to Grotius' conception according to which an acceptance is required on the part of the third party.[305] 'Later writers lacked Stair's clarity of analysis', says David Sellar,[306] 'and added little but confusion to this area of the law.' *Carlill* v. *Carbolic Smoke Ball Co.* offered the prospect of an alternative analysis. And the Requirement of Writing Act 1995 added a new dimension to the existing confusion.[307] Yet, at the same time, the doctrine of promise as expounded by Stair has survived and it remains useful, not only as far as the analysis of promises for a reward is concerned.[308] Thus, most recently, the Principles of European Contract Law state quite simply: 'A promise which is intended to be legally binding without acceptance is binding.'[309]

IV. EUROPEAN LEGAL SYSTEMS AS MIXED SYSTEMS

1. A Legal Tapestry of Many Different Shades and Nuances

We have referred, above, to Scotland and South Africa as 'mixed legal systems', because their development reflects an interaction between the continental civil law and the

[303] For a detailed analysis, see McBryde, (1993) 42 *ICLQ* 54 ff.; Sellar (n. 282) sub IV and VI. Generally on the influence of Canon law in Scotland, see J. J. Robertson, 'The Canon Law Vehicle of Civilian Influence with Particular Reference to Scotland', in Carey Miller and Zimmermann (n. 3) 117 ff.

[304] Stair (n. 302) book I, title 10, 5.

[305] See *Law of Obligations* (n. 40) 43 f.

[306] Sellar (n. 282) sub VII.; cf. also Zimmermann and Hellwege, 1998 *Zeitschrift für Rechtsvergleichung, internationales Privatrecht und Europarecht* 139 ff.

[307] Sellar (n. 282) sub X.

[308] See ibid. sub IX.

[309] Art. 2:107 PECL (on which provision see the comments in Ole Lando and Hugh Beale (eds.), *Principles of European Contract Law* (2000), 157 f.).

English common law.[310] An examination of the specific experiences of the 'third legal family' should not, however, obscure the fact (and our awareness of it) that all our national private laws in Europe today can be described as mixed legal systems. Characteristically, therefore, David Ibbetson starts the 'prologue' of his history of the law of obligations in England with the sentence: 'The Common law of obligations grew out of the intermingling of native ideas and sophisticated Roman learning.'[311] Indeed, the very use of the taxonomic concept of a 'law of obligations' that has been gaining ground in recent years in England,[312] evidences the productive adaptation of such Roman learning.[313]

The same is true of the continental legal systems. None of them has remained 'pure' in its development since the Middle Ages. They all constitute a mixture of many different elements: Roman law, indigenous customary law, Canon law, mercantile custom, and Natural law theory, to name the most important ones in the history of the law of obligations. Even these five elements themselves are not 'pure' in the sense that they would have developed in splendid isolation from each other. Roman law from the third century AD became 'vulgarized', which means that it absorbed elements of Greek law (in the East) and Germanic customary law (in the West). The laws of the Germanic tribes, in turn, became Romanized the longer they settled within what had been the confines of the Roman Empire.[314]

[310] On the relationship between Roman-Dutch and Scots law see, from the point of view of modern law, Whitty, 1996 *Tydskrif vir die Suid-Afrikaanse Reg* 227 ff., 442 ff., particularly 455 ff.; Rodger (n. 270) 225 ff.; Daniel Visser, 'Placing the Civilian Influence in Scotland: A Roman-Dutch Perspective', in Carey Miller and Zimmermann (n. 3) 239 ff.; MacQueen, (1997) 5 *ZEuP* 369 ff.; Jacques du Plessis, 'The Promises and Pitfalls of Mixed Legal Systems: The South African and Scottish Experiences', 1998 *Stellenbosch Law Review* 338 ff.

[311] Ibbetson (n. 240) 1.

[312] This is evidenced, for instance, by the legal education requirements laid down by the professions, i.e. the Bar and the Law Society.

[313] For discussion see Peter Birks, 'Definition and Division: A Meditation on Institutes 3.13', in idem (ed.), *The Classification of Obligations* (1997), 1 ff.; cf. also Peter Birks,. 'More Logic and Less Experience: The Difference between Scots Law and English Law', in Carey Miller and Zimmermann (n. 3) 167 ff.

[314] See the references p. 20, n. 83.

Canon law depended to a large extent upon Roman legal rules and concepts;[315] at the same time, in many respects it influenced the way in which the civil law developed.[316] The medieval *lex mercatoria* had absorbed specific institutions like general average (based on the *lex Rhodia de iactu*) or bottomry loan (*fenus nauticum*)[317] as well as the general notion of *bona fides*.[318] And Natural law theory, too, relied heavily on the Roman-Canon *ius commune*.[319] The various strands of tradition were very closely interwoven and formed a legal tapestry of many different shades and nuances.[320]

2. The History of the Testamentary Executor

(*a*) *A Creation of Legal Practice*

As far as Roman law, Canon law, and the customary laws of late antiquity and the early medieval period are concerned the history of the testamentary executor provides a good example.[321] Classical Roman law had not known this institution.[322] None the less, in the *Digest* we find a number of fragments where a person or public authority other than

[315] See, e.g., A. Erler, 'Ecclesia vivit lege Romana', in *HRG*, vol. i (1971), cols. 798 f.

[316] See, e.g., Udo Wolter, *Ius Canonicum in Iure Civili* (1975); Hans-Jürgen Becker, 'Spuren des kanonischen Rechts im Bürgerlichen Gesetzbuch', in Zimmermann, Knütel, and Meincke (n. 11) 159 ff. Generally on the importance of Canon law for the development of European law, see R.H. Helmholz, *The Spirit of Classical Canon Law* (1996); cf. also the contributions to Heinrich Scholler (ed.), *Die Bedeutung des kanonischen Rechts für die Entwicklung einheitlicher Rechtsprinzipien* (1996); Peter Landau, 'Der Einfluß des kanonischen Rechts auf die europäische Rechtskultur', in Reiner Schulze (ed.), *Europäische Rechts- und Verfassungsgeschichte* (1991), 39 ff.

[317] On which see *Law of Obligations* (n. 40) 406 ff., 181 ff.

[318] See Rudolf Meyer, *Bona fides und lex mercatoria in der europäischen Rechtstradition* (1994), 61 ff.

[319] See the discussion and the references in Zimmermann (n. 33) 265 f.

[320] For the 19th-century German law see, in this context, the observations by Klaus Luig, 'Rechtsvereinheitlichung durch Rechtsprechung in den Urteilen des Reichsgerichts von 1879 bis 1900 auf dem Gebiete des Deutschen Privatrechts', (1997) 5 *ZEuP* 762 ff.

[321] For a detailed account and for all references, see Reinhard Zimmermann, 'Heres Fiduciarius? Rise and Fall of the Testamentary Executor', in Richard Helmholz and Reinhard Zimmermann (eds.), *Itinera Fiduciae: Trust and Treuhand in Historical Perspective* (1998), 267 ff.

[322] Schulz (n. 187) 333 ('a fateful omission').

the heir has to carry out the will of the testator.[323] This was an inchoate executorship which may have been based on the legal practice in the Greek provinces of the Roman Empire. It was used, particularly, with regard to testamentary dispositions *ad pias causas* which had become very common by Justinian's time.[324] In medieval Germanic law, on the other hand, we find the notion of *Salmann* or *Treuhand*: a specific part of the estate, or even the entire estate, was transferred to a person or institution in whom the transferor had confidence, with certain instructions about the final disposition of the property.[325] This transaction constituted a substitute for the testament which was unknown in Germanic customary law.

It was the medieval Church that combined the *Treuhand* concept with the Roman notion of the last will as a unilateral disposition *mortis causa*.[326] The Church, of course, was keen to encourage dispositions *ad pias causas* and therefore equally eager to promote the last will as a convenient means of effecting that goal.[327] Thus, on the one hand, the Church relaxed the formal requirements for the validity of the Roman testament. On the other hand, the testament was converted, essentially, into a spiritual instrument. 'Caput et fundamentum testamenti'[328] was no longer the institution of an heir but the bequest *pro animae remedio*.[329] This bequest had to be saved—in the interest of the testator's soul!—from invalidity at all costs.[330] At the same time, a person, or institution, was needed to implement that disposition: a

323 See Ludwig Mitteis, *Römisches Privatrecht bis auf die Zeit Diokletians*, vol. i (1908), 105 ff.

324 For details, see Eberhard F. Bruck, *Kirchenväter und soziales Erbrecht* (1956).

325 See Alfred Schultze, *Die langobardische Treuhand und ihre Umbildung zur Testamentsvollstreckung* (1895), 37 ff.; R. W. H. Pitlo, *De ontwikkeling der executeele* (1941), 83 ff.

326 Cf., e.g., Alfred Schultze, 'Der Einfluß der Kirche auf die Entwicklung des germanischen Erbrechts', (1914) 35 *ZSS (GA)* 75 ff.

327 Schultze (n. 325) 151 ff.; Pitlo (n. 325) 89 ff.; Coing (n. 197) 564 ff.

328 (The source and foundation of the whole will) Gai. II, 229.

329 See, e.g., Philippe Ariès, *Geschichte des Todes* (1980), 233 ff., 242 ff.; Bruck (n. 324) 257 ff.

330 See, e.g., Reinhard Zimmermann, 'Cy-Près', in *Festgabe für Max Kaser* (1986), 395 ff.

fiduciary who acted in the best interests of the testator. This was the executor. He was referred to as *executor testamenti*, or *executor ultimae voluntatis*, and features prominently in title XXVI of the *Liber Extra*. The popes emphatically insisted that 'in omnibus piis voluntatibus' everything had to be carried out in accordance with the wishes of the testator[331] and they therefore made it their business to see to it that the executor did not neglect his duties. Generally speaking, the Church could be involved on two different levels. The testator might have appointed a cleric as executor; but even if he had not, the Church sought to ensure that the person appointed properly distributed the bequests *ad pias causas*. Moreover, it stepped into the breach when the testator had merely left his property to Christ, or to the Angels, or to the poor, without naming any specific person to implement these instructions.

(b) The Testamentary Executor Today

Thus, the executor was a creation of legal practice that developed at the intersection between Roman law, Canon law, and medieval customary law of Germanic derivation. Not surprisingly, contemporary learned authors found it very difficult to conceptualize this new institution:[332] was the executor a mandatary, or a *procurator/tutor/curator*, or a *negotiorum gestor*? Was he a fideicommissary? Or an *heres fiduciarius*? Centuries of discussion were required to provide a suitable doctrinal framework and to integrate the executor into the general law of succession. The results of these discussions, and of the way in which legal practice developed, were different everywhere.[333] The Austrian Code devotes a single section to the executor. This is indicative of the fact that his position is largely redundant in view

[331] Decretales Gregorii IX, lib. III, tit. XXVI, cap. XVII.

[332] See, e.g., Alexander Beck, 'Historisches und Rechtsvergleichendes zur Stellung des Willensvollstreckers', in Itinera Iuris, Arbeiten zum römischen Recht und seinem Fortleben (1980), 298 ff.; Coing (n. 197) 597 ff.

[333] For what follows, see Wolfgang Siebert, 'Testamentsvollstrecker', in Franz Schlegelberger (ed.), *Rechtsvergleichendes Handwörterbuch*, vol. vi (1938), 561 ff.; Astrid Offergeld, *Die Rechtsstellung des Testamentsvollstreckers* (1995), 194 ff.; Zimmermann (n. 321) 289 ff.

of a system of comprehensive and obligatory official estate supervision. Of marginally more substantial stature is the executor according to French law where estate regulation was regarded as an essentially private matter, even before the French Revolution. In Germany, as in France or Austria, an executor need not be instituted. But if he is—and that is often the case—his position is very powerful. Particularly the institution of a long-term administrative executor leaves the heir with hardly more than a *nudum ius*.[334] He is about as powerful as the executor in English law, the important difference being, of course, that there he came to be seen as a representative of the deceased and was, eventually, equated with the Roman *heres*.[335] Unlike on the European Continent, there was no need to coordinate the position of heir and executor with regard to the estate. None the less, the English executor is rooted in the same historical soil as his Continental counterparts. He might still be referred to, in the learned language of the Middle Ages, as *heres fiduciarius*.

VII. THE TRUST: A COMMON LAW PECULIARITY?

1. A Creation of Legal Practice

The executor is generally regarded today as a trustee. The trust, in turn, is very widely considered today as a distinctive institution of Anglo-American law.[336] There is nothing comparable in the civil law. Historically, it is 'a natural outcome of ancient English elements'.[337] It has developed

[334] Karlheinz Muscheler, *Die Haftungsordnung der Testamentsvollstreckung* (1994), 3, 56 f.

[335] Michael M. Sheehan, *The Will in Medieval England* (1963), 148 ff., 195 ff.; Sir Frederick Pollock and Frederic William Maitland, *The History of English Law before the Time of Edward I* (2nd edn., 1898), 334 ff.; Sir William Holdsworth, *A History of English Law*, vol. iii (5th edn., 1942), 563 ff.

[336] See, e.g., W. W. Buckland and Arnold McNair, *Roman Law and Common Law: A Comparison in Outline* (2nd edn., by F. H. Lawson, 1965), 177: 'It has long been recognised that the trust is not derived from Roman law, nor has Roman law influenced its development to any extent.'

[337] Frederic William Maitland, *Equity* (1909), 6.

in isolation from the *ius commune* and provides perhaps the best evidence of the gulf that separated, and continues to separate, the English common law from the continental legal systems.[338] The contributions that have recently been assembled in a book entitled *Itinera Fiduciae: Trust and Treuhand in Historical Perspective* paint a somewhat different picture.[339] Like the institution of the testamentary executor, trusts in general were a creation of legal practice. The *existence* of trusts antedated by centuries the *concept* of the trust. It was only in the nineteenth century that a concerted effort was made to extract a true law of trusts from countless trust-like devices. Treatises devoted to the trust as a separate body of law began to be written.[340] They finally had to settle what now appeared to be basic theoretical questions, such as determining the exact nature of the beneficiary's interest. Prior to the nineteenth century, attempts at conceptual analysis were much more diffuse.[341] They were as diffuse as (and, at the same time, closer to[342]) the attempts undertaken by the great civilian lawyers to conceptualize the fiduciary relationships with which they were confronted. Like the trust in England, the *fiducia* in France or Italy was used to solve particular problems even though it did not fit neatly into any of the Roman categories.[343]

[338] See, as far as Maitland's views are concerned, R. H. Helmholz, 'The Learned Laws in "Pollock and Maitland" ', in John Hudson (ed.), *The History of English Law: Centenary Essays on 'Pollock and Maitland'* (= *Proceedings of the British Academy*, 89) (1996), 153 ff. Maitland's views on the origin of the trust differed from previous scholarship; see Michele Graziadei, 'Changing Images of the Law in XIX Century English Legal Thought (The Continental Impulse)', in Mathias Reimann (ed.), *The Reception of Continental Ideas in the Common Law World 1820–1920* (1993), 122 ff.

[339] This section and the following two reiterate core conclusions of this project and are based on Richard Helmholz and Reinhard Zimmermann, 'Views of Trust and Treuhand: An Introduction', in Helmholz and Zimmermann (n. 321) 27 ff.

[340] See Donovan W. M. Waters, 'The Institution of the Trust in Civil and Common Law', in *Recueils des cours: Collected Courses of the Hague Academy of International Law*, vol. 252 (1995), 207 ff.

[341] See Michael Macnair, 'The Conceptual Basis of Trusts in the Later 17th and Early 18th Centuries', in Helmholz and Zimmermann (n. 321) 207 ff. Macnair refers, in particular, to Lord Nottingham, Sir Jeffrey Gilbert, and Henry Ballow, who all made significant use of concepts drawn from the civil law.

[342] Macnair (n. 341) 235 f.

[343] Michele Graziadei, 'The Development of Fiducia in Italian and French Law

Conceptual clarity was not the starting point. It became a matter of great concern in nineteenth-century Germany, when Germanists and Romanists competed to construe a theory of *Treuhand* from the historical material available to them.[344]

2. Roman Law, Canon Law, and the Trust

Moreover, most of the trust-like devices that existed for so long in England and on the Continent depended to some extent on Roman law. Roman law itself had not developed the trust as an abstract fiduciary concept, but it had known a fiduciary institution (the *fideicommissum*) and a fiduciary office (the *tutor*).[345] It thus provided impulses towards, and examples of, the workings of the trust and the role of the trustee and stimulated the later legal development on both sides of the Channel. Once again, Canon law played a significant part in the medieval development. It contained texts and principles from which rules useful in creating trust-like institutions could be fashioned which the popes and their clerical deputies, animated by an ideal of *utilitas ecclesiae*, required for a variety of purposes.[346] These institutions were a part of English ecclesiastical court jurisdiction for a very long time,[347] and they were a feature of the English legal landscape at the time when, and even before,

from the 14th Century to the End of the Ancien Régime', in Helmholz and Zimmermann (n. 321) 327 ff.

344 Helmut Coing, *Die Treuhand kraft privaten Rechtsgeschäfts* (1973); Sybille Hofer, 'Treuhandtheorien in der deutschen Rechtswissenschaft des 19. Jahrhunderts', in Helmholz and Zimmermann (n. 321) 398 ff.

345 David Johnston, 'Trusts and Trust-Like Devices in Roman Law', in Helmholz and Zimmermann (n. 321) 45 ff.; cf. also idem, *The Roman Law of Trusts* (1988).

346 See Shael Herman, 'Utilitas Ecclesiae: The Canonical Conception of the Trust', (1996) 70 *Tulane Law Review* 2239 ff.; idem, 'Trusts Sacred and Profane: Clerical, Secular, and Commercial Uses of the Medieval Commendatio', (1997) 71 *Tulane Law Review* 869 ff.; idem, 'The Canonical Conception of the Trust', in Helmholz and Zimmermann (n. 321) 85 ff.; idem, 'Utilitas Ecclesiae versus Radix Malorum: The Moral Paradox of Ecclesiastical Patrimony', (1999) 73 *Tulane Law Review* 1231 ff.

347 Richard Helmholz, 'Trusts in the English Ecclesiastical Courts 1300–1640', in Helmholz and Zimmermann (n. 321) 153 ff.

the Chancery's jurisdiction over uses became established.[348] It is likely that the trusts enforced in the ecclesiastical courts played some role in the evolution of the trust in English law.[349] At the same time they served as a bridge between English and continental law. The resources of the Roman and Canon laws were thus a continuing factor in the creation and regulation of trusts.

3. Trust Purposes

The parents of the trust are fraud and fear. This statement which can be found in English texts repeats a maxim of great antiquity. Some form of it goes back at least to the fourth century,[350] and it captures a continuing and common European feature of the history of the trust: both in England and on the Continent trust-like devices were commonly used in similar ways to circumvent inconvenient restrictions in the law. But even apart from that, it is remarkable to see how close a coincidence in trust purposes is revealed by the early evidence.[351] The passing of family property from one generation to the next[352] and the trust for the benefit of the poor and disadvantaged[353] provide two prominent examples.

4. Principles of European Trust Law

Common patterns of development, similar social conditions, use of the same legal sources, and a coincidence of

348 Helmholz (n. 316) 171.

349 Ibid.

350 Jerome, *Epistolae* 52. 6, cited by Johnston, 'Trusts and Trust-Like Devices' (n. 345) 46.

351 See, e.g., the observations by Karl Otto Scherner, 'Formen der Treuhand im alten deutschen Recht', in Helmholz and Zimmermann (n. 321) 262 ff.

352 See, e.g., the contributions to Lloyd Bonfield (ed.), *Marriage, Property, and Succession* (1992); Klaus Luig, 'Philipp Knipschildt und das Familienfideikommiß im Zeitalter des Usus modernus', in Helmholz and Zimmermann (n. 321) 361 ff.; Jörn Eckert, 'Use, Trust, Strict Settlement: Fideikommißähnliche Bindungen des Grundbesitzes in England', in *Wirkungen europäischer Rechtskultur: Festschrift für Karl Kroeschell* (1997), 187 ff.

353 On the origins of which, see Gareth Jones, *History of the Law of Charity 1532–1827* (1969), 22 ff.; Harald Siems, 'Von den piae Causae zu den Xenodochien', in Helmholz and Zimmermann (n. 321) 57 ff.

purposes pursued: it can hardly be maintained that a wall of incomprehension separated the English trust from the law of the Continent.[354] Rather, the trust appears to be the specifically English variation of a common European theme.[355] It has turned out to be a device that is particularly useful and adaptable to many different needs and circumstances. Thus, it has generated great interest, worldwide. The Hague Convention on the Law Applicable to Trusts and their Recognition declared that trusts created in accordance with its terms were to be recognized and protected by all signatory states.[356] Italy and the Netherlands were the first civil law countries to ratify the Convention. In both countries it has been received with considerable enthusiasm.[357] Liechtenstein has received a form of the trust[358] and even France has advanced to the point of introducing the *fiducia* into its *code civil*.[359] Earlier this year an International

354 Cf. also H. Patrick Glenn, 'The Historical Origins of the Trust', in Alfredo Mordechai Rabello (ed.), *Aequitas and Equity: Equity in Civil Law and Mixed Jurisdictions* (1997), 749 ff.; Stephen W. deVine, 'The Franciscan Friars, the Feoffment to Uses, and Canonical Theories of Property Enjoyment before 1535', (1989) 10 *JLH* 1 ff.

355 The most basic difference being that the English trust gives effect *in rem* to the interests behind a trust whereas its civilian analogues are based, essentially, on a contractarian analysis. However, in modern German law the position of the *Treugeber* as against third parties has been strengthened to the point where it is possible to describe his rights as *quasi-dinglich*: see Helmholz and Zimmermann (n. 321) 35 with references; and see Stefan Grundmann, 'The Evolution of Trust and Treuhand in the 20th Century', in Helmholz and Zimmermann (n. 321) 469 ff.

356 For the English and French versions of this Convention, see (1986) 50 *RabelsZ* 698 ff.

357 See Ilaria Beneventi (ed.), *I trusts in Italia oggi* (1996); Maurizio Lupoi, *Trusts* (1997); idem, 'Trusts and Civilian Categories (Problems Spurred by Italian Domestic Trusts)', in Helmholz and Zimmermann (n. 321) 495 ff.; Frans Sonneveldt and Harrie L. van Mens (eds.), *The Trust: Bridge or Abyss between Common Law and Civil Law Jurisdictions?* (1992); D. J. Hayton, S. C. J. J. Kortmann, et al. (eds.), *Vertrouwd met de trust* (1996); Margareta Elizabeth Koppenol-Laforce, *Het Haagse trustverdrag* (1997). Cf. also Smits (n. 5) 261 ff.

358 See Harald Bösch, *Die liechtensteinische Treuhänderschaft zwischen trust und Treuhand* (1995), 64 ff., 246 ff.; Klaus Biedermann, *The Trust in Liechtenstein Law*, tr. H. Gerald Crossland (1984), 59 ff. For Luxembourg and Switzerland see, most recently, Gerhard Wolter, *Treuhandrecht im Umbruch? Ein Blick nach Frankreich, Luxemburg, in die Schweiz und in den Libanon sowie auf das Haager Trust-Übereinkommen* (1999), 123 ff., 143 ff.

359 See Claude Witz, 'La Fiducie en Europe: France, Suisse, Luxembourg,

Working Group, based at the University of Nijmegen, produced a set of Principles of European Trust Law.[360] Significantly, in the introduction to these Principles, the editors refer to Roman-Dutch law in South Africa and to Scots law as being able to offer especially interesting experiences.[361] Neither of these systems, they say, knew the institutional separation of law and equity. Both have a law of property based on Roman legal concepts. None the less, both Scots law and South African law have today a vigorous law of trusts.

5. Trusts in South Africa and Scotland

In the case of South Africa, it was the English trust that came to the Cape in the course of the nineteenth century. But its rules were only partially received.[362] They were integrated into Roman-Dutch law as an extra institution of the administrative type. 'The rules of South African trust law are thus a mixture of English, Roman-Dutch and distinctively South African rules, with the latter continually growing in relative importance. There is nothing in them flatly inconsistent with the principles of Roman-Dutch law. Analytically if not historically they can be treated as natural developments from the rules of such institutions as the *fideicommissum*, *fiducia*, *stipulatio alteri*, tutorship, curatorship, and common law administratorship. But historically the rules of trust law have at least three main sources, and trust law is all the stronger for being able to draw so

Allemagne, Liechtenstein. Analyse des lois existantes et des projets en cours', in J. Herbots and D. Philippe (eds.), *Le Trust et la fiducie: Implications pratiques* (1997), 63 ff.; Michel Grimaldi and François Barrière, 'Trust and Fiducie', in Arthur Hartkamp, Martijn Hesselink, et al. (eds.), *Towards a European Civil Code* (2nd edn., 1998), 567 ff.; Wolter (n. 358) 27 ff. The standard work arguing that the institution already existed and still exists in French law is Claude Witz, *La Fiducie en droit privé français* (1981); cf. also Wolter (n. 358) 15 ff.

[360] D. J. Hayton, S. C. J. J. Kortmann, and H. L. E. Verhagen (eds.), *Principles of European Trust Law* (1999); also printed in (1999) 7 *ZEuP* 745 ff.

[361] Hayton, Kortmann, and Verhagen (n. 360) 3 f.; (1999) 7 *ZEuP* 746; cf. also Smits (n. 5) 265 ff.

[362] For all details, see Tony Honoré, 'Trust', in Zimmermann and Visser (n. 105) 847 ff.

widely.'[363] The Scottish trust developed somewhat differently: 'An important source seems to have been the fideicommissum of Roman law. English law gave the Scottish trust its name . . . but in other respects exercised . . . little influence until the nineteenth century, by which time the essentials of the Scottish trust were already well established. Hence throughout its long history the Scottish trust has remained an institution of the civil law rather than the common law.'[364] In the end result, therefore, both Scotland and South Africa have produced a civilian form of trust[365] and it is interesting to see that the Scottish model has exercised considerable influence on the Principles of European Trust Law.

VIII. GOOD FAITH: A CIVILIAN PECULIARITY?

1. The Good Faith in European Contract Law Project

Trust law is one of the arguments often advanced to demonstrate the supposedly fundamental divide between

[363] Tony Honoré and Edwin Cameron, *Honoré's South African Law of Trusts* (4th edn., 1992), 17.

[364] K. C. G. Reid, 'National Report for Scotland', in Hayton, Kortmann, and Verhagen (n. 360) 68. For a historical analysis of the development of trust law in Scotland, see G. L. Gretton, 'The Evolution of the Trust in a Semi-Civilian System', in Helmholz and Zimmermann (n. 321) 507 ff. The standard modern textbook is W. A. Wilson and A. G. M. Duncan, *Trusts, Trustees and Executors* (2nd edn., 1995). For an account in German, see Daniela Krantz, *Trusts im schottischen Recht* (1997). Cf. also G.L. Gretton, 'Trust and Patrimony', in Hector L. MacQueen (ed.), *Scots Law into the 21st Century: Essays in Honour of W. A. Wilson* (1996), 182 ff. (discussing the various ways of conceptualizing the trust from a civilian point of view). For a comparison between South African and Scots trust law, see Tony Honoré, 'Obstacles to the Reception of Trust Law? The Examples of South Africa and Scotland', in Alfredo Mordechai Rabello (ed.), *Aequitas and Equity* (1997), 793 ff.

[365] Louisiana and Quebec are other stimulating cases in point. For Louisiana, see Joachim Zekoll, 'Zwischen den Welten: Das Privatrecht von Louisiana als europäisch-amerikanische Mischrechtsordnung', in Reinhard Zimmermann (ed.), *Amerikanische Rechtskultur und europäisches Privatrecht* (1995), 28 ff.; A. N. Yiannopoulos, 'Trust and the Civil Law: The Louisiana Experience', in Palmer, *Microcosm* (n. 104) 213 ff.; for Quebec, see the treatment of *fiducie* in arts. 1256–98 *code civil du Québec* (1994); Justin Thorens, 'Le Trust de common law dans les systèmes de droit civil et l'arrêt Tucker de la Cour Suprême du Canada', in *Festschrift für Walter J. Habscheid* (1989), 325 ff.; Donovan W. M. Waters, 'Unification or Harmonization? Experience with the Trust Concept', in *Conflicts and Harmonization: Mélanges von Overbeck* (1990), 591 ff.; Lupoi, *Trusts* (n. 357) 362 f.

civil law and common law. Another one is the absence, in English law, of a general notion of good faith. Common lawyers tend to regard good faith as 'an invitation to judges to abandon the duty of legally reasoned decisions and to produce an unanalytical incantation of personal values'[366] and to be averse to a general provision such as the one contained in § 242 BGB.[367] Just how big are the differences when one leaves behind the most general level of propositions? This was one of the questions that induced a team of lawyers drawn from fourteen Western European jurisdictions to analyse thirty typical sets of facts according to their national legal systems.[368]

2. Differences in Result

A comparative examination of all the answers provided by the contributors to that study revealed the following

[366] M. G. Bridge, 'Does Anglo-Canadian Contract Law Need a Doctrine of Good Faith?', (1984) 9 *Canadian Business Law Journal* 413 f. Cf. also, e.g., Roy Goode, *The Concept of 'Good Faith' in English Law* (1992); Stephen A. Smith, 'Remarks on Contract' (1994) 47 *Current Legal Problems* 8 ff.; and the contributions by Beatson and Friedmann, Cohen, and McKendrick to Jack Beatson and Daniel Friedmann (eds.), *Good Faith and Fault in Contract Law* (1995), 3 ff., 25 ff. and 305 ff.

[367] See supra pp. 85 ff.

[368] The comparative case studies have now been published in Reinhard Zimmermann and Simon Whittaker (eds.), *Good Faith in European Contract Law* (2000), 145 ff. Such enquiry appeared to us to be particularly topical in view of the fact that all member states of the European Union have implemented the Directive on Unfair Terms in Consumer Contracts and will thus have to come to terms with a general notion of 'good faith' in a central area of their contract law; for England see, e.g., Hugh Collins, 'Good Faith in European Contract Law', (1994) 14 *Oxford JLS* 229 ff.; Hugh Beale, 'Legislative Control of Fairness: The Directive on Unfair Terms in Consumer Contracts', in Beatson and Friedmann (n. 366) 231 ff.; Jack Beatson, 'The Incorporation of the EC Directive on Unfair Consumer Contracts into English Law', (1998) 6 *ZEuP* 957 ff. Moreover, the Principles of European Contract Law contain a general provision according to which 'in exercising his rights and performing his duties each party must act in accordance with good faith and fair dealing' (art. 1:201). Their draftsmen appear to regard it as belonging to the common core of European contract law. For a comparative analysis, see Hein Kötz, 'Towards a European Civil Code: The Duty of Good Faith', in Peter Cane and Jane Stapleton (eds.), *The Law of Obligations: Essays in Honour of John Fleming* (1998), 243 ff.; a very different assessment of the impact of a general good faith provision is offered by Günther Teubner, 'Legal Irritants: Good Faith in British Law or How Unifying Law Ends up in New Divergences' (1998) 61 *Modern Law Review* 11 ff. On good faith in Scots law, see now the contributions in A. D. M. Forte (ed.), *Good Faith in Contract and Property* (1999).

picture.[369] Of the thirty cases, eleven led to the same result in all the jurisdictions covered; nine led to the same result in all the legal systems but one or two (cases of 'general but imperfect harmony'); and ten led to a significant disharmony of result. Interestingly, it was only in one of the nine 'general but imperfect harmony' cases that English law deviated from the civilian system; this was a case involving duties of disclosure in contractual negotiations.[370] Equally interestingly, in the ten 'divergence' cases the differences between the legal systems as to the appropriate result cut across the civil law/common law divide. The differences among at least some of the civilian systems, in other words, were usually as great as those between English and French law, or German law, or any of the other civilian jurisdictions.

3. Differences in Doctrinal Analysis

A very similar picture emerged on the level of doctrinal analysis. Even where two codes contain general provisions rooted in the same historical soil (as is the case in France and Germany)[371] there are significant differences in the way in which they are applied.[372] The interpreters of the Italian Code initially followed the very restrictive French approach and were hostile to the notion of an *exceptio doli*.[373] The draftsmen of the Austrian Code, in tune with contemporary Natural law thinking, had been equally unsympathetic to the equity of Roman law and did not

[369] For a detailed assessment of the project, see the concluding chapter entitled 'Coming to Terms with Good Faith' in Zimmermann and Whittaker (n. 368) 653 ff. For the doctrinal background, see the introductory chapter to that volume, entitled 'Good Faith in European Contract Law: Surveying the Legal Landscape'.

[370] Case 2 of the case studies ('Degas drawing').

[371] On *bona fides* in Roman contract law, see the contribution by Martin Josef Schermaier to Zimmermann and Whittaker (n. 368) 63 ff. On the relationship between *bona fides* and the *exceptio doli*, see supra pp. 83 ff.

[372] Cf. also Hans-Jürgen Sonnenberger, 'Treu und Glauben: ein supranationaler Grundsatz?', in *Festschrift für Walter Odersky* (1996), 703 ff.

[373] From the turn of the century, however, they began to become interested in German legal doctrine: see, most recently, the analysis by Filippo Ranieri, 'Bonne Foi et exercice du droit dans la tradition du civil law', 1998 *RIDC* 1077 ff.

adopt a good faith clause at all.[374] Of course, perceptions have changed considerably over the past 200 years.[375] Nevertheless, neither the practical result nor the various ways of conceptualizing them are always the same.[376] The new Dutch civil code, on the other hand, goes even further than German law in suffusing its law of contract with *redelijkheid en billijkheid*.[377]

The range of application of the notion of good faith, of course, depends on a large variety of factors.[378] One of them is the availability of other doctrines and the scope assigned to them. Among these doctrines which in some legal systems do the job for which in others a good faith provision is available are *culpa in contrahendo, obligations d'information, laesio enormis,* the abuse of rights, personal bar, interpretation of the parties' intentions (whether standard or 'supplementary'), unconscionability, doctrines of change of circumstances or erroneous presuppositions, *force majeur*, and mutual mistake. A number of them are still regarded, in some jurisdictions, as emanations of the principle of good faith. Others have become autonomous legal doctrines or have always had their distinctive contours and concerns. The range of doctrines relied on by the common law jurisdictions is hardly less varied: reference is made to implied terms, estoppel (including proprietary estoppel), part performance of a contract in equity, the *de minimis* rule, qualifications of a legal right by reference to the notion of reasonableness, relief against forfeiture in equity, the

[374] For details, see ibid. 1061 ff.

[375] For Austria see, e.g., ibid. 1074 ff.

[376] In spite of the new, more liberal approach towards good faith in Austrian law (strongly influenced by German jurisprudence) it is often emphasized that not everything acknowledged under § 242 BGB may simply be transported into Austrian law; see the discussion by Peter Rummel, in idem (ed.), *Kommentar zum Allgemeinen Bürgerlichen Gesetzbuch*, vol. ii (2nd edn., 1992), § 863 n. 2.

[377] See arts. 6:2, 6:248, 6:258. For a comprehensive (comparative) analysis, see now M. W. Hesselink, *De redelijkheid en billijkheid in het Europese privaatrecht* (1999); for an English summary, see idem, in Hartkamp and Hesselink (n. 5) 285 ff.

[378] For details, see Whittaker and Zimmermann, 'Coming to Terms with Good Faith' (n. 368) 653 ff. For English law, cf. also J. F. O'Connor, *Good Faith in English Law* (1990), 17 ff.

maxim according to which no man can take advantage of his own wrong, breach of confidence, fundamental mistake, repudiation, and, occasionally, even good faith in the exercise of a contractual power.

4. Good Faith and Terms Implied in Law

Three additonal observations may be apposite. One point that comes out very strongly in our study is the intimate relationship between good faith and interpretation. Even within a given legal system both are often closely interwoven or indeed employed as alternative ways of analysing a case. In England, the concept of an implied term is frequently resorted to.[379] If an English lawyer is uncomfortable with an open-textured provision like § 242 BGB, his continental counterpart is often surprised how readily English judges find (or, as he might see it, pretend to find) a term paving the way towards an equitable solution implied in the contract. If, for instance, if we look at terms implied in law in contracts of sale, contracts of employment, and landlord–tenant relationships, we find a host of ancillary duties to have been recognized: duties of cooperation, disclosure, information, protection, and mutual trust and confidence.[380] To a very considerable extent English courts are thus giving effect to evaluations, increasingly based on the notion of reasonableness,[381] to which a German lawyer would apply the label of good faith. From the point of view of both the practical results and the policy considerations employed in the process of reasoning there are significant parallels between the legal systems.

[379] For a comparative analysis, see Martin Schmidt-Kessel, 'Implied Term: Auf der Suche nach dem Funktionsäquivalent', (1997) 96 *Zeitschrift für vergleichende Rechtswissenschaft* 101 ff.; Wolfgang Grobecker, *Implied Terms und Treu und Glauben* (1999); cf. also Johan Steyn, 'Contract Law: Fulfilling the Reasonable Expectations of Honest Men', (1997) 113 *LQR* 450: 'there is not a world of difference between the objective requirement of good faith and the reasonable expectations of the parties.'

[380] For all details, see Grobecker (n. 379) 186 ff.

[381] See, in particular, *Scally* v. *Southern Health and Social Services Board* [1992] 1 AC 294; *Johnstone* v. *Bloomsbury Health Authority* [1992] QB 333 and the analysis by Grobecker (n. 379) 94 ff., 152 ff.

5. The Rematerialization of Contract Law

This leads to the second observation. The way in which the device of implied terms and other legal doctrines are applied demonstrates that English law, like all the other legal systems included in our study, has moved away and is continuing to move away from a paradigm of contract law which focuses almost exclusively on party autonomy. Instead we find increasing emphasis being placed on party loyalty, the protection of reliance, cooperation, consideration also of the other party's interests, and substantive fairness. It is a path leading us away from the exaggerations of positivism and the will theory prevailing in the nineteenth century. At the same time, this process of 'materialization'[382] can be seen as a revival of the ethical foundations of contract doctrine prevailing in the era before the 'rise of freedom of contract'.[383]

There is some evidence that even English lawyers may not always have been as dismissive of notions of fairness and good faith as they are today.[384] Simon Whittaker, in his

[382] For Germany, see now the comprehensive analysis by Claus-Wilhelm Canaris, 'Wandlungen des Schuldvertragsrechts: Tendenzen zu seiner "Materialisierung" ', (2000) 200 *AcP* 273 ff.

[383] See Gordley (n. 115); Atiyah (n. 123).

[384] However, there are also signs that the attitude may be changing again. See, for example, H. K. Lücke, 'Good Faith and Contractual Performance', in P. D. Finn (ed.), *Essays on Contract* (1987), 181 f.; Johan Steyn, *The Role of Good Faith and Fair Dealing in Contract Law: A Hair-Shirt Philosophy?*, Royal Bank of Scotland Law Lecture (1991), 1; Roger Brownsword, 'Two Concepts of Good Faith', (1994) 7 *Journal of Contract Law* 208, 243; John N. Adams and Roger Brownsword, *Key Issues in Contract* (1995), 211 f., 253 f. The United States of America initially inherited from the common law the English scepticism towards a general notion of good faith but have subsequently recognized it in a particularly important piece of legislation (s. 1—203 Uniform Commercial Code); see E. Allan Farnsworth, 'Good Faith in Contract Performance', in Beatson and Friedmann (n. 366) 153 ff.; Robert S. Summers, 'The Conceptualization of Good Faith in American Contract Law: A General Account', in Zimmermann and Whittaker (n. 368) 118 ff. Farnsworth (157 f.) also draws attention to Australia as another country within the common law world which has started to support a doctrine of good faith; cf. also Sir Anthony Mason, 'The Place of Equity and Equitable Remedies in the Contemporary Common Law World', (1994) 110 *LQR* 249, 254; and see, by way of example, the decision by Finn, J., in *Hughes Aircraft Systems International* v. *Airservices Australia* (1997) 146 ALR 1 (37).

part of the introduction to the good-faith volume,[385] draws attention to the influence of the *lex mercatoria* (Law Merchant), to the views adopted by Lord Mansfield, and to a looser approach to 'fraud' prevailing until well into the nineteenth century. The *lex mercatoria*, a body of predominantly customary rules of commercial law, had been applied in England by special merchants' courts since the Middle Ages.[386] It was imbued by the notions of good faith and common sense; the daily negotiations of merchants, after all, 'ought not to depend upon subtleties and niceties'.[387] This body of commercial law was gradually incorporated into the common law and it was Lord Mansfield who completed the process of incorporation. He saw the *lex mercatoria* as part of a universal *ius gentium*. 'The mercantile law', he said in a decision concerning the law of insurance,[388] 'is the same all over the world. For, from the same premises, the sound conclusions of reason and justice must universally be the same.' This explains the frequent recourse by Lord Mansfield to treatises on the *lex mercatoria*, on Natural law, Roman law, and its contemporary continental *usus modernus*.[389] Lord Mansfield, of course, believed in the importance of certainty in mercantile transactions,[390] 'but fairness, not certainty was his lodestar for the general run of contract cases'.[391] Thus, in the well-known case of *Carter* v. *Boehm*[392] he declared '[t]he governing principle [to be] applicable to all contracts and dealings. Good faith

[385] Zimmermann and Whittaker (n. 368) 41 ff.; cf. also O'Connor (n. 378) 3 ff.

[386] See the references in (1993) 1 *ZEuP* 29 ff.

[387] *Hamilton* v. *Mendes* (1761) 2 Burr 1198 (1214) (per Lord Mansfield), 97 ER 787; cf. also supra n. 318.

[388] *Pelly* v. *Royal Exchange Assurance Co.* (1757) 1 Burr 341 (347), 97 ER 342.

[389] See Christopher P. Rodgers, 'Continental Literature and the Development of the Common Law by the King's Bench: c. 1750–1800', in Vito Piergiovanni (ed.), *The Courts and the Development of Commercial Law* (1987), 166 ff.; cf. also David Lieberman, *The Province of Legislation Determined* (1991), 104 ff.; J. H. Baker, *An Introduction to English Legal History* (3rd edn., 1990), 399: 'Bench and bar became imbued with a new European spirit.'

[390] Cf., e.g., *Vallejo* v. *Wheeler* (1774) 1 Cowp 143 (153), 98 ER 1012.

[391] James Oldham, *The Mansfield Manuscripts and the Growth of English Law in the Eighteenth Century*, vol. i (1992), 242.

[392] (1766) 3 Burr 1905 (1910), 97 ER 1162.

forbids either party by concealing what he privately knows, to draw the other into the bargain, from his ignorance of that fact, and his believing the contrary.' In Roman law the opposite of *bona fides* had been *dolus*, broadly conceived: whenever the behaviour of the party to a contract did not conform to the overriding standard of good faith, the *exceptio doli* or the *actio de dolo* could be granted.[393] It is interesting, therefore, to observe how extensive a concept of fraud seems to have been recognized in early nineteenth-century English contract law.[394]

6. Piecemeal Solutions v. Overriding Principle

Thirdly, a remark about stereotypes in comparative legal discourse. It is often said that English law develops incrementally; it finds piecemeal solutions in response to demonstrated problems.[395] This is seen as part of the pragmatic tradition of the common law. Recognition of overriding principles and general legal institutions, on the other hand, are widely regarded as characteristic of the continental approach. But this is an oversimplification. An overriding principle of good faith, as contained in § 242 BGB, in reality, is hardly more than an invitation, or reminder, for courts to do what they do anyway: to develop the law in accordance with the perceived needs of their time.[396] It would neither require English judges 'to give up the time-tested tradition of going cautiously from this case or that case to the next case'[397] nor does it prevent German judges from doing just that. Apart from that it should be kept in mind that the implication of terms in law under the aegis of a standard of reasonableness, as recognized in English law,

[393] See *Law of Obligations* (n. 40) 668; and see supra pp. 83 ff.

[394] This is apparent from Joseph Chitty's treatise on commercial contracts (first published in 1824). See Whittaker and Zimmermann (n. 368) 43.

[395] See *Interfoto Library Ltd.* v. *Stiletto Ltd.* [1988] 1 All ER 348 (352 f.) (per Bingham, LJ).

[396] On § 242 BGB as an 'open norm' see, e.g., Helmut Heinrichs in *Palandt, Bürgerliches Gesetzbuch* (58th edn., 1999), § 242, n. 3; Hesselink (n. 377) 288 f.; Whittaker and Zimmermann (n. 368) 32.

[397] Kötz, op. cit. (n. 368) 245.

is a device of considerable generality and flexibility, as unconducive to 'predictability of the outcome of a case'[398] as a general standard of good faith. Or we may look at the institution of the trust. It is a unitary conception that is famous for its flexibility and adaptability. Continental legal systems, on the other hand, have to rely on 'a whole panoply of extremely heterogeneous legal institutions'[399] in order to satisfy the needs for which English lawyers use the trust.

IX. SOURCES OF LAW

1. The Relevance of Judicial Precedents

We have been looking at one legal institution which is regarded as peculiar to the common law[400] and at another legal concept that is taken to be characteristic of the civil law.[401] In both cases there is more common ground than is usually assumed. The same is true if we turn our attention to the sources of the law. An English colleague once suggested to me that 'civilian lawyers regard our case law with admiration and our statute book with despair'. He could have added that civilian lawyers tend to be particularly desperate when it comes to the methods of statutory interpretation in England. For conventional wisdom has it that the English approach is pedantic and unimaginative, dominated by strict literalism and, at any rate, fundamentally different from the 'European method'.[402] On the other hand, English law is characterized by mature and refined

[398] Goode (n. 366) 7.

[399] Zweigert and Kötz (n. 90) 37. Zweigert and Kötz use this example to substantiate the same proposition: 'we must not too readily infer that it is only the Continental systems, with their tendency to abstraction and generalization, which develop grand comprehensive concepts. . . . Things may be the other way round.'

[400] Supra VII.

[401] Supra VIII.

[402] For a representative statement, see Wolfgang Fikentscher, *Methoden des Rechts in vergleichender Darstellung, ii: Anglo-amerikanischer Rechtskreis* (1975), 115 ff. and *passim*; more recently see, e.g., Michael Reinhardt, *Konsistente Jurisdiktion: Grundlegung einer verfassungsrechtlichen Theorie der rechtsgestaltenden Rechtsprechung* (1997), 227, 260. The phrase 'the European method' is taken from

techniques of developing the law from case to case. The supremacy of judge-made, unwritten law 'is imprinted deep in the English lawyer's soul'.[403] Similar stereotypes still largely prevail about the continental legal methods.

The reality, however, is different. Even in countries with a civil code, precedents are of very considerable importance today.[404] In Germany, they constitute an independent source of law,[405] albeit one of only 'outweighable force'.[406] Modern legal methodology is thus about to leave behind certain positivistic constrictions which have their origin in late eighteenth- and nineteenth-century scholarship. Characteristic of the older *ius commune* is a more open and flexible approach. The *Corpus Iuris Civilis*, it is true, had been ambivalent. 'Non exemplis, sed legibus iudicandum est' (One must not decide according to precedents but to the laws) was the exhortation contained in C. 7, 45, 13; but in D. 1, 3, 38 it was stated that where the law gives rise to ambiguity 'consuetudinem aut rerum perpetuo similiter iudicatarum auctoritatem vim leges optinere debere' (statutory force ought to be ascribed to custom or to the authority of an unbroken line of similar judicial decisions). By the eighteenth century, however, the *usus fori* was assigned considerable weight.[407] This was due to the authority which courts like the *Rota Romana*, the *Grandi Tribunali*, the *Hoge Raad* of Holland, or the *Reichskammergericht* enjoyed as well

Lord Denning (*James Buchanan & Co. Ltd.* v. *Babco Forwarding & Shipping (U.K.) Ltd.* [1977] QB 208 (213 f.)) who thus describes the 'schematic and teleological method of interpretation'.

[403] Roderick Munday, 'The Common Lawyer's Philosophy of Legislation', (1983) 14 *Rechtstheorie* 201.

[404] Cf. supra pp. 55 f.

[405] For details and references, see Reinhard Zimmermann and Nils Jansen, 'Quieta Movere: Interpretative Change in a Codified System', in Cane and Stapleton (n. 367) 298 ff.

[406] Cf. the terminology adopted in the questionnaire underlying the research project by D. Neil MacCormick and Robert S. Summers (eds.), *Interpreting Precedents: A Comparative Study* (1997), 555.

[407] See Coing (n. 197) 125 f.; Heinz Weller, *Die Bedeutung der Präjudizien im Verständnis der deutschen Rechtswissenschaft* (1979), 43 ff.; Gero Dolezalek, *'Stare Decisis': Persuasive Force of Precedent and Old Authority (12th–20th Century)* (1989), 13 ff.

as to the fact that their precedents had become increasingly available in a large number of collections of decisions.[408]

Also, it must be kept in mind that the *ius commune* during the period generally known as *usus modernus pandectarum* was, to a large extent, judicial law (*iurisprudentia forensis*) developing through lawyers' interpretation and judicial opinions.[409] The *vis praeiudiciorum* was widely recognized as vital for determining the law, the convenience of *conformitas in iudicando* was emphasized, and the typical case-law techniques were taught.[410] On the other hand, it was always recognized that the force of precedents was subject to a better, and more convincing, interpretation of the law being advanced. The weight of the argument was what ultimately counted.

The general approach, in other words, was not dissimilar to that prevailing in England before the introduction of the doctrine of *stare decisis*. Before the nineteenth century, English courts had displayed a flexible attitude towards precedents. Typical for that period were statements like 'if a judge conceives a judgement given in another Court to be erroneous, he being sworn to judge according to the law, that is, in his conscience ought not to give the like judgement',[411] or '[t]he reason and the spirit of cases make law, not the letter of particular precedents.'[412] 'You are not bound by any rule of law which you may lay down', as Lord St Leonards stated as late as 1852,[413] 'if upon a subsequent occasion you should find reason to differ from that rule; that is, that this House, like every court of justice, possesses

[408] Cf. Helmut Coing (ed.), *Handbuch der Quellen und Literatur der neueren europäischen Privatrechtsgeschichte*, vol. ii/2 (1976), pp. 1113 ff.

[409] Protagonists of this law in action were academically trained practitioners as well as professors who had usually spent part of their career as an advocate or judge; see, for Roman-Dutch law, the remarks in (1992) 66 *Tulane Law Review* 1712 f.

[410] 'Si tamen casus decisus a casu decidendo, vel in minimo differat, allegatum praejudicium nil relevat' (If, however, the case that has been decided differs in the slightest degree, the precedent that has been adduced does not relieve): Wolfgang Adam Lauterbach, *Collegium theoretico-practicum* (1707), lib. I, tit. III, XLVIII.

[411] *Bole* v. *Horton* (1673) Vaugh 360, at 383 (CP), 124 ER 1113.

[412] *Fisher* v. *Prince* (1762) 3 Burr 1363, at 1364 (per Lord Mansfield, KB), 97 ER 876.

[413] *Bright* v. *Hutton* 3 HLC 341 (388 f.).

an inherent power to correct an error into which it may have fallen.' A number of factors combined to produce the doctrine of *stare decisis* that had begun to emerge by that time:[414] the declaratory theory of adjudication which had been espoused by Sir Matthew Hale and Sir William Blackstone[415] and which reduced the role of judges to finding rather than establishing the law;[416] the legal positivism culminating in, but not confined to, the writings of Jeremy Bentham[417] and John Austin;[418] the doctrine of separation of powers with its emphasis on the sovereignty of Parliament;[419] the quest for legal certainty within a society dominated by vastly increasing trade and industrialization;[420] and, last but not least, the abolition of the forms of action which had previously provided stability.

The same kind of legal formalism thus gained ascendancy in England which dominated contemporary German legal scholarship except that in Germany it found its focus in 'legal science' rather than precedent. For nineteenth-century pandectist scholars proceeded from the assumption that the law constituted a closed system of rules and general principles on the basis of which the correct decision of individual cases could be reached by purely logical deductions. Each judgment was thus an act of scientific cognition, and each judge had the duty to find the one

[414] See, in general, Baker (n. 389) 225 ff.; Rupert Cross and J. W. Harris, *Precedent in English Law* (4th edn., 1991), 24 ff.; Jim Evans, 'Change in the Doctrine of Precedent during the Nineteenth Century', in Laurence Goldstein (ed.), *Precedent in Law* (1987), 35 ff.

[415] See the references in Cross and Harris (n. 414) 27 f.

[416] See, e.g., *Willis* v. *Baddeley* [1892] 2 QB 324, at 326 (per Lord Esher, MR; CA): 'There is, in fact, no such thing as judge-made law, for the judges do not make the law, though they frequently have to apply existing law to circumstances as to which it has not previously been authoritatively laid down that such law is applicable.'

[417] On the influence of Bentham's positivistic legal theory on the common law, particularly concerning the rule of *stare decisis*, see Gerald J. Postema, *Bentham and the Common Law Tradition* (1986), especially at 192 ff.

[418] John Austin, *The Province of Jurisprudence Determined* (4th edn., 1971), *passim*; cf. also the evaluation by H. L. A. Hart in the introduction to that volume.

[419] Cf. J. W. F. Allison, *A Continental Distinction in the Common Law* (1996), 72 ff.

[420] W. R. Cornish and G. de N. Clark, *Law and Society in England 1750–1950* (1989).

correct decision. A precedent *per se* was obviously of only epistemic value in the process of legal reasoning:[421] it could not constitute an independent source of law. The 'scholarly positivism', just like the statutory positivism by which it came to be replaced, aimed at protecting nineteenth-century civic society from arbitrary judicial interference.

Pandectist legal scholarship, to this extent, merely perpetuated an attitude that had its origins in the eighteenth century. By that time, the great number and complexity of legal sources had given rise to a widespread feeling of both legal uncertainty and inefficiency as far as the administration of justice was concerned. The rulers of the emerging modern territorial states were bound to find this situation unattractive. They had been raised in the spirit of enlightened absolutism and perceived it as their duty to centralize, to rationalize, and to clarify the law within the borders of their states. Again, a number of factors contributed towards considerable rigidity as far as the doctrine of legal sources was concerned: the desire of the absolutist monarch to be the fountain of all law as much as the general quest for legal certainty, Montesquieu's doctrine of the separation of powers as much as the notion of the law as constituting an unchangeable and coherent system of rules and concepts from which legal conclusions could be drawn *more geometrico*, as espoused by the authors of the Law of Reason. Occasionally, in the course of the nineteenth century, even in Germany, strict rules of *stare decisis* were laid down: all courts within a specific territory were enjoined to follow the decisions of the highest tribunal as far as they were published in print.[422] In 1838 the King of Hanover authorized the Supreme Court to publish important precedents in the government gazette.[423]

Predominantly, however, the rulers of the age of Enlightenment had turned to legislation as the most suitable means of providing their territories with a rational system of private law. Their codes were to be the ultimate, and

421 See Zimmermann and Jansen (n. 405) 303.

422 See Regina Ogorek, *Richterkönig oder Subsumtionsautomat?* (1986), 192 ff.; Weller (n. 407) 82 ff.

423 See Weller (n. 407) 85; Dawson (n. 39) 436 f.

conclusive, sources of the law. The famous prohibitions against interpreting, developing, and commenting upon these codes (*Kommentier- und Auslegungsverbote*) enacted in the course of the eighteenth century[424] remain the ultimate monuments to an ideology attempting completely to emasculate judges (as well as academic lawyers).

2. Interpreting Statutes

Another consequence of the then prevailing attitude was the rise of literalism in the theory of statutory interpretation.[425] This literalism stood in marked contrast to the liberal and flexible approach—prevailing until far into the eighteenth century[426]—that had been characterized by an interplay of individual legal maxims (*regulae iuris*),[427] that aimed at 'grasping the force and tendency of a statute rather than sticking to its words'[428] and that was based, ultimately, on *aequitas* and *publica utilitas*.[429] The very same two phases can be found in the history of statutory interpretation in England. The period from the Middle Ages

[424] For details, see Hans-Jürgen Becker, 'Kommentier- und Auslegungsverbot', in *HRG*, vol. ii (1978), cols. 963 ff.; Heinz Hübner, *Kodifikation und Entscheidungsfreiheit des Richters in der Geschichte des Privatrechts* (1980), 29 ff.

[425] See Stefan Vogenauer, *Die Auslegung von Gesetzen in England und auf dem Kontinent*, in preparation, ch. 4, D. I. 1.

[426] For a detailed analysis, see Vogenauer (n. 425) ch. 4, D. I. 1; cf. also W. J. Zwalve, 'Interpretatieproblemen voor de codificatie', in *Liber Memorialis François Laurent* (1989), 447 ff.; Clausdieter Schott, 'Gesetzesinterpretation im Usus modernus', (1999) 21 *ZNR* 45 ff.; Hans W. Baade, 'The Casus Omissus: A Pre-history of Statutory Analogy', (1994) 20 *Syracuse Journal of International Law and Commerce* 45 ff.; Hans Hattenhauer, 'Zur Rechtsgeschichte und Dogmatik der Gesetzesauslegung', in Zimmermann, Knütel, and Meincke (n. 11) 129 ff.

[427] See Peter Stein, *Regulae Iuris: From Juristic Rules to Legal Maxims* (1966), 124 ff.; idem, 'The Digest Title, De Diversis Regulis Iuris Antiqui, and the General Principles of Law', in idem, *The Character and Influence of the Roman Civil Law: Historical Essays* (1988), 53 ff.

[428] 'Scire leges non hoc est verba earum tenere, sed vim ac potestatem': Cels. D. 1, 3, 17; on which see *Law of Obligations* (n. 40) 702 ff.

[429] See, e.g., Norbert Horn, *Aequitas in den Lehren des Baldus* (1968); Peter Landau, 'Aequitas in the Corpus Iuris Canonici', (1994) 20 *Syracuse Journal of International Law and Commerce* 95 ff.; Jan Schröder, 'Aequitas und Rechtsquellenlehre in der frühen Neuzeit', (1997) 26 *Quaderni Fiorentini* 265 ff.; idem, 'Aequitas und rechtswissenschaftliches System', (1999) 21 *ZNR* 29 ff.

until the first third of the nineteenth century may be described as the age of equitable interpretation.[430] The courts availed themselves of a wide range of legal maxims, they aimed at finding 'the internal sense' of the law, and they were guided by the 'equity of the statute' that could prevail even against its words. This was the civilian approach. *Cessante ratione legis cessat lex ipsa; odiosa sunt restringenda; summum ius summa iniuria; ut res magis valeat quam pereat; optimus legum interpres consuetudo; exempla illustrant non restringunt legem; talis interpretatio in ambiguis semper fienda est, ut evitetur inconveniens et absurdum; expressio unius est exclusio alterius*: all these and many other maxims were taken from the civilian literature.[431] *Statuta sunt stricte interpretanda* (or: *sunt stricti iuris*) was applied in England to statutes derogating the common law as it was applied in medieval Italy or early modern Germany to statutes contrary to the *ius commune*.[432] The metaphors of the body and the soul, or the shell and the kernel, used by Edmund Plowden to describe the relationship between the letter of the law and its sense and reason[433] had been exploited again and again in continental legal literature since the days of the *Decretum*

[430] Baker (n. 389) 239 ff.; Baade (n. 426) 65 ff.; Pierre André Côté, 'L'Interprétation de la loi en droit civil et en droit statutaire: Communauté de langue et différences d'accents', (1997) 31 *Thémis* 45 ff.; and see now, for all details, Vogenauer (n. 425) ch. 5, D. I. 1.

[431] For references, see Baade (n. 426) 65 ff.; Vogenauer (n. 425) ch. 5, E. IV. 2.

[432] See Zwalve (n. 426) 447 ff.; Reinhard Zimmermann, 'Statuta Sunt Stricte Interpretanda? Statutes and the Common Law: A Continental Perspective', (1997) 56 *Cambridge Law Journal* 315 ff. with further references.

[433] See *Eyston* v. *Studd* (1574) 2 Plowd 459, at 465 (CP): 'it is not the words of the law, but the internal sense of it that makes the law, and our law (like all others) consist of two parts, viz. of body and soul, the letter of the law is the body of the law, and the sense and reason of the law is the soul of the law, quia ratio legis est anima legis. And the law may be resembled to a nut, which has a shell and a kernel within, the letter of the law represents the shell, and the sense is the kernel, and as you will be no better for the nut if you make use only of the shell, so you will receive no benefit by the law, if you rely only upon the letter, and as the fruit and profit of the nut lies in the kernel, and not in the shell, so the fruit and profit of the law consists in the sense more than in the letter. And it often happens that when you know the letter, you know not the sense, for sometimes the sense is more confined and contracted than the letter, and sometimes it is more large and extensive.'

Gratiani.[434] The 'equity of the statute' derives from the medieval notion of *aequitas* which, in turn, was ultimately based on Aristotle's *Nicomachean Ethics*.[435] Blackstone in his *Commentaries*[436] presents a summary of the chapter on the interpretation of statutes in a contemporary translation of Pufendorf's *De Jure Naturae et Gentium*.[437] Even civilian doctrines like the distinction between *interpretatio extensiva, restrictiva,* and *declarativa* were received in England.[438] Thus, it is no exaggeration to state that, as far as statutory interpretation is concerned, England was for many centuries a province of the *ius commune*.[439]

As in Germany, though about fifty years later, the age of equitable interpretation was followed by an era of strict literalism,[440] in which judges saw themselves as 'philologists of the highest order'[441] and preferred to be 'accused of a narrow prejudice for the letter of the law, than set up or sanction vague claims to discard it in favour of some higher interpretation'.[442] It was mirrored by the rise of the doctrine of *stare decisis* and rooted in the same ideological soil. Today, however, the courts in England have turned over a new leaf.[443] In spite of what many continental observers still believe, there has been, since about the middle of this century, a move away from the purely literal towards a purposive construction of statutory provisions: 'The courts now adopt a purposive approach which seeks to give effect to the true purpose of legislation and are prepared to look

[434] For references, see Vogenauer (n. 425) ch. 4, D. I. 1. a.

[435] Baker (n. 389) 240; W. H. Loyd, 'The Equity of the Statute', (1909) 58 *University of Pennsylvania Law Review* 77 ff.; generally on the idea of *aequitas canonica* in English law see, most recently, Javier Martinez-Torron, *Anglo-American Law and Canon Law: Canonical Roots of the Common Law Tradition* (1998), 70 ff.

[436] William Blackstone, *Commentaries on the Laws of England*, vol. i (11th edn., 1791), 58 ff.

[437] Samuel Pufendorf, *De Jure Naturae et Gentium Libri Octo* (1694), lib. V, cap. XII.

[438] Vogenauer (n. 425) ch. 5, E. IV. 2.

[439] Ibid. ch. 9, A. III. 2. Cf. also Côté (n. 430) who summarizes on p. 45: 'in the field of statutory interpretation, England is fundamentally a civil law country.'

[440] For all details, see Vogenauer (n. 425) ch. 6.

[441] *Ex parte Davis* (1857) 5 WR 522, at 523 (per Pollock, CB; Ex.).

[442] *A.-G.* v. *Sillem* (1863) 2 H & C 431, at 537 (per Bramwell, B.; Ex.), 159 ER 178.

[443] Zweigert and Kötz (n. 90) 266; and see Vogenauer (n. 425) ch. 7.

at much extraneous material that bears upon the background against which the legislation was enacted.'[444] At the same time, the doctrine of *stare decisis* has been relaxed.[445] If we keep in mind the great and general sensitivity towards case law and its problems displayed today in Germany[446] as well as the methodological shift away from a literalist approach to statute interpretation that occurred in Germany around the turn of the century, we see a remarkable rapprochement of thinking patterns: a rapprochement, however, which merely re-establishes an intellectual unity based on a common legal tradition.[447]

444 *Pepper (Inspector of Taxes)* v. *Hart* [1993] AC 593, at 617 (per Lord Griffiths; HL). Cf. also Basil S. Markesinis, 'Learning from Europe and Learning in Europe', in idem (n. 234) 13, 15; and see the observations by Robert S. Summers, 'Introduction', in MacCormick and Summers (n. 406) 4; Robert S. Summers and Michele Taruffo, 'Interpretation and Comparative Analysis', in MacCormick and Summers (n. 406) 462 ff., 508.

445 See Zenon Bankowski, D. Neil MacCormick, and Geoffrey Marshall, 'Precedent in the United Kingdom', in MacCormick and Summers (n. 406) 348 ff.; Cross and Harris (n. 414) 135 ff.

446 Cf. supra pp. 55 f.

447 See, as far as German law is concerned, the observations by Hattenhauer (n. 426) 125, 138 ff. (survival of the methodology of the older *ius commune* under the cover of Savigny's famous *canones* of interpretation).

Final Observations

In my first lecture I attempted to show how legal history lost touch with modern legal doctrine in nineteenth-century Germany.[1] This process of emancipation was enormously beneficial in enhancing our knowledge of classical antiquity. Arguably, however, the pendulum swung too far. There has always been, in the development of the civilian tradition, competition between an 'elegant' and a 'utilitarian' approach. It would be highly desirable if legal history, as well as exploring the details of past times for their own sake, once again set itself the task of tracing the ways in which our modern law has emerged from its historical origins.

The second lecture was devoted to a demonstration that this kind of approach is still possible, and meaningful, in spite of the fact that German law—like all other continental legal systems—has been codified. Codification has influenced our ideology. But it has not cut us off from the common legal past. Adjudication and scholarship under the BGB remain German emanations of the civilian tradition.

Legal history helps us to understand our modern law. It explains why the law has become what it is. It lays open the premisses on which the modern law is based. It constitutes a rich source of experience which is as valuable for the development of modern legal doctrine as for law reform. It may also reveal where a wrong turn has been taken and thus prevent us from repeating an error. Today, however, historical legal scholarship has acquired an added significance in

[1] It is my impression that a similar story could be told about other continental legal systems. In Italy, Austria, and the Netherlands, for instance, legal history and legal doctrine are even further removed from each other. For the Netherlands, see Zwalve, (1997) 5 *ZEuP* 393 ff.

view of the Europeanization of private law and private law scholarship. It enables us to see the common ground existing between our modern national legal systems and to understand established differences. It makes us aware of the fact that the law has not developed in national isolation and can, therefore, not properly be understood in purely national terms. It constitutes the foundation for scholarship in comparative law and paves the way towards re-establishing a European legal culture.

In the third lecture I tried to substantiate these propositions with a number of examples. The focus was therefore on 'the vital connection that ties the present to the past'[2] and on the intellectual link between legal history and comparative law. In addition, nearly all these examples emphasized connections existing between civil law and common law. They were intended to demonstrate that there is no wall of incomprehension, except in the minds of lawyers still imbued by 'the nationalist historiography that originated in the nineteenth century'.[3] It is essential, I think, to foster such understanding in order to re-establish a European legal world marked as much by an interesting diversity as by a fundamental intellectual unity.

In the Holy Gospel according to St Luke, Jesus tells the story of a man who 'went down from Jerusalem to Jericho, and fell among thieves, which stripped him of his raiment, and wounded him, and departed, leaving him half dead'.[4] This is the beginning of the parable of the Good Samaritan, one parable with which every common lawyer is familiar.[5] As in the Authorized Version, so also in the Greek original and in Martin Luther's translation the man was 'half dead'. But according to the Vulgate he was 'semivivus'. Obviously, it is all a matter of perspective. Civil law and common law are not identical. But they do not constitute mutually

[2] Friedrich Carl von Savigny, *System des heutigen römischen Rechts*, vol. i (1840), xv.

[3] Harold J. Berman *Law and Revolution: The Formation of the Western Legal Tradition* (1983), 17.

[4] Luke 10: 30.

[5] See *M'Alister (or Donoghue)* v. *Stevenson* [1932] AC 562 (580 f., per Lord Atkin).

incomprehensible traditions either. We can emphasize that which separates us. But we can also try to explore the common ground. I prefer the second alternative just as I prefer the optimism which, in the language of the Romans, regards the wounded man on the way to Jericho as half alive rather than half dead.

Index